"YOU'RE NOT GONNA BELIEVE THIS...."

MY ECCLECTIC MEMOIR

CHARLES E. KACZOROWSKI

"YOU'RE NOT GONNA BELIEVE THIS...."
MY ECCLECTIC MEMOIR

iUniverse books may be ordered through booksellers or by contacting:

iUniverse
1663 Liberty Drive
Bloomington, IN 47403
www.iuniverse.com
1-800-Authors (1-800-288-4677)

Because of the dynamic nature of the Internet, any web addresses or links contained in this book may have changed since publication and may no longer be valid. The views expressed in this work are solely those of the author and do not necessarily reflect the views of the publisher, and the publisher hereby disclaims any responsibility for them.

Any people depicted in stock imagery provided by Thinkstock are models, and such images are being used for illustrative purposes only. Certain stock imagery © Thinkstock.

ISBN: 978-1-5320-1927-2 (sc)
ISBN: 978-1-5320-1856-5 (e)

Library of Congress Control Number: 2017904686

Print information available on the last page.

iUniverse rev. date: 07/14/2017

CONTENTS

I DEDICATE THIS, MY first book, to my loving and beautiful wife, Margie, and daughter, Noelle, and especially to my guardian angel and all the other wonderful angels who have been by my side since the day I was born. They have taken care of me so all of you could read about the kind of life I had, so far. Maybe one day we'll meet. When we do, you'll know exactly why.

ACKNOWLEDGMENTS

I WOULD LIKE TO say to my lovely wife, Margie, you have been my best friend, my partner, and the person I've been looking for to spend my life with. I think you don't have the slightest idea how much I appreciate everything you've done for me through thick and thin.

Noelle, coming into my life when you did and the way you did was a blessing. Hearing you call me Daddy will always bring a tear to my wild heart. You'll always be the apple of my eye and the core of my existence.

To my mom and dad, who I love dearly for bringing me into this world. Dad taught me to always respect my elders and everyone I meet because, he said, you never know when you might meet them again.

Mom, you brought me into this world, where I've met so many amazing and wonderful people. I was able to bring joy and laughter to them as I have given to you and continue to do so every day.

To my older sister, Charnat, my younger brother, Michael, and my younger sister, Marianne, I want you all to know that it's been a total blast sharing this vast universe with you while I've been on this hell of a ride. I know we'll continue to carry on long after I'm gone because I'll be right there by your side.

To every one of my relatives who are still here especially my cousins, I say thank you for taking up part of my heart and giving me such fond memories ever since we were kids. And to everyone I've mentioned here in my book or whenever I call your name, you are my closest and dearest friends.

To everyone else whether I mentioned you or not and you happen to know me or had the pleasure of meeting me, I thank you for entering my life. To Yolanda Perez at DDC; the entire DDC Disaster Team; the 9th and the Central Park Precinct and all the officers of the NYPD; Doug Kerrigan of the Construction Management company, URS; the architect, Fred Basch; and the contractors and vendors involved in the restoration/renovation of the Central Park Precinct; my good neighbor, Jeff Roberts; my dear friends Gordon and Kathy Haberman, Kathy Ryan, John Feal, Glen Klein, Lee Ielpi FDNY (Ret.), Rich Sweeny FDNY (Ret.), Nancy W, Robert Petroff, Tom Canavan, Bobby Muniz, Tony Lo Bianco, and especially my dear friends Dave Margules and OKC Memorial Park Ranger Mike Washington I truly appreciate your unending friendship over the years. I'll never forget you.

Last but not least, my dear friend, P.O. Chris Jackson with the NYPD whom I met at the Central Park Precinct. We bonded immediately realizing we had this connection; we were veterans of two different wars. You being sergeant in the air force, an air traffic controller/combat controller deployed in the Persian Gulf War, Operation Desert Storm, where you sustained a knee injury in the very first Scud missile attack there. I believe the reason we gravitated to one another is that you and your wife have three children, two girls and a boy, all who were born in the month of September around the same time as my daughter, Noelle. To me, that's quite a beautiful, surprising coincidence.

No matter what happens, or how bad it seems today,
Life does go on, and it will be better tomorrow.
—Maya Angelou

Trust me. I know!

PREFACE

IT WAS SOMEWHERE around 1530 (that's military time for three thirty in the afternoon) on Monday, July 6, 1970, when I boarded a plane to go home from Vietnam, a place that was way hotter than hell. I had requested a window seat over the wing to make sure I was able to see that I was indeed flying out of hell. I also wanted to be able to feel and hear the landing gear being retracted, my only reassurance we had left the tarmac and were in the air.

I decided to wait a minute or two before I gazed out my window. The only thing I wanted to see was the vast, blue South China Sea. Seeing that, I kicked off my shoes and stretched my legs out under the empty seat in front of me. I pushed the button on my armrest to decline my seat making myself completely comfortable. That was when I took my long-awaited sigh of relief knowing I was no longer in Vietnam.

For the past three months, I'd been in a place I wanted to forget, but because of what I had surrounding me, the incredible, beautiful beach I'd had for my backyard would have a way of making me remember it. I'd been at a small base camp two miles south of the DMZ, ATSB Clearwater, where on a clear day you could see the mountains of North Vietnam, which were too close for comfort.

I knew something else I'd have loved to forget, but due to the nature of what took place, I'm doubting it very much; it had been the last night I spent in Vietnam. It had an uncanny way of making me remember it. I'd been deep asleep and had been suddenly awakened by this strange tapping on my forehead. I practically jumped out of my boots when

I opened my eyes and saw the muzzle of a .45 caliber resting on my forehead.

It was in the hand of my commanding officer, a young lieutenant I admired very much. I watched him slowly lower his weapon to my chest with a big smile on his face. He tapped a piece of paper he had placed there and leaned in. He whispered unforgettable words: "Ski, you're finally going home. Your fuckin' orders just arrived!"

I thought he was joking, but when I read that piece of paper, I knew he was telling me the truth. I think he was extremely relieved and happy to know I was leaving before things got worse than they had gotten two nights previously. No commanding officer wants to see any of his men who are about to go home get injured or killed. When he started hearing some of my buddies were starting to call me Charlie instead of Ski, he wanted me out of there a.s.a.p.

Three days earlier, we received word that a handful of enemy soldiers, VC or NVA, were lurking about a village not more than two hundred yards from us. We were told not to leave the camp for any reason until further notice. We were placed on high alert. Our well-made, medieval alarm system around our camp's perimeter may be the reason I'm writing this.

It consisted of razor-sharp barbed wire that was littered with hundreds and hundreds of empty beer cans with the tabs inside. We had this daily ritual of breaking off the tabs of the beer cans and dropping them in before we chugged them down and hoped that we would not swallow the tab. We'd then carefully put the can on the wire. You'd be amazed at the noise that little tab could do inside that can—it gave off a tinkling sound at the slightest movement that would let us know we had a visitor—animal or human—trying to get in. When we'd hear the beer cans tinkling, all hell would break loose because we'd answer with rounds from our M-16s.

Well, two nights earlier, the enemy wasn't too smart about our beer-can habit and tried to get past or go under the wire to sneak into our camp. Luckily, the five guys who were standing watch that night along that stretch of the perimeter were totally tuned in to the slightest tinkling and let loose a barrage of gunfire in the direction of the sound. Three of the enemy—I think they were VC—were killed, two going under the wire and the third going over the wire. Thank God we all did some serious beer drinking up there.

Anyway, getting word I was about to leave this godforsaken place four days' shy of my three hundred and sixty-five day deployment in-country was okay in my book! I'd knocked on heaven's door way too many times there since I had arrived, and I wasn't planning on visiting heaven, since I was only twenty-two and knew my journey on earth was about to begin a whole new life as soon as I got out of that fucking place.

Some forty-odd years later, I came across an unusual quote in a book I was reading at the time. I had placed some twenty or so pages of notes I had made to talk about in this book. I took this quote as another surprising coincidence in my life for it was closely related and very much connected to the way my life had been ever since I was five. "Life is not a journey with the intention of arriving safely in a pretty well-preserved body, but rather skid in broadside, thoroughly used up, totally worn out and loudly proclaiming, Wow! What a ride!" That's exactly how I felt the day I left Vietnam. Eric Blehm wrote it in *Fearless*, a true story about the life of the young man Adam Brown, who had persevered through so much despair in his life.

He had joined the navy, became one of the elite SEALs, and went on numerous missions in Afghanistan. He was always in danger, but he learned how to persevere through it all and do what was required. On his return home, he told Eric about this surprising quote he had come across in Afghanistan. He said it had been spray painted on a piece of plywood that someone had mixed in among several other words of wisdom and other graffiti on an abandoned building in a devastated area of war-torn Afghanistan.

I'm sure that when he came across that quote, it must have swept him off his feet as it had me. When I was flying over the South China Sea, I'm pretty sure I had similar words going through my head having taken ride after ride in 'Nam. I had two or three such wild rides prior to going to 'Nam and so many more when I returned home. I can recall all my near-death experiences going back to when I was five, and I consider myself extremely lucky to have survived each and every one of them. I started to convince myself that it was either not my time to go or maybe something else had kept me here. That's why I mentioned my guardian angel and the wonderful angels who have been with me since day one in my Dedication.

I honestly feel deeply blessed; I think God has a purpose for me being here—to do a special chore for him. I no longer call these events near-death experiences; I call them simply events. Besides these events, I've had what I call experiences that left me feeling deeply blessed. These are surprising coincidences that happen about once a week and sometimes as frequently as three or four a week. I had eight or nine all in one day for whatever reason. I pray to God that they never stop.

This all started in 2001 on a day when I believe my life had changed where God may had a hand in it only because of the surprising coincidences I've had that day were so powerful enough to take my breath away and give me an incredible feeling. It started in my heart, I mean my new wild heart that I now have and enjoy immensely even with the number of problems I've had with my heart.

We've all heard, "Things happen for a reason" and "Be careful what you wish for." Those sayings aligned themselves with one of Mark Twain's quotes: "There are two important days in your life. The day you were born and the day you found out why." That hit me like a lead balloon. I've said it so many times to so many people over the years where I truly believe I found the answer to my, why, and that is....I'm here to write this book!

CHAPTER 1

W HEN I WAS sixteen, I gave a special homage to God one Sunday mass by kneeling at the altar and saying a prayer directly to him. I wanted to say thank you to him before mass started. After mass, I went to the statue of the Blessed Virgin Mary and lit a candle. I said thanks to her by saying two Hail Marys. I asked her to give thanks to my guardian angel for doing a great job on being there for me when I needed him.

I may have had some extra help besides my guardian angel from one or two other angels who were also there with me when this other event occurred in my life. Apparently, I had made an unannounced visit to Davey Jones's locker in the depths of the Atlantic at Jones Beach, one of my favorite beaches in the world; it's on the south shore of Long Island, where I reside. This happened late one Tuesday afternoon, July 2, 1963, where I went through the three initial stages of drowning. I had taken in large amounts of water (and not because I was thirsty), I was below the surface way too long, and I could no longer hold my breath. I panicked.

I had no idea I had reached the final stage until I was dragged on shore by a lifeguard where two of them began working to get the water out of my lungs (from the ocean that I love so much). What I found amusing about this event is that I believe I saw a video of my life play out but never saw the credits and that my brother Michael and our best friend and neighbor, Bob Pagano, were only ten to fifteen feet away from me where they thought I was still clowning around.

We had gone to the beach that day with our junior high math teacher, Mr. Lester Walsh, who was our neighbor. That day, the sand was so hot that you couldn't walk on it barefoot; you had to run as fast as you could to get into the water. The three of us, still wearing our sneakers, began tossing a football around to where I stopped to get a can of soda from a cooler and eat the tuna fish sandwich my mom had made along with a bag of chips. I saw Mike and Bob talking to three girls frolicking in the surf. I yelled to them, "How about taking a slow jog along the shore?" They weren't interested so naturally I said, I'm going, and I took off zigzagging through the people on the shore showing off, and I started jogging backward and laughing my ass off.

Every so often, I'd dive into a wave breaking close to shore and then continue running. I was a weekend warrior back then doing all sorts of crazy things on the beach I wouldn't be able to do back home. The heat never bothered me; I actually loved it when it got hot and I was at the beach. Any sport gave me a high in many ways, and that included running on the shore. I had an unusual affinity for the ocean that I believe started the day I was born (more about that later).

When I got back, Mike and Bob were still talking with the girls, so I ran up to our blankets to grab something else to eat. I ate a banana, chugged another can of soda, and let out a loud belch, interrupting Mr. Walsh's reading. I shouted out, "Excuse me!" and took off back toward the shore. Mike and Bob were frolicking in the surf with the girls; I asked them, "Anyone feel like racing to that red flag up at the next beach?" It was a good two hundred yards away. "The last one there treats everyone here to an ice cream."

They all said okay. I told the girls they couldn't take off if they lost; I told them we all played by the same rules. We got into line, and I yelled, "Go!" I took off like a bat out of hell leaving everyone behind me. I could hear Mike and Bob gaining on me as their feet smacked the shore. One of the girls was also catching up. I yelled, "I'm becoming, Flash! See yas!"

I ran as fast as I could. I was gone in a heartbeat. I touched the flag first, dropped to my knees, and rolled down the sloped shore toward the water. I let the waves lap over me. I got up and ran back in a high-kicking jog to show off. I shouted at them, "I'm going to go body surfing after I eat lunch!"

I saw Mike and Bob come running back toward the blankets. I ate two baloney sandwiches and another bag of chips and chugged two more cans of cold soda. Mr. Walsh gave me this weird look. "Charlie, take it easy with all that food and soda you're been drinking. Don't overdo it by going back in the water so soon!"

"Mathematically speaking, Mr. Walsh," I said, "By eating and drinking what I brought, I'll have less weight to carry back to the car!" I smiled and finished my sandwich and the crumbs of the potato chips in the bag and chugged the rest of my soda.

Mike and Bob showed up ten minutes later; the girls and I were body surfing. I started diving underwater for about twenty seconds, coming up, and going into my craziness acting as if I were a fish out of water. I had plenty of energy. I did some handstands in the waist-deep water; I'd take in a mouthful of water, come up, and spit it at the others. I was in heaven.

The waves were getting a little higher. I rode them in on a slant as if I were my own surfboard. I was a big surfing fanatic and into body surfing; I rode as many waves as I could. Mike and Bob were standing with the girls in the surf. I'd pop up out of the water between them like a striped bass trying to break free of a hook. I was trying to impress them. Mike and Bob were climbing onto one another's shoulders and doing front or backflips into the surf where they began to impress the girls. I asked Mike to let me stand on his shoulders and do a forward flip into the next wave that came our way.

I saw the biggest one I'd seen all day. I waited for the right moment to dive smack into it. I wanted to roll over and kick off from the ocean floor and shoot up like a Trident missile, but I got a sudden, major muscle cramp in my stomach. My legs got charley horses; I couldn't kick them. I was struggling to get to the surface. The pain was so great that I opened my mouth to scream and took in a wholesome mouthful of the ocean. That was stage one. Somehow, I was able to get one good push off the ocean floor and started swimming to the surface. I quickly took in a mouthful of air and started to flail my arms hoping it would get the attention of Mike and Bob, who were looking right at me.

They thought I was still doing my crazy antics and started to laugh. I tried to yell to them that I needed help, but I was smacked by a wave and took in more water. Down I went. I tried to keep my legs straight to be ready to kick off the bottom, but I was hit with more muscle cramps and spasms in my stomach and legs.

I thought about swimming underwater to Mike and Bob, but my pain wouldn't let me. I couldn't kick. I was getting nowhere. I needed air. I was hoping I wouldn't go down again. I was hoping Mike and Bob could see I was no longer joking around. I was out of strength; I didn't think I could even flail my arms if I surfaced. While all this was going on, miraculously, a very observant lifeguard must have seen me doing something that didn't look right to him. I must have given him the impression that I was completing stage two of drowning and about to go into stage three.

I had my last good look at the wonderful world and slowly sank into Davey Jones's locker. Thank God, the lifeguard must have jumped off his perch and ran as fast as he could into the surf, heading in the direction to where he saw me go under. I guess he was right on the money. He found me on the bottom, brought me to the surface, and took me to shore where another lifeguard was waiting. They dragged me onshore. The other lifeguard was trying to get the water out of my lungs. It must have taken a while before I began to throw up the ocean and came back to the life I loved.

"Take it easy. Relax. Breathe," the lifeguard said. I tried to explain to him what had happened, but he said, "Don't worry about it. You're okay now!" The only thing I had to worry about was the fact that my jammies, a long bathing suit surfers wore, had ended up halfway down my ass and I was showing the people who had gathered to gawk what I had "cracked" up to be.

I had no idea that Mike and Bob had no idea where I had gone until they saw the commotion onshore. When they ran up and saw me coughing up water and half my ass showing, they pretended they didn't know me. They raced to tell Mr. Walsh what they had seen. The two lifeguards helped me sit up. I pulled my suit up to where it should have been. I wished I had had a towel to bury my embarrassed face in.

I saw Mr. Walsh heading toward me with Mike and Bob trailing behind. I became a little nervous seeing how much Mr. Walsh was already shaken up knowing what had probably happened to me. I quickly asked him for his shirt. He took it off and handed to me. I got up and thanked the two lifeguards for saving my life. I put the shirt over my head and started to walk to the blanket. I lay down. I put the T-shirt across the back of my jammies so my butt wouldn't be recognizable as the one that had shown up onshore.

I told Mr. Walsh I wanted to leave. He agreed. We collected our things and headed to the car. No one spoke until we left the parking lot. I told them what had happened and left it at that. I told myself I was never going back to that section of the beach and was never going to joke around in the ocean again. I'd learned my lesson the hard way.

After that, I'd wait a good while after eating before going back into the water. I've stuck to it ever since that day. This was my second near-death experience, eleven years after the one I had at five years old which I'll be telling you about later.

I believe I deserve to shout out something so much more deserving than "Wow! What a ride!" when I have my last event in my life. Maybe it will be "Oh shit!" or "What the fuck?" that will have me laughing my ass off whether I'm in pain or not before I take my final breath and leave. Don't you agree it should be somewhat colossal and outrageous?

CHAPTER 2

W ITH ALL MY experiences of having 'knocked on Heaven's door', I believe a portion of my dash was taken up where I could have been doing something much more enjoyable. The dash I'm talking about is that short line between someone's year of birth and year of death on a tombstone. That little dash represents your whole life, and for me, all the times skidding in sideways and used up.

But every time, I was able to find a way to carry on. My journey has been somewhat extraordinary. I'm not sure if I was getting good mileage with the way the price of gasoline has been whether I used regular or premium. It's beyond me that I must have stopped at least a hundred times and asked myself, *What if I had gone right instead of left? Or up instead of down? Or back instead of forward? What if I had said yes instead of no?* I'd wonder if things would have been different.

But I know my life was changed forever on that day in 2001, the same day when I had my first amazing, unbelievable, and surprising coincidence. Since that day, I've had so many other surprising coincidences occur especially in September, where on two consecutive weekends I had so many surprising coincidences on a Saturday morning and an unbelievable and powerful occurrence take place on the following Sunday morning.

I felt like I had another blessing in my life where God had personally had a hand on both days because of the way they had occurred. Something was definitely around me, a presence that gave me this amazing and powerful feeling. I even wrote a simple short story about it. Somehow, that story became this book. The way it came about is amusing, and I'll get to that, but I have something much more important to tell you.

Before I take you on the amazing journey through my life, pretend you're sitting next to me on a bright shiny, mystical metal and wood, kiddy roller-coaster (similar to what I tried to draw for my book cover). Before I tell you some pretty interesting rides I've taken, I will tell you about my childhood and teen years. I also have a few things to tell you about my time in the navy and in the business world, including some surprising coincidences that will explain this book's title. It took me five minutes to come up with it and about five years to write everything I wanted to say in this book, bouncing from past to present, over and over again, and wanting a book cover and a back cover to be symbolic of my two fears in my life which I'm sure you'll find quite intriguing.

I take credit for my photo on the back cover. I've been told by some of my closest friends that I look fuckin' great knowing what I went through the past few years. I think the photo makes me look mysterious and captivating; maybe I should have been in a James Bond film. I'll bet all the loose change in the bottom of my wife's purse that people will buy my book just for the photo that they'll have framed so people will ask them, "Who's the good-looking guy in your family?"

Enough about my photo. Let me get back to something more stunning, like my book. Ripley's Believe It or Not Museum in New York (I've been there twice) has a vast amount of strange artifacts, oddities, and amazing photos. Numerous people had questioned Ripley on the authenticity of his stuff. He proclaimed that every one of his articles had some kind of historical interest. What I'll be relating in this book won't even come close to what Ripley had in his museum, but it does have lots and lots of historical interest and plenty of hysterical interest too.

Let's get this show on the road. Hang on. You're in for one hell of an interesting 'ride'.

CHAPTER 3

D ID YOU EVER get in the habit of adding a quip on to whatever you've just said? I did that with the phrase "and never the twain shall meet." I ended up saying it so many times for two whole weeks; I somehow ended up by changing it to "unless it's Shania Twain herself" just to humor myself.

I started saying the earlier version two weeks after I witnessed the unthinkable. I was standing directly across the street from the North Tower on the morning of September 11, 2001. What made me come out and rattle off that ridiculous saying God only knows, but I began saying my newer version the day I stepped foot on the hallowed ground of the devastated site of the World Trade Center. It was being referred to as Ground Zero. I think my new version of that quip came about as I was overseeing the unimaginable recovery/cleanup operations in the aftermath of 9/11.

What I witnessed that fateful morning was worse than what I had seen and experienced in Vietnam. I'd survived another devastating event in life; it's gripped my heart so much that I find it hard to talk about. Whenever I met a family member of a lost loved one, my feelings tore me up. I didn't sustain any injury when I went running for my life when the South Tower started to collapse just as I had run for cover in 'Nam so many times from rocket attacks.

It wasn't until early 2003 that I realized I had been injured by the attack. I had worked for 2,274 hours at Ground Zero and had inhaled and absorbed toxins that caused me major health problems. I began to feel like shit. I still had drive; I wanted to carry on with my life the best

I could and hoped I wouldn't lose my incorrigible sense of humor. I've been told numerous times that I have a gift for making others laugh, that I have extraordinary wit, which is much better than incorrigible humor. I'm gonna flaunt it in this book whether you like it or not. I've become completely comfortable in making fun of all the events in my life that I have survived including all my close calls in 'Nam. I'll be sharing some of this with you later on. Other vets have written about their miserable experiences in 'Nam, but I'm not taking that route in my book. My journey through life could have ended any number of times. Maybe I have super powers; I'm still here.

But back to my quip about never the twain shall meet and Shania Twain, one hell of a good-looking woman I hope to meet one day. If so, I would love to ask her what it was like being related to Mark Twain until I found out that Mark Twain's real name was Samuel Clemens, who probably couldn't hold any kind of musical note whatsoever. And I found out Shania's real name is Eileen Regina Edwards. I've been admiring two well-known people in my life for quite some time and they end up being completely other people. I sure hope that Ripley is the real name of the museum owner.

Speaking of quotes, I came across another that struck a major chord in me (which is not as painful as a lead balloon): "If there's a book you really want to read but it hasn't been written, go ahead and write it." Reading that was one of my surprising coincidence because when I did, I was in the early stages of writing this book. I think I was meant to see that quote. I was on a bus going to work. I took a seat in the back of the bus that happened to have a newspaper sitting on it. It was opened to the page I normally went to first in that paper. Someone had started the crossword puzzle. I looked at the Jumble word puzzle, the sudoku, the horoscopes, and my favorite, the Quote of the Day.

That day's quote was staring right at me; I read it repeatedly just to make sure my eyes weren't playing tricks on me. I was at a loss for words. I just stared out the grimy window. I wondered what the odds were of my reading that quote that day. It brought on a truly beautiful vision. I squinted my eyes to focus on the words. They were connected to an author on the *New York Times* best-seller list who was being quoted. Yeah, I know. That's one hell of a vision to have of myself especially when the woman who was standing in front of me on the bus had no idea her shoulder bag kept rapping my head every time the driver tapped the brakes.

I was a little pissed off not at the woman but for not being able to see who the author was of this wonderful quote. Someone had stuck a wad of grape chewing gum right over the author's name, and the gum looked still sticky. Whoever that author is deserves a handshake and a thank you from me. He or she made my day by giving me another surprising coincidence.

I got off the bus and got onto my train. I was lucky enough to get a seat. I found myself paying attention to the number of times the train was stopping at stations. That got me thinking about the number of times I had stopped writing my book and the number of people who had come and gone in my life whom I wanted to mention in it. I'm sure some of them will be totally surprised and amused to find themselves in these pages. Who knows? Maybe you'll come across your name or that of someone you know. If you do, call me. We could do lunch. My number will be noted somewhere later on in the book, but please try not to schedule lunch with me on the second and third Thursdays of the month. I play mah-jongg both days from 11:00 a.m. to 4:00 p.m., and yes, I'm extremely good at that game.

CHAPTER 4

I'D NEVER THOUGHT I'd write a book about my life or anything else. I wrote that short story, about a dozen or so pages. It had a powerful message, it was inspirational, and it had a classic, humorous anecdote at the end, but it went nowhere. I felt so closely connected to what had occurred to me on those two consecutive weekends in September 2008 that I felt I needed to write down what had taken place both days. I experienced an amazing number of surprising coincidences at a friend's cozy beach house that I'd stay at in September. I called the place my little piece of paradise though it wasn't mine. It's eight miles off the coast of New Jersey on Long Beach Island.

The surprising coincidences that occurred to me that morning came about with a woman who I have seen from time to time since I'd been going to the island. She and her family owned a huge beach house next door. We happened to meet that Saturday morning instead of just waving to each other across the yards. What happened to me the following Sunday morning when I experienced a very unusual occurrence was on a beach on Long Island. I believe the two of them are so closely connected because of an incredible and unbelievable feeling they gave me. I believe the man upstairs had gotten involved in them. I felt deeply blessed just like the day I was born.

Allow me to explain. I was born on Monday evening, December 8, 1947, one of the holiest days in the Catholic religion besides Christmas and Easter. It's the Feast of the Immaculate Conception of the Blessed Virgin Mary. I believe she took a minute from her busy schedule to bless me as I entered this glorious world of ours somewhere around suppertime (not mine but my mom's) in the San Diego Naval Hospital.

In parochial school, the nuns and priests would take me aside every so often and ask, "Charles, did you know you're a very special child being born on December 8? You've been blessed by the mother of Jesus on the day we honor her." I had no idea how they meant that, but their comment made me think I might be a little luckier than all my classmates. At times, if I was told the same thing by a new nun or priest at the school, I would make a quick stop in the boys' room to see if I had a halo. I thought only the mother superior or the monsignor had the gift of seeing it. I wonder if that was the reason I was given the lead part in the class Christmas play and was asked to lead the procession down the church aisle for my first Holy Communion and Confirmation.

I still have that photo my dad took of me having to wear a shiny white suit with a huge, shiny, white bow tie under my chin for my first Holy Communion. Dad had put some beer on my head to keep my cowlick down so I wouldn't look like Alfalfa of the Our Gang comedies going down the aisle. I have to laugh every time I think of having all that beer in my hair and having to carry a lit candle as I led the procession. I believe the vapors from my hair mixed with the smoke coming off the candle had a huge effect on me because I passed out when I reached the altar right in front of the monsignor and the mother superior. The congregation yelled and gasped as I was going down. This may be the reason why I never had the urge to smoke, to become a priest, or to drink beer that has a lot of head.

Years later, my mom told me the ushers who were tending to me thought I'd been drinking. The nun I had that year, Sister Lucy, repeatedly asked me over the next two weeks if my dad had given me something to drink that day. All I could do was to tell her the God's honest truth: "No, only a glass of milk, and it wasn't that cold. I don't like drinking warm milk!" To this day, I don't like warm milk or warm beer.

I believe I was blessed one other time when I had my first job after graduating high school. I went to work for a well-known famous architect Wallace K. Harrison. He and his partner, Max Abramowitz, had a large architectural firm on the fifth floor of the International Building, 630 Fifth Avenue in Rockefeller Center. Mr. Harrison's and

Mr. Abramowitz's offices overlooked Fifth Avenue and had huge garden terraces. The remainder of the office for all the architects, designers, and draftsmen extended across the floor all the way toward the other end of the building that overlooked Sixth Avenue.

On the Monday morning of October 4, 1965, when I came to work, I was summoned to Mr. Harrison's office by his secretary. When I arrived, I was told to step out onto the terrace where I could see Mr. Harrison pacing back and forth and stopping to look out past these huge planters. It looked as if he were waiting to tell me something important. I had no idea why I had been summoned. I walked onto the terrace through a glass door. "Hello, Charlie!" he said when he spotted me. "Good morning Mr. Harrison." He waved me over. "Charlie, how would you like to share a moment with me today and be a part of New York City history?"

"Okay!" I said. I mean, he was my boss.

I went over to where he was leaning slightly over the parapet and looking across Fifth Avenue. We saw a huge crowd on the steps of St. Patrick's Cathedral and along the sidewalk. We saw some TV vans and crews with cameras. A large contingent of New York City police cars were parking on Fifth Avenue in front of the cathedral. The officers came out of their cars and went heading up the steps toward the front doors and spreading themselves out among the crowd. I figured they were waiting for whoever was to step foot out of the cathedral. Mr. Harrison's secretary called me over and gave me a Kodak camera. She told me, "Take as many photos as you want. Mr. Harrison says it's yours to keep!"

The second I got back to where Mr. Harrison was, he said, "Looks as if he's about to make his presence known!" We saw the two huge main doors open. Four people came walking out. Mr. Harrison and I laid eyes on Pope Paul VI. He waved to the crowd in short gestures that looked like he was making the sign of the cross for everyone in front of him. He had a warm, pleasing smile. I couldn't believe I was seeing the pope.

I took three pictures of him—one making the sign of the cross to his left, another one doing the same out in front, and the third toward his right. He looked up at the buildings to the right and left of him; people were yelling out the windows, "Your Holiness, up here!" or "Pope Paul, we love you!" to get his attention and hopefully a papal blessing. I put my camera in my left and was ready to make the sign of the cross with my right if he looked our way. When he did, I was about to yell out "Hi, your Holiness!" but I decided not to. I snapped a picture, the best one I could take. It was deeply moving to witness the historical event and know I had been blessed by him. His presence made my day.

I took one more picture as he blessed others. Mr. Harrison asked if I had taken enough pictures of this unbelievable moment. I gave him a hearty handshake and a smile and said, "I thank you from the bottom of my heart for letting me be here with you for this special moment. I feel doubly blessed today!"

What are the odds of having to stand next to a world-famous architect in a very famous building on Fifth Avenue and be blessed by a famous, well-respected world leader, his holiness the pope? I leaned over and saw the world resting on the shoulders of Charlie Atlas, a huge bronze statue in front of the building. I was a part of history in the greatest city in the world, New York.

On my way home that evening, I was still thinking about what had occurred that day and wondering if my life warranty had been reinstated for another fifty years or five hundred thousand miles, whichever came first. That once-in-a-lifetime opportunity was one amazing, unbelievable, surprising coincidence in my life. Whenever I see or hear anything about whoever is the pope, I always think back to that day. Maybe one reason I'm still here is due to such blessings and having one hell of a guardian angel and maybe a few more at my side. I thank God for his kind generosity.

CHAPTER 5

T HE DAY I finished writing my short story about what had occurred those two weekends in September 2008, I was all set to send it off to *Reader's Digest*, a magazine that has been a part of my life since I was seventeen. I had read practically every issue without fail and religiously every month up until I arrived in Vietnam in July of '69.

My dad handed me a copy of the magazine and said, "I think you should take a look at two stories in this magazine. I folded the corners of the pages they start at. I'd like to know what your thoughts are about each one for they remind me of what you've gone through the past two years."

Both stories related to me—one to my near-drowning experience and the other regarding a major operation a young girl had gone through that was similar to an operation I had had when I was seventeen. I had a huge goiter on my thyroid and had been given a radioisotope pill to get rid of it. It did get rid of it, but it came back two months later and was bigger than the first time. I was told I'd need surgery to remove it. My surgeon explained he'd have to make a long incision in my neck to remove it completely. He said the operation would take about two to three hours. I wasn't looking forward to it one bit, but it had to done.

There were some tense moments during the operation not for me but for my parents because of what took place during my surgery. There was a very serious car accident about half a mile from the hospital; three people were brought in with life-threating injuries. The entire blood supply of O negative was used up on them, and that was my blood type.

My parents had to wait to have more blood be delivered from nearby hospitals.

My operation took close to five hours. I apologize for saying this to anyone who might be reading this who was involved in my operation because I believe a slight mistake was made during my surgery. They had to move or slightly relocate my left phrenic nerve to remove the goiter. In 2014, I learned that it was over my heart and was severely damaged probably from all the hard blows I'd taken to my chest in Vietnam and then being involved in three major car accidents where I was slammed into the steering wheel. I had serious breathing problems due to what I had inhaled at Ground Zero. I had fluoroscopy imaging done on my lungs. That was when I learned that my left phrenic nerve was directly over my heart and severely damaged and my left diaphragm was totally paralyzed.

Let's get back to the *Reader's Digest* stories. They were moving and inspirational, but I also enjoyed the funny stories in each issue. Knowing the kinds of stories I'd been reading over the years in the magazine got me thinking my short story, which was also moving and inspirational as well as humorous, would be attractive for the magazine. I envisioned my story captivating all who read it. I had found it easy to write about what I had experienced on Saturday morning, but writing about what had happened on that Sunday morning hadn't been easy. I had seven witnesses to what had happened on Saturday, none on Sunday except the *man* upstairs where I'd gotten a lump in my throat when I wrote about it.

I think about both days because I don't know why I had had those experiences and probably never will. They had swept me off my feet. The more I thought about what had occurred to me on those days, the more I kept telling myself that it would make one hell of an inspirational story. I still wasn't sure that God had not had a hand in it because it occurred in September, and I've had quite a few things occur in my life in September more than any other month. The top of the list was my surviving the September 11, 2001 terrorist attacks (more on that later). I think my heart was trying to tell me there was something missing from my story. I had to speak to a very close, dear friend of mine, Janice Cilento, to have her honest opinion on what I had written.

It just so happened that Janice and her husband, Larry, were there

18

on that Saturday in 2008 after everything had already occurred. I mentioned to her later that evening what had taken place before she arrived and how much it had affected me. She didn't know, however, what had happened the following Sunday morning. I called her at work and asked her if she could meet me for about thirty minutes. She agreed.

On the day I went to meet her, I saw her stepping outside her building for a smoke. I called out her name, gave her a wave, walked up, and gave her a quick kiss on the cheek. I told her I needed her complete attention. I could tell by her look that she was interested. I told her I'd written about my experiences on that Saturday I had told her about and my experiences on the next day. I said I wanted her opinion before I mailed it off to *Reader's Digest*. She caught me off guard. She started blasting me with some very vile comments (only joking, Janice—they weren't vile) accompanied by cigarette smoke.

"Are you fucking kidding me?" she asked, sounding really pissed.

"What are you mad about?" I asked.

"I'm not mad! But did you just hear yourself?" She looked at me as if I had two heads. She started giving me some motherly advice even though I thought I was two years older than her. I listened to her every word and coughed and choked on every other word; I was getting both barrels from her—smoke, that is, which was coming out of her nostrils. I tried to calm her down before I called a cop on her for assaulting me with tar and nicotine. I told her I'd finished my story.

"Oh no you're not finished! You're not doing anything of the sort until you go back and mention some of the things you've told me!" She was alluding to the fact I had failed to mention some very important information she knew about me.

"Janice, I wrote only about what had occurred on Saturday and Sunday morning, nothing else!"

She gave me another odd look. I think she went slightly cross-eyed, but that could have been her cigarette smoke affecting my vision. "Charlie, what about how much 9/11 and what you saw at Ground Zero has affected you? What about all the other surprising coincidences you had? What about all the designs you submitted for the various 9/11 competitions? Did you happen to mention anything about the time you spent in and around the WTC long before 9/11 or when you were there for the first terrorist attack? That would make your story that much more interesting and inspirational!"

She stopped to take a breather, though how anyone can take a breather by taking a long drag on a cigarette is a mystery to me. "Wait a minute! Oh my God, tell me you mentioned you were in Vietnam!"

I got another good dose of her cigarette smoke. She chucked the butt into the street and spoke in a calm, sympathetic voice. "Charlie, did you mention you're having to deal with all these numerous health ailments affecting you especially your breathing from being at Ground Zero?" I told her no, but I knew she was right that I should have. But hell, it had taken me fifteen to twenty pages just to write my short story on what had taken place on those two days, and she wanted me to write about all those other things that had occurred in my life. That, I was sure, would take a whole book. I wasn't sure I had the time for that. But I told her I'd think about it. She gave me a kiss on the cheek. I thanked her for hearing me out. She always found ways to hear what I had to say when it was something as important as that.

As I headed home, I tried to think of ways to rewrite my story and include the things Janice had pointed out. I figured that would take another ten, fifteen pages. My subway car was rocking side to side, and my brain was doing the same. I was seeing my short story going up in smoke, but that might have been just the remnants of Janice's smoke clogging my brain and escaping out my tear ducts. I closed my eyes, took a deep sigh, and tried to think of another way of doing this. I got this strange vision of an amazing book that included everything Janice said I should mention. It seemed it would end up over five hundred pages. But what I couldn't see was its title.

The next thing I saw was me holding my book in the air in a bookstore trying to explain to a crowd all the events that had happened to me. Hell, I even saw someone have the audacity to ask, "Why the fuck are you still here? What makes you so special? Are you from some other world?" I saw myself standing there lost for words. The vision ended when my train ride did. I had to transfer to a bus. I had a lot of thinking to do.

CHAPTER 6

MY ANGELS HAVE been with me ever since I was five years old. I don't know if there's a law that says we get to knock on heaven's door more than twenty times, but I must have been very good to have gotten that many chances. I think my wonderful angels have done me many favors. I only wish my wonderful angels would install a doorbell on heaven's door to spare my knuckles, which could use a break.

I did some heavy knocking during the summer of '69. It started on July 10 that year and ended on July 6 the following year—twelve long months all filled with mini-events. They all occurred in a place I didn't want to be in. I was extremely lucky to have received some good advice even before I got there. This advice was strictly about survival, and I was coached on the matter by a former navy instructor I've known for most of my life. He patiently taught me how to develop a survival mentality that would see me through my time in 'Nam.

He told me to make the word *survive* my closest, best friend over there. He said that would eventually give me a different outlook on life, one I wanted to have when I came home. He said that if I didn't take his words of wisdom to heart, I might not come home. He knew what he was talking about. He'd been involved in the landing on Omaha Beach in World War II. His life-saving advice was probably the best advice any father could give his son before going off to war.

I also received training four weeks before I went to 'Nam from a few more navy instructors who taught me about survival in a much different way. I can honestly say their training probably saved my ass.

Now if you're thinking, *Oh no! Here we go—another 'Nam vet wants*

to share his miseries about what he went through, surprise, surprise—
you're totally fucking mistaken! I won't be doing any of that, but I
will tell you a few things I did over there and possibly give you a brief
account of one or two of my mini-events. I'm sorry, but that was an
unimaginable time in my life; I was twenty-one then. You will never
understand what I'm talking about unless you were in my shoes. I came
home from 'Nam with a new attitude about life; I wanted to enjoy the
rest of my life and have a comfortable lifestyle and a good-paying job
doing something I loved doing. I didn't want any major heartaches or
injuries physical or mental. But I must have forgotten that life is full of
surprises—good and bad.

I had two surprises back to back within a month of each other. Two
of them sent me to the same hospital leaving me asking myself, *Why am
I still here?* For some reason, I've never gotten a clue, so I accepted that
I must be one lucky son of a bitch.

When I got home after each one of these events still in some pain, I
looked in the mirror and said, "Been there, done that and knocked on
heaven's door. Thanks, God, for not answering. I'll let you know when
I'm ready." I'd step aside right then in case lightning struck where I'd
been standing.

CHAPTER 7

W HEN I WAS growing up, I wanted to proclaim to the world that I was Superman, but I decided not to. Instead, I gave some pretty good performances to my friends of my super powers by reading all the Action comics I could get my hands on.

Besides Superman, I had my dad, whom I totally looked up to for the reassurance I needed to do certain things. I was beginning to acquire one of Superman's powers—super vision but I never saw this coming, years later, when I was about to lose this huge collection of Action comics and baseball cards—mostly Dodgers and Yankees—from the late '50s and early '60s. You're not gonna believe this, but my mom accidently threw them out when she was cleaning the attic when I was in Vietnam. I had hidden them there so Michael, my younger brother, wouldn't trade them with our friends. I had put them between some of my mother's things I knew she wouldn't throw out. I simply wasn't there to tell her, "Oh, no! That's my stuff!"

I didn't get mad about an honest mistake. It wasn't until I came across a guy who was selling vintage baseball cards on Fifth Avenue and 42nd Street and I happened to see some cards similar to ones I'd had that were worth big bucks. I never told my mom about what she had done; I didn't want to hurt her feelings after seeing how happy she was that I had gotten home to her from Vietnam as I had promised her I would.

Let me get back to my hero. I started thinking Superman was a real person. I saw him on TV. I learned it was the actor George Reeves who played him and would stand there with his cape blowing in the wind. Pound for pound, inch for inch, strength for strength, there was

Superman looking at me. I was convinced he was as real as me except when he dressed up in a suit and tie and wore those heavy, black-framed glasses as Clark Kent. I'd wonder if his cape would get stuck in the crack in his ass when he wore that suit. I think that's a reason I never wanted a Superman costume. I hated getting wedgies. I'd definitely need super powers to get rid of them.

I honestly thought I had some of his super powers to the point I would even mimic getting weak if I saw anything that resembled kryptonite, I mean, any of a vast assortment of green objects. I'm dead serious about this, so don't laugh.

My mom took my two sisters, my brother, and me to the family doctor for our yearly check-ups. I told my mom the doctor had said I was a pretty special boy because I had 20/10 vision; I had read the bottom line of the eyechart without squinting. And I had extremely good hearing; I asked the doc if he had heard that fly sneeze in his office. Well, someone had sneezed, and it wasn't him or me. I was also told I had very good muscle tone for my age and compared to most boys my age. I did push-ups and sit-ups for the fun of it. That made me think I might be stronger than my friends. I never had to grunt or moan when we played tug-of-war or if I picked up something that was way heavier than me. I would give it my best shot without breaking a sweat

I had one super power that I had fun with. Once, I explained to Mr. Lester Walsh, the teacher who had taken us to Jones Beach on the day I almost drowned, why I hadn't finished my math homework for his junior-high class. The assignment carried a lot of weight that semester. He gave me an unbelievable expression when I finished with my tale that made me crack up laughing inside and brought tears to my eyes. I guess he and the class thought I was feeling sorry for myself. I was told to wait after class so he and I could have a one-on-one chat about my explanation. I felt I was actually being complimented for my reason.

He emphasized I was really good at math because I'd managed to squeeze ten pounds of bullshit into a five-pound bag. The way he said it made me think I was amazingly strong in other ways I didn't know about. I wish you could have been there to see his many facial expressions and hear his other verbal expressions. He told me the number of times he had seen me over the weekend playing football in the street with my friends; he lived right up the street from me. He reminded me of the number of times he'd blown his horn and waved at me. Bottom line, my neighborly math teacher gave me a C for my grade and an A+ for my explanation. I chuckle whenever I hear anyone refer to a bag of shit of any size.

Was I faster than a speeding bullet and able to leap tall buildings in a single bound? Maybe I could leap a trash can here or there when playing keep-away with my friends. Once when we were playing that game, I was having to run after one kid (whose name escapes me, but if he's reading this, he knows I'm talking about him) who had the ball that we wanted to drop into a basket to score—first team to get three points wins. He'd run up the street, and I'd jump over hedges and trash cans to get the ball back.

I was considered the fastest kid in the neighborhood. "You can catch him, Charlie!" was all I would hear from the other kids on both teams. He got a sizeable lead when I had to stop from being run over by a car. I called the driver a real jerk before I took off again. I leaped some puddles as I ran the fastest I had ever run. I was sure the soles of my shoes were starting to smolder. I could smell a faint but disgusting odor as I finally caught up with the kid and grabbed the ball from him. I started running but stopped after going only ten or twenty feet to check on the soles of my sneakers. They weren't smoking, but they looked as though I had stepped in dog shit. It was all over the bottom of my sneakers and up along the sides. It squished when I stepped.

I didn't want anyone to know what I had done and laugh at me. I yelled out something about a dentist's appointment. I ran home through front lawns rather than on the sidewalk. My mom was outside sweeping by the backdoor. She asked me why I was sweating so much. I told her I'd been playing keep-away. She looked at my sneakers and said, "You, mister, better keep away from coming any closer to this backdoor. Is that mud or doggie-do on your sneakers?" You know how moms get about tracking stuff into the house.

I wasn't allowed in until I could show her the sides and the bottoms of my sneakers were squeaky clean and smelled like roses. Nothing was ever mentioned about this. Good thing, because Michael would have blabbed it all over the neighborhood. But everyone knew I wouldn't take anyone's shit no way no how for no reason.

As I mentioned, anything green (except for lawns, trees, and bushes) would make me act as if I'd come in contact with kryptonite. This included green clothes and even furniture. I'd pretend it was having a major effect on me and fall to my knees, and that would crack up my friends to the point of tears. At meal time, I'd go for the corn, carrots, and potatoes and avoid any green vegetables. Eventually, my mom and dad got wind of my shenanigans from Michael, and they made it known that I'd be eating the same as everyone else at the table—no substitutions.

Today, I steer clear of corn and carrot dishes but I don't like baked potatoes because they're so fucking hot that I have to wait for them to cool off a bit. And I eat green vegetables except for asparagus, which I consider a sorry excuse for a vegetable even with hollandaise sauce. I need some answers here, folks! Why cover them up? Is there something about the weird look of the upper portion of the stalk that makes it tough to eat? Asparagus scares the hell out of me.

When it comes to things that scare the hell out of me, another one is roller-coasters—doesn't matter what kind, shape, speed, or thrill, I'm deathly afraid of all of them. Hell, there's no amount of money that would get me on one. Yes, I rode one when I was seven at an amusement park. It was lit up with flashing, colored lights, and I heard some strange music blasting out from somewhere that tried to be in sync with the lights but never seem to be able to. The cars looked like silver bullets. It was a Labor Day weekend, and school was starting the next Tuesday. My parents were treating us kids to a last hurrah of summer. We were told to make the best of it because there wouldn't be any playing outside after school during the week so that night we got to go on as many rides as we wanted.

When I saw the roller-coaster, I knew it was the ride for me. I wanted to 'fly through the air' like Superman. It was the ride of all rides, and I was excited. I saw the kids waiting for the man to lift the metal bars so they could get out after the ride. I figured that was to make sure they didn't fly out. The roller-coaster seemed to go faster each time it looped around.

I begged my dad to let me go on the ride, which I felt was calling out to me. I asked Michael and my sisters, Charnat and Marianne, to go on the ride with me. They initially agreed, but by the time it came our turn to get on, they had changed their minds. I told the operator I wanted to sit in the middle car. I sat, and he lowered the bar. I saw my brother and sisters were walking to a different ride. My dad yelled, "They changed their minds. They're going on a different ride. Stay on and enjoy it!"

I was the only youngster on the ride. The three cars in front of me and the two behind me were empty. I realized there would be no one yelling or laughing with me as I had seen the kids do on the ride before me. I wasn't sure I wanted to stay on. But it was too late. I felt a jerk. The cars started rolling forward. As we headed for our first climb, I got a vision of myself being on the ride and the bar going up. I saw myself flying out as if I were Superman in his cape and running head-on into the frame of the ride. I was sure I was knocked unconscious if not DOA.

Well, that vision did a number on my brain, which started telling me to get off as soon as I could. Look, didn't we all have wild imaginations growing up? Didn't some of you think there were monsters under your beds? I started screaming that I wanting off. I went into convulsions. I was crying uncontrollably. I think my mom spotted me. My screams must have sent chills up her spine. She must have alerted my dad, who was keeping an eye on my brother and sisters on a small Ferris Wheel. My dad made eye contact with me and came running over yelling at the operator to stop the ride. He ran up on the walkway alongside the cars and got me out before the ride even stopped. He tried to calm me down and console me as the operator was yelling at him that he shouldn't be up there. My dad kept asking me what was wrong. Nothing seemed to help. The damage had already done. I begged him to take me home.

We headed to where my mom was. I told my dad that I wanted to get as far away as possible from that horrible, mean ride! I'm sure he had no idea why I was so upset about a kiddie roller-coaster. My brother and sisters came off their ride and saw me still crying; they asked me what had happened, did I get hurt, did something hit me. They'd never seen me cry like that. There were so many tears running down my face and into my mouth that I began to form bubbles. Yuck. Can anyone tell me why God made tears so salty?

My mom and dad said we were leaving. My mom tried to console me, but her efforts went nowhere. My brother and sisters didn't say a word to me. When we finally got home, I ran to my room and dove under my blanket for safety. Michael came into our room and asked why I was crying so much. I didn't answer. I think I cried myself to sleep.

Ever since that day, I consider roller-coasters the work of the devil. I also developed a fear of heights I still have today. That was my one and only roller-coaster ride. And it will forever remain my one and only roller-coaster ride.

So now you know my two biggest fears—kryptonite and roller-coasters—and my attitude about asparagus. I did have a third fear—of tornados—when I saw four of them in person but from a good distance away. I was at the navy's Great Lakes Training Center outside Chicago for boot camp in May of 1967 when four tornadoes were reported a few miles away. We were ordered to go inside, take cover, and stay away from the windows. I guess I thought I still had some super powers in me. I got up on a bunk to take a look. The whole sky was a spectacular black. I must have unconsciously clicked my bare heels because I lost my footing when my drill instructor yelled, "Get down now!"

I fell to the floor and started laughing, but I quickly climbed up for one more look though I knew that I'd suffer the consequences. I wanted to see those four spiraling funnels once more. I watched them spin out of the area. They really didn't seem that bad to me because they somewhat reminded me of myself. They had minds of their own; they went and did whatever they wanted wherever they wanted. Havoc always seemed to have a way of finding me and spiraling in and out of my life.

Chapter 8

I DON'T WANT another "event" to occur in my life because I have a strange feeling it might be my last. I'm not saying I will have another one; it's just that I don't think this body of mine would be able to stand it. My journey on this wonderful planet is slowly winding down. I'm at the point that I want to buy a comfortable rocking chair and rock any stress right out of me. The only stress I want to deal with is trying to open those small packets of soy sauce for my beef lo mien. I always have to go search for a knife or scissors to accomplish that task. You know what I'm talking about.

Having survived what I have survived, this fine specimen of a body is about to call it quits. Not with life but with having to deal with any injury. I'm near the "Enough is enough!" point in my life. I focus on staying alive and steering clear of mishaps. I want to see the dark side of the moon in NASA photos and learn they've discovered a cure for the common cold besides bedrest. I can't see being in heaven and telling a sneezer, "God bless you!" when he would already be there. I'm venting.

Lately, I've had to deal with a number of health issues that are plaguing thousands of other workers who spent time at Ground Zero. For me, it was 2,274 hours. Hell, I never thought I'd end up limited in doing things I loved and cherished doing. At times, I've thought about giving up, doing nothing, and becoming a couch potato as long as I had a good supply of double-A batteries at my side for the remote.

Every so often, if I had the time, I'd get up and visit St. Patrick's Cathedral in Midtown Manhattan to light a candle and say a prayer or two in the far-right corner toward the rear where they have a small altar.

That church has been a big part of me since I was blessed by the pope in 1965 when he came outside the church on Fifth Avenue.

I visited the place the day before Thanksgiving in 2010 to have a chat with the man upstairs after I lit a candle and said a few prayers in front of the statue of the Blessed Virgin Mary, whom I know listened to every word I said to her. It was the day before the festive holiday of giving thanks, and I wanted to express my thanks, gratitude, and deepest appreciation to God for having me here alive and kicking after having almost died in Oklahoma City in April of that year.

I was planning on breakfast at the house of a dear friend of mine, Joanne Hutchison, and some of my New York City friends. We were there to make our yearly visit to the city's beautiful museum and memorial to those who had died in the Murrah Building bombing on April 19, 1995. It was a shock to everyone in the house (except for me) when I didn't answer the breakfast call. I'd been lying on the living room floor for about fifteen or twenty minutes. I'd experienced two solid punches or bolts of pain straight to my heart. I was told later that Joanne's husband, Gary, had cuffed my arm with a blood pressure gauge and found my blood pressure was off the charts. He and the other guys got me to the car and to the ER, which fortunately was close. I was in bad shape.

When I got to the ER, I saw Joanne and Dot looking at me with concerned, serious faces. They told me that I was being admitted. I had had a heart attack and was having acute kidney failure. I spent three days in the hospital.

That was what I wanted to chat with God about at St. Pat's. I figured since I was there and would be having a one on one with God, I might as well get something off my chest that had been bothering me for some time. I wanted to tell him, "I've had it! If you're trying to find out how much I can take, give me a warning next time before you pull something like that. I still have some items on my bucket list, amen."

Either my request was denied or he didn't hear me. He was probably on the west side of Central Park watching some of the huge balloons being filled up for the big parade. Hey, anything is possible with him.

I was beginning to wonder if God had me here for a much bigger purpose considering what I had survived. I never really complained about them; I figured, "It is what it is." I guessed I'd just have to wait and see. Since I wrote, "I never really complained," I'll mention something that I could and would complain about if you wanted to get technical about it. They may seem minute to you (that's minute, not, minute, as in, time), but they irk the hell out of me, and I want to get to the bottom of this before I leave. Will someone please tell me God's honest truth about the dairy product, half & half, and what exactly is, one-hour martinizing service at the dry cleaners? I've always been hesitant to put half & half into my coffee because I'm not sure what's in it. Half cream and half milk? A splash of one and a bunch of the other? I know it's spelled out on the container, but I don't want to waste what time I have left reading the ingredients of what I consume, and I don't want to be standing in line in heaven and not find half & half on the table. That would be a definite sign that it was not what they said it was. I guess I was either half right or half wrong.

As for one-hour martinizing, I've never met anyone who's asked for that special cleaning service. Whenever I've taken clothes—dress shirts, slacks, blue jeans, and suits—to be cleaned and pressed, I've never asked for that service not having any idea about that process and what it entails. Would I look and smell better? Would it make my clothes look or smell better? I've never placed my clothes at such risk whether I needed them back in under an hour or not. I've always been willing to wait the usual amount of time. Knowing my luck, I'm sure that if I asked about one-hour martinizing, the manager would probably tell me, "One-hour martinizing? We stopped doing that a few days ago because of global warming." If by chance you've ever had this process done, please call me. It's one of my pressing issues.

The two things I just mentioned have given me a few grey hairs to add to those I've gotten from some of the surprising coincidences I've had. Some were amazing, and the rest were unbelievable just like the one that occurred to me not long ago. I was at a 7 Eleven for a newspaper and some milk when I heard someone tell the clerk he wanted to play the three-number and the four-number lottery games for the midday drawing. I heard him say, "Let me have one dollar straight on 446 and 5580 and fifty cents box on 1966." He said they were his lucky numbers. When I got to the cashier, I handed her a ten for the newspaper and milk and said, "I'd like to try my luck too. Let me have fifty cents straight box on 611 and 929 and the same on 6911 and 1991, my lucky numbers, also for midday."

I got my tickets, my change, and my bag of goodies and left. If any one of my numbers had come in, I would have won a good chunk of change somewhere between $80 and $2,500. Outside, I said a quick prayer and wished my tickets good luck by raising my right hand and showing them to the heavens. You're not gonna believe this, but as I was placing my tickets in my pocket, I experienced a surprising coincidence. I heard brakes screeching and saw a delivery truck coming to an abrupt stop at the light at the corner where I was about to cross. On one side of the truck were one of the four numbers I'd just played—6911—the last four numbers of the truck company's phone number.

What was even more surprising was that my three numbers 929 won me $80 being that I had boxed it. Come to poppa! I found something else that was strange; whenever a certain number would pop into my head, I'd always see it, usually on a license plate or something. Go figure! Now, if I spot a certain number on a license plate, numerous times in one day, for whatever reason, I play it for fifty cents box. I think it's my angels having fun with me and trying to get a step closer to earning their wings. If that's what's happening, for the remainder of my gregarious life here, I'm gonna welcome such surprising coincidences with open arms and every so often collect my winnings on the numbers I play.

CHAPTER 9

ONE BEAUTIFUL FALL evening, I planned to do something I had talked about doing for quite a few years—achieving a personal goal I had set in 1979 that would make people remember me for the rest of my life and beyond.

I was all set to take a walk, and I do mean a walk, from Lower Manhattan to the 59th Street Bridge, also known as the Queensboro Bridge, some eighty city blocks, and do it just for the fun of it. I planned to weave down certain streets and avenues. I didn't care how long it would take me, but I figured it could be under two hours. I wasn't worried about it taking longer because I was in the greatest city in the world.

Because of my workload and my hectic schedule, I'd had to put that trek on hold many times. I had been hoping to get it done while I was in my thirties and in good physical shape. The only person who knew I'd been thinking of doing that walk was a hotdog vendor I'd known for three or four years who had a designated spot right across the street from the bridge on the Manhattan side. I'd frequented his stand numerous times and had told him about my dream. I said that the day I asked for "Two hotdogs, easy mustard and onions and two cans of Coke," he would know that I'd done it and that I wouldn't be lying to him. I knew the way he was with his usual customers—always talking about things he had done and wished to do. He more than likely had told a few of his customers about me and had probably told them he wished I'd forget the walk and take a fucking cab to his stand and talk to him about walks in other cities. I'm guessing that being a hotdog vendor in the city is a very lonesome job especially if you cook your dogs in hot water instead of grilling them. The wait alone must be boring.

On Friday, September 11, 1981, I did my walk. I'd heard that the weather would be good. It was all systems go. Margie, my wife, and her sister, Mary Ann, were headed to the Berkshires to stay at their favorite hotel, the Red Lion Inn, and enjoy the fall colors on the drive up. They considered that breathtaking. As for me, I chose the southwest corner of Liberty and Church Street as my starting point. It was one of the four corners that make up the sixteen acres of the famous WTC complex, and it was right across the street from where I worked. All I had to do was walk across the street to begin my walk.

At the time, I was working in One Liberty Plaza. I had an office on the fiftieth floor with a spectacular view of the city looking north toward the Empire State Building. I was able to see the area that I had plan to go through to get to the bridge. One Liberty Plaza was the world headquarters of Merrill Lynch, at the time the largest brokerage firm on Wall Street. One Liberty Plaza was my home for eight years till I helped Merrill move across to the west side into B and D buildings in the new World Financial Center. I worked out of the B building for two more years before I resigned having ten years with the company in 1989.

My office there was a view along the Hudson River. There I was, first across the street from 2WTC, the South Tower, for eight years, and then spending my last two years across the street from 1WTC, the North Tower. In all the years I worked there, I walked through the concourse of the WTC maybe a thousand times. I knew every retail shop, all the places to eat, and all the ways to get to all six buildings in the complex. (One of them, 7WTC, was across the street with no underground connection.) I knew every exit up to the street and the way to some of the subways there including the Path train to New Jersey.

My view of the city from One Liberty let me plan my hike. I saw myself going straight up Broadway to about 42nd Street and then zigzagging my way onto certain streets that would bring me well over to the East Side and quickly onto Second Avenue. From there, it would be a straight walk up to the bridge with minimal pedestrian traffic.

I recall what I was wearing that day—blue suit, white, buttoned-down collar shirt, yellow paisley tie, maroon shoes that matched my attaché case (typical corporate uniform) when I started my walk that evening. I wasn't going out of town the next morning, and I had no need to rush home. I planned on treating myself to a nice dinner out and sleep in the next morning.

I'd tell those I'd meet on business trips that the senior executives, the president, and the members of the board at Merrill Lynch all looked up to me for the work I was doing for the company. That was because they were four floors below me on the forty-sixth, but I never told people that part. I was a headquarters facilities project manager; my work involved a lot of travel. I'd design new floor plans for existing branch offices being renovated anywhere in Indiana, Illinois, Ohio, Michigan, and Wisconsin. I had taken a short break for about a week to take a seminar in real estate development at NYU. I was told I'd be getting involved in site selection, lease negotiations, design, and the construction for twelve new, fifty-thousand-square-foot regional operational computer centers known as ROCs that were going into some pretty nice buildings in twelve major cities throughout the country.

I'd get letters from office managers or executive directors of the regions and some top executives back in headquarters congratulating me on my accomplishments when these places opened for business. I could tell you more about my work, but that would be another book. Let me get back to my walk.

I started out at 5:00 p.m. and started looking for gargoyles high up on buildings. I wasn't going to call it quits with my walk; I was sure I'd never have this opportunity again, and I wanted to brag about accomplishing it. I made pretty good time getting up to Lexington Avenue and 43rd Street over by the beautiful Chrysler Building. I started heading in a more northeasterly direction by zigzagging toward the East Side and Second Avenue. I told myself that once I got to my destination, I would give myself a great big "Atta boy!" and stomp onto the roadway of the bridge confirming my conquest to myself.

I arrived at 7:02 p.m., having done my walk in two hours and two minutes. I think I did pretty well. I stood there for a minute to take it all in. I wasn't one bit tired. I had enjoyed my walk so much that I didn't pay attention to the distance. I didn't see my friendly hotdog vendor, so I had a nice Mexican dinner. Ole!

I have reminisced about this walk many times, and I wondered what had become of Freddy and his delicious hotdogs. I'd had memorable chats with some of the people I met along the way. I asked Merrill Lynch's public affairs representative if I could get my name mentioned in the annals of the city's history of people who had completed amazing walks.

I once saw the most famous walker of all, Philippe Petit, do his tightrope from one WTC tower to the other seven years before I took my walk. I happened to be in the neighborhood that morning. I had just come out of the subway at Vesey and Church Streets and heard all kinds of ruckus on the street. I looked up and saw this crazy guy walking a cable from one building to another. I wondered how they had strung that cable, and I asked myself, *Why the fuck is he doing that with no net?* I knew he was crazy when he stopped midway and for the love of God simply lay on his back on the cable (that was probably not more than an inch in diameter) and then place his balancing pole across his chest. I assumed the guy was fucking nuts; I wasn't going to watch him fall to his death.

He became world-acclaimed for his stunt even though he was arrested for doing it for breaking numerous city laws. He had had to watch every step of his way while I was much more carefree on my walk but was nonetheless wired myself. Plus, I had a much better view of the buildings I passed while Philippe saw only the rooftops.

I'd remember his feat when I was in one of the conference rooms on the 106th floor of the South Tower. I had an office there back in 1989 that overlooked the harbor and the Verrazano-Narrows Bridge. So when I would be waiting for a meeting to start, I would sit there and kind of envision myself trying to do what Philippe had done. I'd lean back in my chair, stretch my legs out, and balance a pencil on my nose. I'd gaze over toward the North Tower and see myself lying across the cable as he had done. Wow. That was definitely a vision I'll always remember.

Well, you're not gonna believe this, but there I was in September on the same date but a different year early in the morning. The skies were as blue as my eyes. I was practically in the same location—just two short blocks farther north of Liberty Street but still on Church Street and closer to the North Tower. I believe I said something that morning that was totally different from what I had said in 1981 when I was about to start my walk, saying, "I'll never forget this day as long as I live!" after I finished running rather than walking up Church Street. It was 9:59 a.m., Tuesday, September 11, 2001.

CHAPTER 10

I MENTIONED THE WALK I had taken on September 11, 1981 because it had all the makings of being another surprising coincidence. The walk I did in 2001 was in the same month and on the same date, and I started out and ended up in the same places but under very different conditions and circumstances.

In 1981, I was surrounded by people trying to get home that Friday evening. In 2001, a mass of humanity was all around me when a huge dust cloud came raging and roaring up Church Street as the South Tower collapsed. My walk turned into a sprint. I was looking for cover. I was back in combat mode. I headed for a building on Chambers about three blocks away; it had a habit of leaving the front doors opened toward the street. I was fifty-four and playing the adult version of keep-away from that roaring sound behind me that accompanied that huge cloud of dust. I got into the lobby of that building and closed the doors a second or two before this greyish cloud came tumbling past. The sight of it made me reel back farther into the lobby and seek refuge under the stairway. It was the first chance for me to catch my breath. What the hell just happened? I couldn't imagine what it would have been like if I had made my eight thirty breakfast meeting in the concourse of the South Tower. My mind and heart were meeting in the middle. I couldn't swallow.

It took a minute or two for me to realize I had just survived another event in my life. I remembered having seen Piper Cubs or Cherokees fly past my 106th-floor office in the South Tower in 1989 to 1990 and wondered what were the chances of two such planes hitting the tower within a half hour of each other. I didn't know then that it had been two huge airliners that had crashed into the towers.

I heard someone yell that the North Tower was coming down. It was 10:28 a.m. All my good memories of working in and around the WTC for the previous thirty-five years left me and were replaced by a horrible feeling in my gut and unusual taste in my mouth. It was as if I had left this world and entered another. It gave me an unbelievable chill I couldn't shake.

I slowly ventured outside after eleven. I needed to know what was going on. I had to call my wife to let her know I was okay but had no luck getting through to her. I saw others outside trying to make calls as well. I saw people who had been obviously caught up in that dust cloud. They looked like a bunch of zombies in a horror movie; they were covered with an ashen-white powder that covered the streets and sidewalks as well.

I remembered seeing fog roll in off the ocean when I was in the DMZ. It made me want to get out of Dodge—Lower Manhattan—by getting up to the bridge. I wanted off that frickin' island! I had horrible visions of what I had witnessed there and did not look back as I headed north. For whatever reason, I was mesmerized by a display of men's clothes in a store window near Church and Chambers. My reflection was staring at me so powerfully that it took me back to my 1981 walk. I was dressed pretty much as I had been that day twenty years earlier— blue suit, white shirt, yellow tie, and shoes that matched my attaché case. I was frozen in time and lost in my reflection, a surprising coincidence.

I'd never imagined seeing worse carnage than I had in 'Nam. I thought that the two experiences—the demons of 'Nam and the demons of the WTC—were mingling. I was sure my wife was home watching TV and had seen what had happened. The last thing I had told her was, "Margie, I have an eight thirty breakfast meeting in the WTC. See you later. Love you!"

Seeing my reflection in the window made me feel completely lost inside and out as if I were in a strange new world. I was already grieving for all the people who had perished in the WTC, my home away from home. I wanted it back the way it was. My mind was all over the place. A good Samaritan had to pull me back on the sidewalk after I had stepped onto the street into the path of a fast-moving delivery truck that had run a red light. Maybe he was one of my angels. I thanked the person repeatedly. I realized I must have been in a trance. I needed to snap out of it.

I hadn't realized how far I had walked until I saw that I was only two blocks from the bridge. I had gotten there in an hour and forty-seven minutes. I wanted to get over that fucking bridge, off that island, and get to my office that was only a few blocks away where I could use a landline to call my wife. I heard a lot of commotion. The NYPD wasn't allowing cars or pedestrians over. They were setting orange traffic cones in place to block all traffic. I was royally fucked.

CHAPTER 11

"LISTEN UP ... THE bridge is closed! All the bridges and tunnels in and out of Manhattan are now closed, and the subways are no longer running. The city is locked down!" Those words put an immediate end to my journey. My chances of getting off the island had been shot to hell even though I had gotten so close. I was stranded on an island with millions of people.

I figured that since I was stuck in Manhattan for who knows how long, I would give blood, something I did three, four times a year. I was a universal donor in that my blood type was very rare—O negative. The nearest blood center was close by. When I got there, I was amazed to see so many people lined up to give blood. I thought I accidently got onto the wrong line when I turned the corner, thinking it was the line for a movie theater where they were showing *To Hell and Back*. It was a movie I believe was meant for me to see.

As I stood in line, I tried calling Margie. I even asked others who seemed to be talking on their cells if they would mind calling my wife but they weren't get through, either. The blood line was moving slowly. I was feeling hunger pains and I was extremely thirsty and I needed to sit down. I was physically and mentally drained. That was at about 2:15 p.m.

I was about at the door of the place at four thirty. I was looking forward to stuff my face with Oreo after Oreo and drink apple juice while seated. That was until someone announced over a bullhorn that the building was way beyond capacity. The fire department wanted to end the blood donations. "We truly appreciate you coming here and standing around and waiting. But if you could, please come back later this evening, if not then tomorrow to give your blood. We can surely use it. I thank you for your patience and support."

I thought it was a fucking joke. I was so close to donating blood. Hearing this fucking clown tell me I should take a hike and come back later was totally asinine and unreal. I took it personally. Seriously, who pulls a shit stunt like that? I responded louder than his bullhorn, "Excuse me, shithead! Are you fuckin' kidding me? I just walked here from the WTC. I have O negative blood. I've been waiting on this fuckin' line for close to two and a half fucking hours. I'm tired, hungry, and thirsty, but I stood here and waited! Now you're telling me come back later or tomorrow? Go fuck yourself and the horse you rode in on! You're not getting one stinking drop of my blood, not later, not tomorrow, and maybe never again!"

I started to walk away. I'm sure people thought I had lost it. I walked off the line and headed for the bridge. I was hungrier, thirstier, and more tired. I headed for a diner I knew about at 2nd Avenue and 57th Street. I hoped that by the time I was finished eating, the bridge would have opened up. I heard some people say that the bridges had reopened but only for pedestrians. Some said that a third plane had crashed into the Pentagon and a fourth somewhere in Pennsylvania. *What the hell is going on? Who the fuck did this? Did we retaliate on whoever the fuck did this? Declare war on them now!*

This news made me walk faster though my legs were telling me to take it easy. I didn't want to get a leg cramp, but I was pounding the pavement trying to bury my anger. It was four forty-five, the time my normal workday usually came to an end. I was making my way over the bridge.

CHAPTER 12

I STOMPED MY feet on the bridge at the same spot I had done that twenty years earlier after my walk. I left ash and dust on the bridge. Police officers told us we could walk on the road over the bridge as they weren't allowing vehicular traffic. I aimed for the middle lane so I could pass those walking slower. I was so caught up in the moment and thinking of the lives lost that I forgot about stopping at the diner.

I remembered seeing two helicopters go down in 'Nam. One had a singing troupe onboard that was to perform with Bob Hope and his entourage, and the other had four army soldiers. They were blown out of the air by satchel charges that two teenagers pitched into the helos at the last second before they took off. Everyone onboard was killed. What made me think of this at that moment, I have no clue, whatsoever.

By the time I got about a third of the way over the bridge, I realized I really should have eaten something, drank something, and rested my legs, but I wanted to get to a phone. I put my legs in low gear to get up the bridge's incline without cramping up my legs. I repeatedly stopped to catch my breath and try calling Margie. Dead silence. I felt I was far out in the universe and unable to communicate with anyone.

And then my legs seemed to lock up. *Shit! Don't tell me I'm gonna get a muscle cramp.* I was entirely mistaken. Instead of having a muscle cramp, something else was occurring, but it was deep inside my head—nowhere near my legs. I had a strange vision that caused me to twist my head around to fine-tune this video that was about to start. I saw myself in fourth grade. I was in the Christmas play in the school auditorium. The next thing I saw, I was at an amusement park being guided by someone unseen to a shiny kiddie roller-coaster (yes, similar to what's on the cover and what had scared me to death many years earlier).

I could swear I felt someone's hand on my shoulder; it was a warm and comforting touch that let me know it was okay, not to worry. I sat in the roller-coaster and was ready to enjoy the ride. I saw myself going slowly up the track till I couldn't be seen any longer. That's where the video came to an end. It somehow unlocked my feet. I could walk again but only slowly. I got only about six or seven steps before the video started playing again. That time, it was much clearer. I saw three classmates dressed as the three wise men.

You're not gonna believe this, but it was yours truly who got to play the baby Jesus. My mom had told me the nuns wanted to have the perfect child playing that part because of my birthday connection to the Blessed Virgin Mary. Everything went blank. This fuzzy feeling went from my legs to my stomach and stopped at my heart. I believe the Holy Spirit entered my body. I felt I had received a new heart, a wild heart that was so alive. It had me kicking in all directions as if I were kicking something. That wore me out. I had to sit.

I was almost halfway across the bridge. I decided to get over to the railing in case I cramped up. I held onto that railing for dear life. I saw something. It seemed like a mirage. Someone who was seated in a folding chair was waving me over to another chair. *Seriously? How the hell did he know I needed to sit down?* I walked over, sat, and thanked him over and over. He patted me on my shoulders. And then this other guy came up and offered me a hotdog and a can of soda. "Eat. Drink."

Turned out that a couple of food vendors had pulled their carts onto the bridge and were setting up on the other side of the roadway. The guys who gave me the chair and the food went back to their cart and opened their umbrella. I could see the word Sabrett's. And the hotdog was exactly how I liked it—easy mustard easy onions. "Drink, drink," he said as he gave me another soda. He must have seen me chug the first one.

A woman came over and handed me a bottle of cold Poland water. I tried to tell her I didn't drink water, but she said, "It's okay. You're gonna need it!" I guess she knew what she was talking about because as soon as she left, that second can of soda got the best of me. I upchucked and messed up my shirt, tie, and pants. I used the water to wash myself off.

"How much do I owe you?" I asked the vendor.

"Nothing."

Other pedestrians who were hustling across the bridge were probably wondering why I was seated in a folding chair eating, drinking, and cleaning off a mess from my clothes. And the bottom of my pants and my shoes were still covered with that ash. I saw a woman and a few kids handing out bottles of water to whomever wanted one, and I saw more vendors opening up their carts.

I felt a huge lump in my throat. I loosened my tie and undid my top shirt button. A crazy question went through my head: *How did the three of the people on this bridge have exactly what I needed? Why did they give them without my having asked for them?* They were like the three wise men with gifts my friends had played. *What are the odds? A thousand to one?* I felt blessed.

I still had the likes of hell playing in my mind from the carnage I had seen downtown that reminded me of Vietnam. The water I'd received washed away the mess on my clothes but not the image of the fourteen people I had seen jump to their deaths from the North Tower. A thousand bottles of water couldn't have washed away that memory.

I also thought about being okay with that roller-coaster in my mental video. Was that some kind of sign I could get on another roller-coaster of any kind? But at the time, I just wanted to hear my wife's voice and let her know I was alive. I took out my phone. The battery was about to go dead.

I reached the end of the bridge and I looked back to where my three angels were who had given me food, drink, and rest and gave them all a comforting smile even though I knew they couldn't see me. I felt an unbelievable rush go through me, a feeling of enlightenment. *Did I just have an epiphany? Or was it divine intervention?*

When I finally got off the bridge, I kept on walking to my office. I saw my boss, Luis Mendes, outside the building in some kind of hazmat truck loaded with hardhats, flashlights, orange vests, and other equipment. I told him where I had been and what I had done to avoid that huge dust cloud. "I need to call my wife to let her know I'm okay."

"I may be calling you later," he said. "I remember you telling me you know the Trade Center pretty well having worked there for so many years."

"No problem. But my phone is dead. Call me later on." I went in and called my wife but got a busy signal. Same thing when I called my parents. I wanted to get home. I headed for the subway knowing I had at least a two-hour subway and bus ride out to Nassau County. I thought about trying to hitch a ride, something I'd done in the navy. I figured I could explain to any cop what had happened to me and why I needed to get home as quickly as I could and wrap up any conversation with, "So if you don't mind, I'd like to get going. I got another twenty-three miles to go!"

CHAPTER 13

D O YOU THINK it's possible for anyone to accidently cut a finger (it being his middle finger) on a piece of sharp cheddar cheese? What about the same person coming up to you a few days later and telling you he had cut the same finger and one more that had gotten stuck in Swiss cheese holes when the knife came down? Before you give me your opinion, what if this same person told you he was an illusionist—he was heading down the street and would turn into a drugstore?

But what if the same person ranted and raved about something he had experienced the previous weekend, something he called surprising coincidences? Would you be interested in hearing what he had to say? I hope so. I'll tell you all about them because they happened to me when I had this casual acquaintance with the woman who lived next door to my friend's vacation house that I've been using for years.

On this day, a Saturday morning, I asked to borrow the gas grill she had on the deck of her beach house. I got into a conversation with her you're not gonna believe. I believe that if the place I was staying had a gas grill, I would have never had these surprising coincidences with her and this book would never have been written. I think what happened to me was meant to happen. Come hell or high water (still don't know what that means, but I like the sound of it), I'm hoping all this will captivate you. If it doesn't, I don't know what would.

CHAPTER 14

M AYBE I SHOULD have started this book with "Back in the day," but I think the majority of you weren't born yet back in my day where perhaps you were just a glimmer in your moms' and dads' eyes (or the headlights or the spotlight from a cop car, shining into your 'future parents' who were canoodling, parked somewhere).

I was born on December 8, 1947, and I almost acquired my sea legs that night—a term that implies you were born on a ship. According to my mom and dad, it was a pleasant evening where she went into labor. She was aboard a naval destroyer, one that my dad served on, being in port at the San Diego Naval Base in California and having dinner with my dad.

He rushed off the ship to get help to where she was taken up to the naval hospital to give birth to me. I think being that close to the Pacific, I was born a fish out of water. I fell in love with the ocean. I loved swimming, fishing in the surf, and sailing or being on a fast motorboat. I especially like body surfing.

One of my surprising coincidences occurred when I was home with the flu and lying on the sofa propped up by pillows. The only surfing I was doing then was channel surfing. I stopped at a Seinfeld show. I'd seen all the episodes of this popular sitcom about two or three times; they all have zany twists thanks to the actors' comedy skills.

But I'd never seen this particular episode—I thought that was amazing. I believe I was meant to see this episode. In it, crazy Kramer said, "The two streets in Manhattan, First and 1st [meaning First Avenue and 1st Street] are the 'nexus' of the universe." The smug look that accompanied his comment cracked me up. I thought, *Why not come out and proclaim something about my book this way?* My first Boy Scout merit badge was in astronomy. I yelled the first thing that came to mind: "My book is definitely the pinnacle of the planet of this entire universe!" and that gave me a high.

You're probably thinking, *Who in his right mind would make such an outlandish statement like that unless he knew what he was talking about?* I'm talking about my comment here, not Kramer's. And since I happened to mention our universe, let me say I never knew so many books have been written about it.

I watched the next two episodes of Seinfeld but must have fallen asleep. I dreamed about going through the shelves in the library for books about people who had experienced surprising coincidences including near-death experiences and who also said, "You're not gonna believe this …" Most skeptics refer to this phenomenon as synchronicity. Only a chosen few such as myself (who is not a skeptic) have experienced both. The majority of my surprising coincidences and near-death experiences have been more like blessings. I knew that if anyone ever asked me, "Do you know of a good book to read, one that goes beyond your wildest dreams?" I'd say that they'd just have to wait till my book came out. It would be the best book on gravity (yes, gravity) and that they'd have a hard time putting it down.

The two quotes I mentioned earlier—the one by Mark Twain and the other by a nameless author—are connected to my surprising coincidences. I came across two quotes by Maya Angelou, a highly acclaimed author and celebrated poet: "I've learned that people will forget what you said, will forget what you did, but people will never forget how you made them feel," which is so true in my life. She also said, "There is no greater agony than bearing an untold story inside you," which really got a grip on my throat. It let me know I was meant to write this inspirational and motivational book.

You could very well come across something I have mentioned or will mention that may relate to you whether it was an event you survived or a surprising coincidence. If so, you and I should definitely meet for brunch that I'm sorry to say would have to be your treat. I don't like driving home on a full stomach and an empty wallet. Call me. Maybe we can just go for a cold beer, my treat.

CHAPTER 15

T HE DAY I started writing my story about what had occurred on the two days in September 2008, I wanted to make sure I had the who, what, where, and when to make it inspirational though I didn't have the why. Something told me to hold off mailing it to *Reader's Digest* until I had talked with Janice Cilento, who knew me pretty well.

The short chat I had with her may be the reason why I'm up to only chapter 15 in my story. I'll need to cover everything she told me to mention, but my life has become an open book from this point on, which is something I never expected it to be. But since I've told you more than my proctologist knows about me, I hope I'm not making an ass of myself.

One night, I was rolling over in bed, and the light from my alarm clock was bright enough to illuminate the book I'd been reading, *Up-Country*, by my favorite author, Nelson De Mille. I thought about how long it must have taken him to write it. His characters were captivating. I gave mental faces to them all. It got me thinking of some of the characters I'd be mentioning; some of them, particularly my buddies, are real characters. I hope some of them will captivate you as they have me. (I'll be including photos of some of them in this book.)

I turned my bed lamp on and wrote a note to myself to visit the library. I wanted my book to be as good as Nelson's books. I skimmed through some and realized I didn't know the difference between forewords, prefaces, prologues, and introductions. I never knew that a foreword was never written by the author, that a prologue is used when the book is fictional, an introduction tells the readers what the book is mainly about, and a preface is always written by the author. I'll wait till I'm done with this book to write a captivating and motivating preface.

I did one hell of a job of captivating and motivating a lovely couple I met from Iceland when I was at the 9/11 Memorial in Lower Manhattan one week. Helmut and Helen asked me a few questions about the memorial. Apparently, they must have read what was on the back of my jacket and down the left arm; it revealed I was involved in the recovery/ cleanup with my city agency at Ground Zero. They asked about a good place to eat, and I told them O'Hara's across the street; I'd been going there since 1978. They thought I was joking. I told them I wouldn't joke with anyone from Iceland being that their country was so small they probably had only one restaurant. They thought that was quite funny.

They were on vacation; it was their first time to New York. I gave them an odd look and said, "Hey, did I ask you if you were here on vacation or why you came here instead of Fargo, North Dakota? Is everybody like this from Iceland?" But I gave them a big smile. "Forgive me. I'm not from here either. I'm originally from San Diego. My mom and dad got lost coming out of so many tunnels and crossing so many bridges to get to Long Island that they decided to stay here because all these islands looked the same to them." They thought that was funny.

Helen told me she was a cartoon artist; she said she enjoyed my sense of humor. I asked her to tell me something about Iceland that was not humorous. With a precious, cute smile, she proudly said that Iceland comprised 40,000 square miles and that she and Helmut wouldn't want to live anywhere else. I asked, "Since your country is smaller than my mom and dad's house out on the island, does everyone know each other, and is there a need for alternate side of the street parking?" Their laughter made me laugh too. I hadn't offended them.

I told them about my being a survivor of 9/11 and other near-fatal experiences. I mentioned the book I was writing and told them I had a powerful story to tell. They were amazed that I had an insatiable sense of humor after everything I'd gone through. Helen told me not to visit Iceland during the months that had twenty-eight days. They were trying to match or outwit my witty humor, which I was enjoying.

After a few more comical comments, I told them I had to get going home. I gave them one of my business cards and told them to call me if they ever came back to New York so I could warn DOT, DEC, DEP, and Burger King and not necessarily in that order. They gave me their e-mails and said they wanted a copy of my book when it came out. I told them I'd think about—don't hold your breath.

I believe our conversation got them interested in what I had told them. This convinced me that my preface should be powerful enough to capture readers quickly. They told me they were honored to have met someone who had been through so much and had done so much for the city and had a love for life. I was deeply touched by their words. We gave each other hugs, and we parted.

On my way home that evening, I had another vision about my book that came about after browsing through *From Dust till Dawn*, a book I had purchased at the 9/11 Museum earlier that afternoon. It was written by a dear friend of mine, David Margules. In it, he talked about the recovery efforts; it included photos he had taken at and around Ground Zero such as the Ground Zero Cross, the Final Column, and some of the families who had lost loved ones. His words touched me. He conveyed his feelings about what he had seen. His book could be considered as being among the annals of historical literary writings about New York regarding 9/11 that will put you at the edge of your seat.

CHAPTER 16

I GAVE A few of my closest friends one or two chapters to read; I wanted to hear their reactions. So far, I was surprised to hear everyone asking to read a few more chapters and saying, "This stuff of yours is great!"

Most of them told me that I had an uncanny way of telling my story and that if they had bumped into me on the street not knowing anything about me and got into a meaningful conversation with me, they said more than likely I would have made a definite impression on them.

I was impressed by their comments, which gave me more reason to believe that I was on the right track and that I had them captivated. I've bumped into a lot of people over the years but don't recall having left any sort of injury to any parts of their bodies except for leaving an amazing impression on them where they wanted to know the title of my book. I'd say, "You're not gonna believe this." They'd say, "No, I'll believe you. What's its title?" The looks on their faces are absolutely priceless when I tell them, "No, that's the title." That was when they started laughing and let me know it was a grand title. I'd then tell them one or two of the events I'd had and that I'd survived a tour in 'Nam, the '93 bombing of the WTC, and 9/11.

All that would make me recall a Seinfeld episode that I'd seen numerous times. Elaine is walking down a street. It's pouring. She's soaking wet. No umbrella. She's sobbing uncontrollably. She bumps into a guy who is under a huge umbrella. She says in a very irritable and whining voice, "I don't know where I'm going!" He says, "That's the best way to get to where you've never been!" That sounded like something I would have said in that situation. His words of wisdom were closely connected to me as to what I'd been feeling ever since these surprising coincidences started happening. They'd make me wonder where I was going. The only answer I could come up with was that they seemed to relate to "It is what it is."

So before I tell you about this humdinger of a surprising coincidence that happened to me some twenty-five years ago that still baffles me today, let me mention something else that has baffled me. Some of my friends don't know why I'm constantly complaining about the problem I have with M&Ms. They're so hard to peel. I don't care for the colored coating. If I can't get one peeled, I just dump it in my mouth. The letters come off there, and I have to deal with this other problem where the letters come off as soon as the candy gets into my mouth. I then find myself choking on those letters for I guess the heat and the moisture in my mouth causes the damn letters to slide off and onto my tongue. Then they get stuck in my throat and cause me to cough. My eyes tear up. I try to talk, but all I can say is "m ...m ... m." I've resorted to lollipops because they have sticks I can hold onto purely for my safety. I hope I didn't make you hungry or start craving chocolate; forgive me.

CHAPTER 17

I'M ABOUT TO take you back to a day of Saturday May 14, 1988, when I had this incredible, surprising coincidence. I wonder now if I had had surprising coincidences before that but hadn't been aware of them as I had been since 9/11. My life has been full of surprises in so many different ways that I'm not really sure if the wheels had been set in motion for this surprising coincidence to occur to me late that Saturday afternoon by what had taken place two days earlier.

I was at Chicago O'Hare airport wanting to board my flight home. I was looking forward to spending time with Margie before heading to Manhattan to see a concert at Madison Square Garden. Over the years I'd been to other concerts in other places where I've seen the Beach Boys, the Four Seasons, Elvis Presley, Paul Revere and the Raiders, Peter Frampton, and Billy Joel, but nothing of the magnitude of what I would see at Madison Square Garden on the night of May 14, 1988. I was sure it would outdo Woodstock, which I'd missed because of a previous engagement in a muddy hellhole on the other side of the world listening to AK-47s (which of course had wood stocks).

I was going to be two rows back from the stage dead center for the greatest concert in my life. A buddy of mine who knew someone in the music business had gotten two tickets. He rattled off the names of whom we'd be seeing and listening to, and he had me at Led Zeppelin; that gave me an unbelievable rush. From that moment on, I was in a state of restless joy for the whole month preceding the concert.

That morning, I'd had a room-service breakfast, showered, and gotten dressed. I headed to the airport, where I had more coffee. Talk about being a nervous Nellie! I hated waiting to board flights. Doing so would force me to come up with some sort of frivolous game to take my mind off the wait. I looked up and saw a number 2 pencil stuck in a ceiling tile. I thought it would be a challenge to count the holes with the pencil as my starting point. I decided I might have to count them again as a double check. (And to answer your question, no, it wasn't me who had pitched that pencil up there. And the count was 371.)

I'd been going to Chicago for so long that it felt like it never wanted me to leave. I've stayed in every hotel in the downtown area from 1979 to 1987 when I worked on altering and renovating Merrill Lynch offices there. Hell, I knew so many people on a first-name basis at O'Hare that we almost felt like family. But on that trip, I'd stayed at a hotel near the airport to make sure I made it out in spite of any hell or high water.

I'd picked up an abandoned magazine that had a page dog-eared at the start of an article. I started reading it and couldn't put it down. I was interrupted by a stranger. A woman had the audacity to ask me, "Is this seat taken?" pointing to the empty seat next to me. Come on! If it's vacant, why would she ask me if it was taken? But I just said no and went back to my article. She sat, cleared her throat, and asked, "Excuse me, but is this newspaper by any chance yours?" I said no and again went back to my reading. I didn't want to make eye contact with her. But then I started feeling bad about my curt attitude. I took a deep breath and closed my magazine. I looked at her and saw she was a very attractive woman in her fifties. I cleared my throat to get her attention and gave her a smile. I told her I was sorry for my childish attitude and behavior.

"Oh no!" she said. "I'm sorry for my interruptions. I could see you were deeply involved in whatever you were reading. You seemed like you didn't want to be disturbed."

I told her I'd been through a lot over the past two days and couldn't wait to get home. She said she hoped the rest of my day would go better. She got up when they announced boarding for a flight to Miami at the next gate. She said good-bye. I said, "Have a safe flight." I smiled and went back to my reading.

I came across something in the article that was quite surprising after what had just taken place with that woman. My mind jumped back and forth to what had occurred to me on Thursday, then on Friday, and again that morning. I'm referring to what was being said in the paragraph I'd just finished reading about the connections that take place in a person's life. It had me thinking about all the trouble I had had to go through earlier with another kind of connection I had. I'd been in Detroit when I was suddenly called to go to Denver to settle some matters for Mother Merrill that had to be handled in person with the developer, contractor, and architect for an out-of-the-ground Merrill building. That had thrown my schedule way off. I desperately wanted to get home for the concert on Saturday. All the Denver–New York flights had been booked, so I had to go through Chicago. But I would have flown to as many cities as needed to make it home Friday night and be well rested for that Saturday concert.

So I was scheduled to arrive at LaGuardia early Saturday afternoon. I'd have to get home, spend some time with my wife, shower, get dressed, and take the train into the city from Long Island for the 8:00 p.m. event. Penn Station is right below Madison Square Garden. I was psyched at the thought I'd be seeing Led Zeppelin, a group I'd idolized since my teen years. I knew all the words to their songs on their two first albums. I still couldn't believe I'd be close enough to see Robert Plant's and Jimmy Page's eyes. It was a dream come true.

I'd been traveling the country every week including weekends for the previous four months for Merrill Lynch. I'd missed family functions such as births and deaths and countless family get-togethers. Margie (who I wish could have gone with me on some of those trips) was an absolute saint to put up with my being away and having to be home alone and go to those functions.

Besides the concert on Saturday, there was a wedding on Sunday; the daughter of my wife's closest friend was getting married. I'd given Margie my word I'd go to the wedding with her. Besides, I loved to dance my ass off at receptions. If Margie was tired and needed a little break, I'd ask anyone to dance. I'd been on the road for almost four weeks straight, and I missed her dearly. As for this concert I was going to, it was Atlantic Records' fortieth anniversary in the music business. I'd never been to a concert of that magnitude, though I'd seen the Rascals, Iron Butterfly, Crosby, Stills, Nash, and Young, and seventeen other well-known groups. Need I say more? I needed to leave Chi-town and get my ass home.

CHAPTER 18

A FTER ALL THESE years, the lyrics of one Led Zeppelin song "Good Times, Bad Times" would put a spark in my brain just by hearing the first four musical notes. It has become a part of my physical makeup all because of where I was, what I was doing, who I was with, and how much I wanted to be somewhere else that had left this image implanted in my brain. I listened to that song almost every day from April 13, 1970, to July 6, 1970. It would rip my heart out of my chest when I thought that at any moment, my time on earth could come to an end.

I don't know of anyone born after July 4, 1970 who would have been able to spend one day in the place I was and be there till the day I left on July 6, 1970 (or any of the days when I arrived 'in country'). In April 1970, I had pleasure of hearing every song from the first two albums by Led Zeppelin on a cassette player that my good buddy, Raymond "Flash" Gordon had in 'Nam. We'd blast these songs out as loud as the player could go. That had started on the day we traveled north along the coast of Vietnam for about twelve hours. We continued to do so for the next eighty days at a place worse than Da Nang. If there was a place worse than hell, we were in it! We were in Cua Viet at the DMZ two miles south of North Vietnam.

So I was about to hear Led Zeppelin some eighteen years later, and I wouldn't have to worry about my life. I called John, my buddy with the tickets, about my coming home through Chicago. I wanted him to know that I was itching to be there with him to see the concert. I had done good work for Merrill on that trip that had taken me to Atlanta, San Francisco, Cincinnati, Detroit, and Denver. I'd met my target dates and handled all the problems that had cropped up. Merrill was ready to ship equipment to the sites I had worked on so they could open for business. I was proud of the role I had played in helping Merrill get to that point. I was looking forward to hearing, "Nice going, Charlie!" But I was exhausted mentally more than physically, and I needed to rest up for the concert if I wanted to enjoy it to the fullest.

I had called the limo company that was going to pick me up at LaGuardia and take me home to Long Island. I'd told Margie about my schedule as well. I checked to see how much time I had before they would start boarding. Just as I was stashing my magazine in my attaché case, I heard my name being called. I was to go to the nearest white courtesy phone. I picked it up and gave my name. I was told that Sarah, who was with Merrill Lynch, was coming to see me at the gate. I was not to board my flight until she handed me a very important package to take to New York. I had no idea how she knew I was there. I heard someone calling my name and saw an attractive girl who reminded me of Jessica Hahn, who had made the news for having had some kind of love affair with a Baptist minister. She had a Merrill envelope under her arm. "Are you Sarah?"

"Are you Charlie Kacz from headquarters?"

"In the flesh!" That made me think how lucky that minister had been. She told me that my boss needed the envelope for a 10:00 a.m. meeting on Monday. It must have been pretty damn important because she told me I had to leave it at his office today. What the fuck is this all about? Did my boss forget I was off Monday and Tuesday and had big plans for later that day? I thanked her. She said, "I guess I'll be seeing you when I see you this Wednesday. I hear you're back in Chicago for a meeting and leaving Friday." Where did she come off using my line that I always said to my boss?

The idea of taking the envelope all the way downtown before I went home truly sucked. And as for her telling me that she'd be seeing me in Chicago on Wednesday for a meeting (which I knew nothing about) was ridiculous. I was scheduled to be in Los Angeles on Wednesday. I always made my own traveling plans. Sarah wasn't my secretary. Okay. How long could it take me to shoot into the city from LaGuardia, go up to my boss's office, drop off this package, jump back into my limo, and head out to the island?

At the time, Merrill was relocating its headquarters to two new buildings in the World Financial Center on the West Side across the street from the North Tower of the WTC. The department I worked in was up on the fiftieth floor in One Liberty Plaza. I had to add this extra time on the elevator up to that floor and then back down before I would be on my merry way home. Okay, maybe it would probably take about fifteen minutes.

Certain things happen for a reason when you least expect it. Wow. Is that the fucking truth or not? It was truer than true because what had occurred to me after I found the magazine. Everything was happening for a reason. I wanted to shred that magazine to pieces. I thought that whoever had left it for me to find had gotten as far as I had and had gotten pissed off. The remainder of that paragraph stated that our lives are 90 percent what we do and 10 percent what happens to us or something along those lines. It seemed to be the reverse with me. I called Margie about my detour downtown. She sounded frustrated. But I would still make the concert.

I got to LaGuardia and headed downtown. I wasn't expecting anything else to come up once I got to my boss's office, but a certain Mr. Murphy was waiting for me. He's the one who came up with Murphy's law. I saw something taped to my boss's door that looked like a brightly colored sign pasted onto a large mailing envelope with the company's logo. It had four large letters in various colors that clearly spelled out my name—Kacz. That was a nickname that had been bestowed on me by an executive vice president who later became chairman, and it was how I became known across the country. I thought something else was about to come up and it wasn't going to be good. I read a note: "Charlie, read the contents in the white envelope on my desk for you marked Important." I felt as if I had been hit with a .45 caliber round. I went in, saw the envelope, opened it, and read it. I read it a few times.

Was there ever a time in your life when you felt you were being stuffed into a large, wooden barrel that was headed over the Niagara Falls? No, I wasn't told to fly to Buffalo. What would make you come up with that stupid, idiotic thought? Who would ever fly to Buffalo on a Saturday afternoon in May rather than attend a Zeppelin concert?

I tried to gather my thoughts. I tried to pretend that what I'd just read was not what had been written. I began to laugh. If I had read the note correctly, I wished I were going to Buffalo to go over the falls even without that fucking barrel. *This has got to be a joke.* The note was dated Friday the 13th. No way am I superstitious except about walking under ladders, black cats crossing my path, or stepping on a crack and breaking my mother's back.

I started thinking it had something to do with that (don't laugh) damn magazine article I was reading. The note read, "Dear Kacz, whatever plans you might have for this Saturday evening, I'm asking you to put them off and do me this one big favor. I need you to be at this very important appointment this evening. It's more of a dinner meeting, and I do mean it's very important. I need you to attend a casual-attire dinner at the Oak Room in the Plaza Hotel at eight. Due to a family emergency, I had to go out of town, and I won't be back until late Sunday evening. I'll be stopping by my office to pick up that package you brought from Chicago. I desperately need to look at and review it Sunday evening since you already know about the meeting I have to be at Monday morning. This is a meeting I think you should be at, but it's okay. Take your two well-deserved days off. Kacz, you'd be an absolute lifesaver to sit in for me for dinner Saturday evening. I will not forget this! A.Y."

I think he knew I'd do it not just for him but for anyone in the company I reported to; I always said business before pleasure no matter the cost. I know you're thinking, *You must be some kind of fucking jackass to pass up a concert you'd been dying to go to for a dinner.* I was trying to figure out ways to kick myself in the ass without hurting myself. I walked out of his office saying, "Shit! Shit! Shit! Fucking shit!" all the way to the men's room.

According to the note, I'd be meeting with the three executives from Chicago, the same top-notch directors I had just helped move into a brand-new suite of offices in Sears Tower. I started recalling something I'd heard in San Francisco about a certain group in Chicago being ready to expand their offices. The last bit of info that my boss left me in his note was that dinner reservations were under his name, the bill was taken care of, and I'd be heading out on Wednesday to Chicago, not Los Angeles. I'd be staying at the Ambassador East.

It was nearly four thirty. I didn't have time to go home to shower, change, spend some time with Margie, and head back into the city for dinner, so I made two important calls. I broke the news to John that I wouldn't be going and why. I begged him to get some good photos of Plant and Page performing. I called Margie with all the bad news. I told her I wouldn't be home until late. I told her that luckily I still had one clean dress shirt to wear. "See you later. Love you!"

I freshened up in the men's room. I donned my last shirt and splashed some Obsession on my face in place of showering. I went down and told my driver, "Take me to the Plaza Hotel." I tried to tell myself I was doing the right thing even though I was also telling myself, *You're a fucking shithead!* I punched my luggage. My driver must have thought I had just lost a bundle in the stock market.

At the Plaza, I checked my bags with the concierge and said I'd be back around midnight. I picked up a courtesy phone and asked the operator to relay the same message to three people: "Kacz will be meeting you for dinner at 8:00 p.m. at the Oak Room. A. Y. will not be joining us due to a family emergency."

Then I needed a drink. Or two. As was usual for me at the Plaza, I went to the famous Oyster Bar for a Bloody Mary and a platter of raw oysters. I took the first seat I saw at the bar and plopped my ass down. Normally, I'd never leave my back to the door (after what had occurred to me on Christmas Eve in 'Nam). A friendly bartender came my way and gave me a jolly hello and a big smile. "What's your pleasure, my friend?"

"Please bring me a platter of your succulent oysters and a stiff Bloody Mary, and make sure I never see the ice in my glass be all by itself. What's your name?"

"Albert, but I prefer Al."

"Al it is."

He placed my order and went to make my drink. I scanned the room. It was empty except for two couples at different tables laughing and having drinks. The bar was the place Margie and I frequented often. We'd spent the first two nights of our honeymoon in the Plaza's honeymoon suite. We'd come to the bar for dinner on our second night and drank champagne. We wished ourselves a wonderful life together. We were driving to Montreal for a week of bliss.

I thought about what I'd be missing that night. That left an empty feeling in my stomach and a sour taste in my mouth. *What are the odds of something like this happening? I'm getting fucked not being able to see my two favorite rock 'n' roll performers, Robert Plant and Jimmy Page.* I hoped someone would walk into the bar, shove my head under it, and kick me in the ass. I'd buy him a Bloody Mary and sing "Good Times, Bad Times" to him. *It never seems to end.* I forced myself to make the best of the situation by humoring myself with my new friend, the bartender. I told him who I was, whom I worked for, what I did, where I'd been, and why I was there. I was trying to drown my sorrows in Bloody Marys and oysters. I didn't mention the concert; I didn't want to change the mood he was in after telling me the next two drinks were on the house. If I had told him, I think he would have told me I was one big, stupid, fucking shithead.

"Al, make my next drink a gin and tonic, the best gin you got! Forget the Bloody Mary! I need a change in my life." I told him the oysters were delicious, as good as the job I did out in Denver, and I mentioned how much I truly loved my job. I'm sure by then he was thinking it was the alcohol doing all the talking. Anyone else listening to me would have thought I was venting about my job. I figured the two couples in the bar were tourists. I mean, who else would be in my favorite bar on a Saturday afternoon in the greatest city in the world? I started wishing I had invited Margie to come in and join me for dinner; my boss wouldn't have minded.

"This drink is also on me, but the oysters are on your tab," Al said.

"Wonderful! Then bring me a platter of crab cakes, my good man!"

While I was enjoying the gin and tonic, I sensed that someone had just walked in. I felt a slight draft on the back of my neck. Someone pulled out two chairs to the left of me. I heard a second chair being pulled away a little farther down the bar. I took a quick, casual glance. All I could see was the back of the woman who had sat next to me. She had a flowing, beautiful, long, curly, brown hair sprawling on her shoulders. I couldn't see who was with her. *Yup, more tourists.*

Al came over. "So what's your pleasure, gents?"

Gents? Did he just say "Gents"?

CHAPTER 19

T HE NEXT THING I heard was a request for two cold beers on draft in a voice I would have recognized anywhere. I leaned back, looked over, and yelled, "I don't fuckin' believe it! Can't be! No fuckin' way!"

The two gents turned to me. "What's wrong?"

Staring me in the face was Robert Plant, the one with long, curly, brown hair, and Jimmy Page. They were astonished. "Are you okay?" they asked. What are the odds of that happening particularly on that day? My two favorite idols sitting next to me in living color. I was in shock, which was probably why I had shouted those foul comments. I apologized to Al, to the two couples, and my new drinking buddies. I told Al, "Whatever my friends here want to drink or eat, it's on me. Whatever my friends over there want for their next drink is also on me, and get a drink for yourself too, Al!"

Robert turned to face me. He smiled. "Thank you very much, but it's okay, we got it."

I stumbled on my words. "I know you got it. You've always had it! You've never lost it, but right about now, I'm losing it! I insist you let me do this. Please, have some oysters, the best in the city. Al? Two more orders of oysters for my friends here!"

Jimmy asked me, "So what are you celebrating?"

"The two of you of course!" I said. I introduced myself and told them whom I worked for, what I did, and so on. I didn't say a word about the concert. For a fleeting moment, I thought of calling those I was to have dinner with and telling them, "You're on your own an unexpected situation came up don't have time to explain see you Wednesday enjoy your dinner" with no punctuation. Maybe they could have handled the truth. Maybe not. I lifted the last oyster on my platter to the heavens and said, "Shucks!"

I was thinking how lucky I was to be sitting next to them compared to being at the concert having them smack in front of me on stage. Our conversation went from the weather to the hustle and bustle of the city. I wanted to tell them something but figured it could wait until they were eating oysters. The two platters arrived. I said, "Enjoy!"

I started telling them about April 14, 1970 and my buddy Flash Gordon. I said we had done something way out of the norm, but being where we were—the DMZ—we really hadn't given a shit about it. I asked Al for another round of drinks and quickly finished my story.

"So why are you celebrating us again?" Jimmy asked.

"No hurry, Al," I told our bartender, who wanted to hear the answer. I told them what had happened that day and why I had ended up in the Oyster Bar on a Saturday afternoon.

Robert and Jimmy said almost in unison and perfect harmony, "That's a real bummer, Kacz. Good times, bad times, right?"

"Fuckin' a!" was the best response I could come out with.

Jimmy, Robert, and Al started laughing. Jimmy said, "So Charlie, your plans of going to the concert tonight went down in flames? You did know we were performing this evening, right?"

"Of course I knew! I've known for months and even had a ticket!"

Jimmy gave Robert a knowing look. "Charlie, if you do finish early with your dinner, Robert and I want you to have this." He reached inside his leather jacket. Robert said to me, "We loved your story, Kacz—truly amazing!" Jimmy handed me what looked like a ticket. "Here you go, Charlie! We want you to have this. It's our way of thanking you for fighting for your country and for spending your time and money with us and celebrating us. Your hospitality is well appreciated, and we're proud to know you. I'm glad we've met!"

Jimmy cut in. "This ticket will get you in backstage as our guest. Come and join us after your dinner. We'll be doing a little partying, and we'd love to see you there."

My heart stopped. *Are they kidding?* I told them how much I had been looking forward to seeing them perform two rows up from dead center, but I said I would probably have a long night with my guests from Chicago—work before pleasure. It wouldn't be right to split early. I got up to go to the men's room and accidently almost knocked over Robert's Bloody Mary, but he was quick with his hands and grabbed it. He started singing, "Now that would have been a real Bloody Mess!" cracking up Jimmy, Al, and me.

When I came back, we clinked our glasses and toasted each other's good health and a life filled with laughter whether it was good times or bad times. Just then, Al tapped my hand and gave me this grim look that informed me that some people had just walked in. I turned and saw my three Chicago dinner guests. I gave out a big sigh thinking it was eight. I checked my watch and saw it was only five after seven. I was safe for the time being. I told Robert and Jimmy that my guests had arrived early but that I still had about an hour before I had to go.

Robert said they had to head for the Garden for their show. I grabbed a napkin and asked them for their autographs, something I normally wouldn't have done, but this was the exception. They both did so wholeheartedly and without the slightest hesitation. As Robert was signing his name, he said, "For you, Kacz, it would be an honor and our utmost pleasure!"

I saw Jimmy pull out his billfold and reminded him that I'd get it. He said, "I know, but I want to give Al a well-deserved tip from Robert and me for being a good sport and a damn good bartender. I'm glad to hear you considered us your friends because you're definitely a true buddy to us. You're quite an amazing fellow, Kacz and a fine gentleman too. By the way, what's your favorite three songs of ours?"

"'Good Times, Bad Times,' 'You Shook Me,' and 'Kashmir.'"

They gave me two big shit-eating grins and replied, "Fuckin' a!"

We all had another good, hearty laugh. Jimmy said, "Enjoy your evening. We had an absolute blast. Thanks for one great memorable afternoon here in your great city." They smiled and gave me quick embraces.

We shook hands, and I said, "Hope to see you again!"

Robert smiled and said, "Fuckin' a! And next time it's on us!"

I motioned Al for my tab. One of my dinner guests waved me over. Before I did, I ran to the door and shouted out down the corridor to my new buddies, "I'll be listening to your music till the day I die!" I headed back into the bar to my dinner guests, who were enjoying their drinks. "Hey Kacz, fancy meeting you here! How the hell are you? Are you still jet-setting around the country, or do they have you staying put here in New York?"

They knew me quite well. "Yes to all of the above. I wish I were traveling to some other place right about now, but that's a different trip altogether. What's your pleasure? My treat, my city!" I told them why I was there instead of my boss.

One of the directors asked, "So were those guys your friends from back in the sixties?"

I chuckled. "Yeah, they've been my friends since the late sixties, and they happened to be in town. We got together for drinks and laughs and to compare some of the good times and bad times since then." They obviously had no idea whom I'd been with, so I left that alone.

I changed the conversation by asking why they were in New York though I knew about the meeting on Monday morning. They gave me the lowdown as to what was taking place in Chicago and why they were having to get back there on Tuesday if all went well here. I said I'd be seeing them in Chicago on Wednesday. One of them said, "When you get there, we'll return the favor. We'll take you to a restaurant of your choosing as long as it serves good steaks."

"Fuckin' a!" I said with a chuckle.

We talked about the meeting on Monday, but all I could think about was my amazing meeting with Jimmy and Robert. I felt blessed. Maybe that was meant to happen. Maybe it wasn't just a surprising coincidence. I framed that autographed napkin. It sits in my den on top of their first two albums. Whenever I hear "Good Times, Bad Times", "You Shook Me", or "Kashmir," my heart jumps back to that day I met my two favorite rock 'n' and roll singers and that day in 1970 going up the coastline of Vietnam. Most of all, I will never forget that fucking magazine article.

The concert got rave reviews. Led Zeppelin closed the show. And my buddy John got some great pictures of them performing. I told him, "Well, John, you're not gonna believe this, but I ran into Jimmy and Robert at the Oyster Bar in the Plaza that afternoon."

CHAPTER 20

I'VE HAD OTHER such surprising coincidences like the one I had at the Oyster Bar not with rock stars but with movie stars. I'll list only a few—Cary and Barbara Grant, Frank Sinatra, Cesar Romero, Helen Hayes, Lee Marvin, Dudley Moore, Susan Anton, Tony Lo Bianco, Susan Sarandon, Liza Minelli, Lee Marvin, Robert Redford, Kirk and Michael Douglass, Danny DeVito, and Julianne Moore. The details about having dinner and drinks with them vary, but it was a surprising coincidence meeting Robert Redford. I met him at the Marriott Hotel when I was having dinner at 1:00 a.m. when I was working at Ground Zero.

Have you ever had dinner or drinks with a famous person? Did others say, "That's fucking unbelievable!" when you told them about it? I have perfectly good reasons for using foul language or other fuckin' curse words; I'm trying to get my damn points across with my deepest feelings. I really don't like using any kind of fuckin' curse words. I had my share of them in 'Nam. But my surprising coincidences have been blessings because of what they've done to my wild heart especially those that involved Margie or my daughter, Noelle. They sucked the air out of me and gave me a magical, mystical breath of fresh air that ended up in my wild heart. I'll cherish them forever.

I'll take a short break here and ask you to look at my photo on the back of this book. Maybe you'll remember having seen me on the street or in some restaurant. I have this strange attraction to people when our eyes meet. *Be careful what you wish for*, I tell myself, *because it might come true!* I hope that day comes and we do meet, so keep on wishing!

CHAPTER 21

I NEED YOUR attention for a few minutes. Writing this book has been hard because I have problems with punctuation, when to start a new paragraph, when to put some info in parentheses, and were those damned commas are supposed to go. And you've seen how I bounce around a lot. That's because I write whatever comes to mind when it comes to mind.

I've gotten help in my writing from a thesaurus; it's helped me select the right words in order to keep you captivated. Hell, if Nelson DeMille could do it, why can't I? I thought about using words such as *furthermore* or *henceforth* to grab people's eyes whenever I've written a letter or an e-mail to an editor. Over the years, I've gotten calls asking, "Are you the author of a letter on [whatever subject it was]?" I'd say yes, and they'd say I had submitted a fine letter; to me, that meant "a fine piece of journalism." I'd be told it would appear in the next day or two. But all I was doing was writing about what I felt. I'd always end my letters with a bit of humor to help get my point across.

I've seen my name in print so many times that I thought about writing something longer than letters, but that would have required additional fuel—pertinent information and more substance—to get my point across. So I just stuck to letters to the editor. So why am I writing a whole book? Maybe what I should have done was publish a collection of my letters and entitle it, *Well … In My Opinion*. Stay tuned.

CHAPTER 22

I BELIEVE I'VE acquired a brand-new, beautiful heart I call my wild heart. I received it late the afternoon of September 11, 2001. I believe because of what I witnessed across the street from the North Tower the moment I arrived, 9:06 a.m., until 9:59 a.m., when I went running for my life, I was given this new heart of mine from my wonderful angels.

I can still see in my mind everything I saw that morning. I remember walking around and through the WTC the way it was before it became the way it is due to the events of that fateful morning. I could rattle off where every store in the concourse of the WTC was. I knew the place like the back of my hand. I could tell you what it was like on the promenade level or on the roof with a 360-degree view of the city. I could tell you about what it was like having an office on the 106th floor of the South Tower. I could tell you things about the Windows of the World, which I had frequently visited for lunch, dinner, drinks, functions, and parties.

I could tell you about the time I spent in the Vista Hotel, 3WTC, that would astonish you, and I could tell you about the South Tower and a few things about the famous sphere in the fountain. I could tell you about all the buildings in the complex. I remember seeing these two monolithic towers depicted as two dark-brown, tall, wooden blocks on a beautiful scale model—twelve feet by twenty feet altogether—of Lower Manhattan that I helped carry into the conference room at the architectural firm where I was working. That was my first involvement with the WTC.

When I flew home in July 1970 from Vietnam, I went there to take a better look at the WTC. Every so often, my work would take me there.

In 1978, I started working for Merrill Lynch across the street from the South Tower. The horrible feeling I had on 9/11 stayed with me for years. The complex became nothing but mountains of debris in one hundred and two minutes.

I went there to help oversee the removal of all the mountains of debris—warped and twisted steel beams and columns covered with the dust of all the concrete. I saw first responders sift through it for any traces of loved ones. I was there for ten months of cleanup mostly on the graveyard shift. WTC went from being my home away from home to a memory. You're not gonna believe this, but all the memories I had starting with that scale model up until WTC's destruction—thirty-five years—were somehow wiped clean from my heart and mind as if they had never existed a minute after the North Tower collapsed at 10:28 a.m.

I proudly stood with the first responders and construction workers at Ground Zero as the remains of a member of the Uniform Services for the City of New York was being removed in a black body bag draped with an American flag. I was standing on hallowed ground shoulder to shoulder with many others saluting as the remains went past me. I started to see and feel my wonderful memories of the WTC slowly returning. They were a mixture of loss, sadness, and joy, a feeling similar to the one I had the day I left 'Nam.

I could swear I saw some of those demons I still had lurking inside of me from 'Nam leave me. I rattled off a prayer that they would never come back. Everything that was going through my mind and body found its way into the designs I submitted to all the design competitions for the 9/11 Memorial. I watched the memorial being constructed. Something always seemed to occur to me while I was there. I'd feel a slight gust whispering across my face as if it were saying hi to me. She's been there for so many years; I'm sure we met many times before 9/11. It always brought a tear to my eyes. She would take me back to the way it was where I had all those memorable moments there in the WTC complex knowing perfectly well they would never leave me again.

CHAPTER 23

I was excited to hear I'd been invited to a breakfast with Attorney General Elliot Spitzer at his headquarters in Lower Manhattan when I was a member of September Space, an organization of volunteers who worked at Ground Zero in numerous capacities. At the breakfast, we were told we'd attend the tenth anniversary memorial service in Oklahoma City to remember that city's fateful day—April 19, 1995.

About fifteen or so of us went there with our team leader, Lisa Orloff, who is now a very dear friend of mine. We arrived on April 17, 2005. I had this immediate connection with some of the survivors of the bombing being a survivor myself. I had the deepest respect and admiration for the first responders there. The feeling weaved its way into my wild heart and soul. The people I met felt the same as I did—full of love and devotion. They became my extended family rather than just friends, and I think the feeling was mutual.

I have been attending their memorial service ever since 2005 to show my support and respect for the survivors and some of the families and especially the members of the 4/19 Outreach Organization. I usually go there with a few close friends from New York; we share quality time with some of the survivors. We tour the beautiful city and attend commemorative events. The time I spend there is very precious to me. I believe I was meant to meet these wonderful, loving people there.

I give Lisa a world of thanks for reaching out to me to join her organization, now known as, World Care where she continues to work hard just as she did when I met her volunteering at Ground Zero. I never would have met all those wonderful people in Oklahoma City otherwise.

CHAPTER 24

I WANT TO tell you about some of my buddies with whom I worked at Ground Zero for New York's Department of Design & Construction, DDC. I was surprised to learn I'd go to work for the department on February 26, 2001, the eighth anniversary of the first bombing at the WTC. I had been there that day. I'm still working for that agency today and am enjoying it.

We had two joyous occasions to celebrate our camaraderie that developed among us after having worked together at the WTC site after its destruction. The first one was going to a restaurant in Long Island City in September 2002. The second celebration was at another restaurant across from the WTC site in 2003. I (we) needed something different to do for the next celebration and to strengthen our bond. I was lucky to get a beach house on Long Beach Island, New Jersey, for a weekend after the 9/11 anniversary ceremony in Lower Manhattan. The beach house belonged to a dear friend of mine, Susan Howland, whom I had met in April 2004.

After a lengthy conversation with her after I had just completed a four-day seminar with her organization, Sky Help, she knew I worked for DDC, where I was, what I did, and what I'd seen at the WTC site. She said she was honored to know I was also a Vietnam vet. I was given the okay to use her house for a weekend any time after the Labor Day weekend. That was fine with me and five other guys from DDC who wanted to celebrate our job well done for the city of New York.

We left NYC on a Thursday afternoon for the beach house and had a nice dinner on the island. Friday morning, we checked out the beach.

Some of us did some fishing hoping to catch something for dinner. We sat on the deck drinking and talking about the good times and bad times we'd been through at Ground Zero. We enjoyed a great dinner and planned to start really celebrating the next day at noon and continue until the cows came home though we knew there wasn't one fucking cow on the whole frickin' island.

We talked about the emotional roller-coaster ride we'd been on at the WTC site. We became more than friends; we were brothers in a close-knit family. We called ourselves the Original Six (not bad, eh?), and we called our event the Festivus—for the rest of us. We'd come on Saturday and kick in $20 each for food and drink. We'd bring family and friends (at no charge to them) and have a good time. We've been doing that yearly since 2004 close to the 9/11 anniversary, and one year, we had over forty-two people. It's gotten better and better and more memorable too.

We chartered a spacious schooner once for thirty-five of us for a sunset cruise on the Hudson. We headed south toward that famous lady in the pond, the Statue of Liberty. The skipper got in close so we could take pictures of her in all her splendor. We all knew that to our backs was Ground Zero. It brought tears to my eyes, but I wasn't ashamed a bit.

We had a great Mexican dinner after that; we had the restaurant line up tables for us, a big, happy family, and we must have ordered everything on the menu as well as drinks of all types. We had a great view of the Hudson River and Journal Square in New Jersey. I could see a portion of where the WTC once stood. My wild heart remembered all the memorable things I had done and seen there. I'd been at Ground Zero with the greatest guys in the world from DDC despite the conditions we faced. They were my brothers just as much as were the guys I served in 'Nam with.

None of the guys I knew at DDC had ever been in war; I'm sure none of them had been prepared for Ground Zero and had to bury what they saw deep in their hearts and minds. I hope and pray they don't get the demons I did in 'Nam come back to haunt them.

If any of you guys are from DDC, I tell you I have the utmost respect for you and the way you handled yourselves at the site. We have a special, mystical thread that connects us all. I have a favorite design of all the designs I submitted relating to 9/11; I call it my Living Memorial.

CHAPTER 25

T HIS IS THE perfect place to tell you how I came up with my title for
      this book. It was by accident, but not one involving a crash or a fall
off a ladder. I was on the phone with two dear friends of mine out in
Oklahoma City—Joanne Hutchison and Dot Hill. They work downtown
in the same government office. I had called Joanne to tell her about this
book I was writing and asked her to conference in Dot so I could tell
them both. I also wanted their opinion on what I was planning to say
about them in my book. I knew a lot of people in Oklahoma City who
are just as wonderful and as loving as they are, and I had fallen in love
with their memorial. I also wanted to find out what they thought about
a surprising coincidence that had happened to me at their memorial in
2005.

   When we were all conferenced in, I started to describe the one that
took place with them and was immediately interrupted by them. They
started asking me lots of questions—why was I writing a book, where
I found the time to do so, and why I wanted to include them in it. I
tried to avoid their questions by telling them I was also including most
of my near-death experiences and said that I might be using my sense
of humor to describe them. I told them I'd be stating the God's honest
truth about how much I felt connected to them and the other people
I'd met in Oklahoma City. But they persisted in asking me all kinds
of questions to the point I asked them if they were working for CNN.
I asked them if they would mind if I mentioned the number of times I
used my henway joke when I was with them in restaurants. I'd ask the

waiter or waitress for a henway and would be asked, "What's a henway?" I'd say, "Oh, about three or four pounds." *Da da boomp.*

We were all talking at once. They were still persisting with their questions and asking me about my surprising coincidences. It got to the point where I actually said, "Well, you're not gonna believe this …" and then hung up. I hoped they saw the humor in that. But I wasn't getting anywhere with them at the time.

I called back. Joanne reconnected us all. I didn't have a chance to apologize for so rudely hanging up before Dot asked, "So Charlie, what's the title of your book?"

"I don't have one, but I'll come up with one by the time I finish it." I told them what had occurred with them at their memorial, and they wanted to know more about the other surprising coincidences I'd had. I knew if I started to tell them more of the details, they'd probably interrupt me again and I'd be saying "You're not gonna believe this" again. Just then, I circled those five words I'd just written down and thought, *Why not?* I said, "Thank you!"

They asked why I was thanking them. I explained that they had helped me come up with the title for my book. Joanne and Dot said that they loved my title and that they knew that whatever I'd write about them would come from my heart. I was tempted to tell them that I had a new wild heart but didn't.

Don't judge a book by its cover—we've all heard that. What went through your pretty little head when you saw my book? Did the title catch your attention? Maybe you care less about a cover of a book than what's inside. I hope what I've written so far has struck your fancy and what I write from here on in will make me your favorite author. I'm already thinking of another book about my life. I know I'll come up with another brilliant title for it, one with greater artistic value—an absolute masterpiece.

Speaking of masterpieces, I had an unbelievable moment in my life (possibly a surprising coincidence) when I met an artist famous for his masterpieces. When I was working with Wallace K. Harrison, the architect of the Metropolitan Opera House in New from 1965 to 1967, I made numerous trips to the opera house with him while its construction was going on. On one trip, he wanted to talk to someone about the two huge murals that would be visible through the massive windows on the east side of the building. That's when I met Marc Chagall.

He asked me why I didn't pronounce my last name the Polish way—"Katcka-*roff*-ski" instead of "Kazza-*rou*-ski." My jaw dropped. I had a great time talking with him. I think that if he were alive, he'd ask me, "Why didn't you start your book with your surprising coincidence of meeting me?"

That had to one of the most memorable days in my life.

CHAPTER 26

I T IS WHAT it was. That phrase came to me the first night I set foot on Ground Zero—Tuesday, September 25, 2001. I hadn't been back to downtown Manhattan since that fateful morning of Tuesday, September 11. Everything I had witnessed that morning was fresh on my mind as I came out of the same subway I had come out of on that fateful morning. On that Tuesday evening, I went there to take part in the recovery/cleanup operations at Ground Zero.

I reported to our temporary DDC field office at PS 89, two blocks north of the WTC site. I walked into this classroom on the second floor. I was told to take a seat. I saw only these little wooden classroom chairs. I sat from 7:45 p.m. until 9:00 p.m. listening to specific instructions, the whereabouts of everyone assigned to the site, and the temporary headquarters for the NYPD, FDNY, and OEM. I felt like I had to raise my hand to be excused to go to the little boys' room.

After class, I had to receive credentials at a trailer to access the sixteen acres that made up what was referred to as Ground Zero. Prior to going to the trailer, I sat outside the school for a few minutes to reacquaint myself with the site that no longer resembled the WTC site I had known. I wanted to get my mind, heart, and soul in sync with one another. I wanted to think clearly about my new job. The destruction people saw on TV couldn't compare to what I saw in person. I'd learned that in 'Nam.

I was told to pick up a radio to communicate with other DDC team members at the site. I was asked if I would mind working the graveyard shift—midnight to 8:00 a.m.—as one of two site supervisors for DDC.

My job was to make sure no one got hurt and nothing went wrong. I made my way down the Westside Highway and saw a ten-foot-high chain link fence encompassing the former WTC's sixteen acres. The devastation was beyond belief. Various sections of both towers were leaning in different directions. I gripped the woven metal links tightly. I was holding on for dear life. I cursed those fucking terrorists who had committed this horrible act. I wanted to rip their throats out with my nails. I took a deep breath. I began to cry for all the lives we had lost there.

The skyline no longer resembled the Manhattan I knew and loved. The two powerful, iconic images that once stood there leaning in ways you would never have imagined left an image in my mind and heart forever. I was hit by this gust of wind that drove a stringent, acrid smell up my nose and left a taste in my mouth and on my lips. No matter which way I turned, that smell was there. It reminded me of something I had smelled and had stuck in my lungs and heart in downtown Da Nang. It made me feel I had never left 'Nam.

In July 1970, just after I'd returned from my tour in Vietnam, I drove to the South Tower and smushed my face to the façade. I looked straight up the tower, which looked as if it were stretching up to heaven. I became part of the building I'd seen as one of the two proposed structures just four years earlier on a scale wooden model. I remembered flying over the tower as we approached LaGuardia when I flew home from 'Nam. It had a magical hold on me.

Back to September 25, 2001. I'd gotten my credentials and was making my way toward the east side of the site. I was walking very gingerly over what I realized was hallowed ground. I had an unbelievable, overpowering feeling. I felt lost. *It is what it was!* I cried. I had a huge lump in my throat. I had to snap out of that mode. I took some huge steps over some beams. I was hit by this strange bolt of light that smacked me in my eyes. I thought the sun had burst through from out under the debris. I kicked ash-white powder mixed with pieces of metal and chunks of concrete. That strange flash of light burned my eyes. I got a godawful headache. I know that must sound ridiculous, but it occurred. I'm having to take two, three steps back just to avoid not wanting to be hit again by it as I write this.

The pain was so intense that I turned around. I needed aspirin before my shift started. Back at the school, I saw a first-aid bag on top of a bunch of school books on a five-drawer file cabinet. Hell, I even remember seeing the handle on the fourth drawer of the cabinet hanging very loosely to the side. Maybe this bag spoke to me. "I'm here when you need me." I found a bottle of extra-strength Tylenol and took two. I sat and rested my head against the wall. *What caused that brilliant flash of light that had me blurt out that totally ridiculous comment? Did I see something I wasn't supposed to see, or did I do something I wasn't supposed to do? Or was it something that's been weighing so heavily on my mind that struck a sensitive and emotional nerve?* (Don't engage in that line of questioning without your doctor's permission especially after taking two extra-strength Tylenol that might have been beyond the expiration date and washed down with cold coffee.)

That something that had been weighing on my illustrious mind was me trying to come up with a new idea to do something different that year on the coming Saturday, September 29, a very important day in my life. I needed to clear my head to figure out what I could do since my initial plans I had made for that day might not have occurred. I needed to come up with an alternative to *What should I do?*

I looked up and saw this beautiful picture of an ocean scene—one beautiful wave rolling toward the shore. The water was so clear that you could see the horizon through the waves. It made me think I could see through all that throbbing pain in my head. I was able to get up and think straight. I went back to the site. I checked the time. Eleven. Duty called at midnight.

I've never forgotten that first night at Ground Zero. I remembered my first headache. I was young. I left a movie theater late one afternoon I'll talk about later. There are no surprising coincidences.

CHAPTER 27

M Y ORIGINAL PLANS for Saturday, September 29, was supposed to be a major surprise for my wife and Noelle. Margie and I were celebrating our twenty-eighth anniversary, and Noelle was celebrating her eleventh birthday. Double your pleasure, double your fun. I love them both. My plans were different from the usual—taking them to a fancy restaurant and going for a scenic drive to somewhere Margie had never been to before. We'd go home for cake, ice cream, and gifts. Just having my daughter call me Dad was the best gift I could ever have or want. I always considered myself deeply blessed to have Noelle for my daughter.

I was listening to a Stevie Nicks cassette on my way from home to work. I'd take a bus and then the subway, the E train, to the last stop, the WTC. I must have listened to one song on that cassette, "Wild Heart," at least twenty times. It just got into my head and brought about my new wild heart I've mentioned. The song's hold on me became very noticeable as I reached the top of the stairs to Church Street. I felt as if I'd been hit with a barrage of arrows that hit my heart. "Something died in my heart last night … that's when I needed you, I needed you most." Feeling this new heart allowed me to deal with everything and anything I saw on the site; a tremendous void had been created in me due to what had occurred that fateful morning fourteen days earlier. That void was letting me know it was still there; my fond memories of my time in and around the WTC were buried deep. But my resilience and perseverance allowed me to carry on. I know that I'd been there and done that and that too.

I spent just about every weekend for a whole year—Friday afternoon to Monday morning— at the Vista Hotel (3WTC) as I worked on some major alterations for Merrill's Investment Banking Division that has moved into the WFC (World Financial Center) that we handled on the weekends. Merrill was growing rapidly back then in the '80, and we were rebuilding the cubicles and offices on the weekends and making sure people could go to work there come each Monday morning.

I wanted to come up with a way to celebrate with Margie and Noelle, but I didn't know if I'd be working at Ground Zero because our schedules were in flux. I took a call from my boss and heard myself say, "Sure, no problem. I'll be there before four o'clock." I'd made my boss happy by agreeing to work as one of two section supervisors when one of them had been called away. I solved my boss's problem but created one for myself. Margie and Noelle were just feet away staring at me. Margie, Noelle, and I had planned on going to dinner that evening. But I'd have to leave home at 2:00 p.m. to get to work by 4:00 p.m. Margie gave me this look after hearing my reply to whomever had called, but she knew my work ethic. "I'm needed at the site. I'm going in to work," I told her. I think she knew that half my heart had been down there since 9/11 and the other half was catching up. But I wanted to be there for them and celebrate our day. I came up with a great idea, but Margie beat me to the punch. "Come on, Charlie, I know you're tired. Why don't I drive you in? This could be our scenic drive to Lower Manhattan, and maybe you, Noelle, and I can celebrate in a different way."

You're gonna have to wait for the details on that; I have much more important things to tell you as they come popping into my head.

CHAPTER 28

W RITING ABOUT 9/11 and the time I spent at Ground Zero was therapeutic. It helped me find the resilience and perseverance to carry on. Maybe I'll inspire someone else to write about his or her astounding experiences. I've told others about my surprising coincidences because I found them interesting and thought those I spoke to could be my wonderful angels in disguise.

I recall meeting a young chap (whose name escapes me at the moment) on Fifth Avenue in front of the Museum of Art. He had on display and for sale some amazing photographs he had taken all over the world. The colors were stunning. One in particular caught my eye. It had no price tag. I wanted to know why. It reminded me of a photo I had taken at Ground Zero that I thought was intense and powerful. It had won an award. I asked him a couple of questions about the photo and noticed him rubbing his arm as he beat around the bush about it. I asked him why he was rubbing his arm. I told him that I'd taken a photo at Ground Zero that made the hairs on my arm stand up when I looked at it. I told him about the book I was writing about my surprising coincidences.

He said, "You better include that photo of yours if you're going to mention some of your powerful surprising coincidences." He said that whenever you talk about real important things, you get this unbelievable, strong feeling deep in your heart that sends a message to your left arm. He called it "seeping."

"Sit back and enjoy it," he said. "You were meant to write that book just like I'm meant not to part with that photo. Your readers will be captivated by your photo as much as you are."

I told him about one of my surprising coincidences and one event I'd experienced.

"I can't wait to read your book," he said. I wrote the title on a business card for him. "I love your title! It's perfect!" he said.

After hearing him talk about captivating readers, I thought about Nelson DeMille's (my favorite author) books or those by James Paterson, Lee Childs, and Eric Blehm. Their books and characters had captivated me. I'm hoping my book captivates you in the same way.

CHAPTER 29

I've often asked myself, *What if I had done something completely different a second before one of my events or surprising coincidences had occurred? Would they still have taken place?* Lee Childs's books make me feel as though he wrote them for me. I thought he was giving me a message that related to what I was going through.

I compared myself to Lee's main character, Jack Reacher, who was having a moment of reflection in one storyline that had to do with his older brother. Jack was thinking back about what his older brother had told him: "Before you criticize someone, you should walk a mile in his shoes. Then when you criticize him, you're a mile away and he'll have to run after you in his socks." It was something my younger brother, Michael, would have said to me.

Once when I was having dinner with some friends, someone asked me how my book was going. I told him. Others said that they thought most readers wouldn't have a clue about what I'd been through in life. Their remarks reminded me of Reacher's brother's remark. So if you feel like criticizing me, start walking in my shoes and do me a favor—get lost. But get lost after you've put some Dr. Scholl's Odor Fighting Insoles size 10–12 in them. Forget about the socks. I'm picky about my socks. I'd be more than happy to meet you for dinner (I happen to enjoy the Four Seasons restaurant in Manhattan, so bring your credit card) where we can continue our little talk about your reasons for criticizing me. Okay, that's off my chest.

But hell, it's taken me over four years to get where I am now in this book. I've cut and pasted using Microsoft Word, a real chore. I should have written it out, made my changes and corrections, and then typed it into my computer. I probably would have been finished way earlier than I did if I had. I'm telling you this because I do all my typing with just my middle fingers. I'm not joking! My left middle finger would hit the caps lock and shift key while my right middle finger would hit the letters. Talk about a slow process.

My dad had bought a Remington typewriter back in the '60 for my sisters, who were taking typing in school. I tried it once and got my fingers stuck between the keys. Just typing this out has caused my middle fingers to overheat. I have to put them in ice water for a bit and then warm them up in lukewarm water before they'll relax. While the water baths are going on, I read what I've typed to see I've used the proper and correct verbiage. I'd never heard the word *verbiage* until I got lost in a small town near Cincinnati. I was there waiting for some furniture to arrive for a Merrill Lynch office I was working on. Somehow, I took a wrong turn when I went for a drive and driven way south and didn't realize it until I saw a sign that read Welcome to Kentucky. I continued driving with no direction in mind until I was deep in the countryside. I was in my glory. I was just trying to keep the sun to the left. I came upon this fork in the road, got out, picked it up, and threw it into a field. (A little bit of my wit here.)

I took a left where normally I would have taken a right. After twenty minutes of passing dilapidated barns and homes, I crested a hill and saw a beat-up pickup stopped in the middle of the road. Three old geezers were sitting on the tailgate looking real pissed off. "What's the problem, gents?" I asked.

"Who are you calling gents?" they asked. "You planning on helping us? We're out of gas!"

"Listen up, gents! I'll help you if you help me. I'll take you to a filling station if you'll kindly direct me back to Ohio." They were agreeable to that. I needed to get back before my furniture arrived.

The gentleman who got into my car asked, "What you smiling about being lost? And how come you tawk so funny?"

That made my day. We found a gas station about twenty minutes later and filled his five-gallon can. On our way back, he asked me again, "Hey son, ware didya learn how to tawk?"

I tried to be polite, but I couldn't resist saying, "I learnt to tawk dis way by goin' to lotsa skools up nord."

His reply was immediate. "Why din't your momma and poppa jus keepya in one skool so you culd tawk right and people cud understand you better by using proper verbiage? Haf da time, I can't undastan wat yur sayin!"

I thought his comment was absolutely priceless even though I'd never heard the word *verbiage* before. I thought it must have been a local term.

Back at the truck, I shook hands with them and asked for directions back to the interstate. They told me that if I ever got lost in their town again (Oddville, Kentucky. Go ahead—look it up), that I should stop to say hello. They gave me excellent directions back to Ohio. I felt good having gotten lost, meeting those three nice gents, and picking up a new word for my vocabulary.

I got back to where I was supposed to be about ten minutes before the trucks arrived. I planned on finding a library so I could look up *verbiage*. I hope I've made any of my readers from Oddville proud. I was, however, surprised to learn that you Oddvillers use that word only in months with twenty-eight days. Go figure.

CHAPTER 30

ONCE UPON A time, I caught an awesome-sized striped bass off the beach at Long Beach Island, New Jersey. The hit my pole took was exhilarating. That bass danced in the surf as I reeled it in. I was one happy man landing my first striped bass. I was thrilled enough by my catch to give it a big kiss (no, not on its lips). I carried it back to the beach house I always stayed at up the street. I left my pole on the beach figuring I'd go back for some more fishing considering how lucky I felt.

As I was walking past my neighbor's house, my dear friend, Helen Hoffman, was out front talking to one of her younger brothers and asked me what I planned on doing with my beautiful fish. I told her I was thinking of having it mounted and hanging it on Susan's dining room wall. She knew I was joking. She introduced me to her brother, who was considered a fine chef who worked in a very popular restaurant in Philadelphia.

He told me he'd love to prepare it for our Festivus dinner that night; he said that grilled striped bass would be the highlight of our meal. He did just that, and it was a hit. That year's Festivus topped some of our previous celebrations. I'm thinking of including a photo of me and my striped bass, but if I don't, just take my word about this. If need be, I'll get *Dateline*, *60 Minutes*, and *20/20* to do stories on the recipe and the chef behind it. Everyone thought it was delicious; they raved about it hook, line, and sinker. (No, they weren't left inside the fish!)

My reason for telling you this fish story is to let you know that what you've read so far in this book is no fish story. I'm a first-time writer who's having a hard enough time just telling you the truth about everything; I don't have to put a spin on anything to captivate you more than I already have. I can imagine how much more painful it would've been for me to write bullshit. If I had tried, my two poor fingers would have rebelled and cramped up possibly permanently.

I prefer to blame my finger cramps on global warming. I think my middle fingers and global warming have had a connection ever since the day I was born. It was revitalized in the summer of 1969 to the summer of 1970 because of where I was and how often I had raised my middle finger at 'Nam and charlie, the VC. The temperature over there and the heat from the rockets and mortars must have warmed my fingers, and this was long before Al Gore. I believe I was born with this already in me. There, I said it, born with it!

I might have to drag my older sister, Charnat, into this mess. She may not be aware of this. She was also born in San Diego fourteen months before me, but she's not as much of a sun worshiper as I am. My dad was stationed in the navy there after the war. Only about two hundred miles away in New Mexico, they tested atomic bombs. I believe the testing there and in Nevada must have blasted particles into our squeaky-clean atmosphere and saturated it. Those particles must have been blown by the Santa Ana winds over San Diego, and no one in DC had any clue about it. "We the people, in order to form a more perfect bomb" conducted the tests in the remote west. I think all the underground testing we were doing by setting off megaton explosions could have major rifts in the earth's surface that caused earthquakes.

I thank you for hearing me out regarding my two theories here. I'm ready to take you back to a time when I had only one great concern—trying to stay alive.

CHAPTER 31

I MAGINE WHAT IT was like to having to survive every second of every minute every day for a year. It was a year that lasted from the summer of '69 to the summer of '70, July to July, in Vietnam. Picture yourself being in one of those photographs you have seen from that time in a paper or on a news report.

Shit! Wait one fucking minute. There's no way in hell those who haven't been there can imagine it. Survival is a very powerful word. Especially when it relates to your own life. If you've never had a reason to worry about surviving any one day and worry about it the next day too, day after day, wake up and smell the coffee. You'd be in for one hell of a surprise.

I want to tell you about a time I hardly ever talk about. It was a time when I was probably closest to heaven but thought I was heading for hell instead. I was on a flight that took me to where the Pacific and the South China Sea become one. I was on a Continental Airlines plane the military used to transport personnel from the states to Vietnam. We had just departed from our last pit stop on Guam and were headed for South Vietnam.

We took an unexpected plunge about forty minutes into that flight. We had dropped dramatically and had taken twisting turns right and left without any warning. I didn't have time to say a prayer, kiss my ass good-bye, or ask anyone to do it for me; I was preoccupied with latching my seatbelt. Some guys who had been standing got knocked around a bit. It took a while for the pilot to bring the aircraft back to normal flight. The flight attendants tried to compose themselves and us passengers.

I'd been replaying my last three weeks of survival training in my mind hoping to remember everything my instructors had told me. "You're gonna make it through this shit even if it tries to kill you!" I almost told myself that I'd even get on a roller-coaster again if that would get me out of this near-death experience.

The captain enlightened us as to what had just happened—we'd plunged in a matter of seconds from 37,000 feet to 30,000 feet having flown into a typhoon with no warning. That convinced me I was fully prepared for whatever came my way in 'Nam. But I do like a good heads-up once in a while. Don't like surprises. Never did. Especially the life-or-death type of surprises. I like being prepared and being around to thank God later.

Before I joined the navy, I was working in New York and was reading stories about Vietnam. It started to get to me. My dad, who had served in the navy and fought in World War II in Europe, would ask me every so often what my feelings were about the war in Vietnam and how would I feel if my draft number came up. I didn't want any part of it whatsoever! In a roundabout way, I kind of got my first taste of what war was like from my dad's description of what he saw and what it was like being there on D-Day.

His stories about being onboard the closest ship to Omaha Beach on that famous morning and the idea of going to 'Nam were scaring me shitless. I heard a few weeks later that some of my classmates had been drafted and ended up there in four months. That had me thinking of taking a trip to Canada, a place that looked so peaceful and beautiful compared to Vietnam, but I couldn't speak Canadian. I gave up on that idea and had a heart to heart with my dad.

Turns out his dad hadn't wanted him facing the enemy one on one and had convinced him to join the navy. I took my dad's advice and my (God rest his soul) grandfather's advice to follow in my father's footsteps and join the navy too. I was sworn in on February 27, 1967, my dad's forty-sixth birthday. I'm sure he didn't like seeing me leave for the Great Lakes Naval Training Center outside Chicago with eight others. It wasn't what I had wanted to give him as a birthday gift. He'd worry about me for my four years' enlistment and pray I didn't get sent to war.

CHAPTER 32

I ARRIVED IN Chicago and heard an announcement that anyone going to boot camp at the Great Lakes Training Center should get on a yellow school bus outside the terminal. My eight amigos and I headed for the bus. At the training center, we stood in line to sign in. Our papers were stamped and signed. We got a short synopsis about the weather in Chicago. It sounded like I'd be spending the coldest three months of my life there and wouldn't thaw out until May, when we'd leave.

It would have been nice to have seen a lake at the Great Lakes Training Center. I recalled we had five big ones somewhere in the Midwest.

Boot camp consisted of a lot of marching, saluting, and getting orders shouted at us almost 24/7. I was amazed at how many guys didn't know their right from their left based on their actions when they were told "Right face!" or "Left face!" (No, I wasn't one of them.)

We were told we'd get one day off, a Liberty Pass. We could take trains to either Milwaukee or Chicago. I wanted to go to Milwaukee so I could step foot in Wisconsin and get some cold Budweisers. When I got there, I saw a crowd gathering across the street at some movie theater. I walked over to see what the commotion was. Lo and behold. Sonny and Cher exited a limo. I figured my navy dress blues would garner me some respect and let me get closer to the doors. My hunch was right.

Sonny and Cher walked right past me. Sonny was shaking hands with all those he passed. I wanted to tell Cher, "I got you, babe!" Well, I did, and I got this weird look from Sonny seeing me in a navy uniform. (Yes, I was ogling his woman, but wouldn't you have if you'd been in my shoes?) He quickly made his way over to her and put his arm around her waist. I stepped out of their way. When they reached the doors, they turned and waved to the crowd. I'm pretty sure the kiss Cher blew off her hand was directed at me, and it seemed to be okay with Sonny, who gave me a parting smile. (Rank does have its privileges.)

I took a long walk along the lake, had a nice meal with three Buds, and then I headed to the train station so I'd get back before being declared AWOL. I told some of my roommates where I'd been and what I'd seen. I believe I may have started off saying, "You're not gonna believe this …"

Graduation came a few weeks later. I got my orders. I was heading for some naval air station on Florida's Gulf Coast. I was told to go home and thaw out for two weeks and get to my next duty station on time. My dad picked me up at the airport, and I saw a big banner outside our home that read, Welcome Home Charlie. At dinner, my mom and dad said they had scheduled various outings to my relatives before I left for Florida. My sisters and brother told me there was another outing we'd be going to on Sunday that was a secret.

It was great just hanging out with my younger brother, my sisters, and my friends doing as many things possible before I left. I told them I'd spend the next two years in Florida for my next duty station, not Vietnam. But I didn't know what I'd be doing in Florida.

I was looking forward to the last outing we'd be going to. It was Mother's Day, and we were going out to dinner, a special treat in my family. Sunday arrived. My dad made pancakes for breakfast, and we went to church. On the way home, my dad told us what the big surprise was—a major league baseball game. He'd gotten six tickets for a Yankees-Orioles game at Yankee Stadium. Now that was some surprise!

Dad had gotten great seats—a little beyond first base and about ten rows back from the field. We had a great view of home plate and right over the Yankees' dugout. My dad said after the game, we were going across the street to the famous Yankee Clipper Restaurant for dinner. That was my first game in a famous stadium. It was mother of a day. I saw Mickey Mantle hit his 500th home run in the bottom of the seventh inning with two outs and the count of three and two. The stadium was in complete pandemonium. Yanks won 6 to 5. That day will always stick out in my mind as a truly memorable day for my family and me. And on Mother's Day too. I love my mom so much!

We had a great dinner. We left the Bronx and went back to Brooklyn. I couldn't wait to tell my friends where I'd been and what I'd seen later that night; I was leaving early the next morning. They couldn't believe I'd been to the game until I showed them the ticket stub. I told them I might see them at Christmas if things worked out.

I packed my navy sea bag and spent some time with my family in the living room talking about everything that came to mind. The next morning, we had breakfast. It was hard saying good-bye because I wouldn't be back until Christmas. My dad drove me to the airport, where he told me to make him proud, keep my nose clean, and don't do anything stupid while I was down there. He said he'd keep praying I didn't get sent to Vietnam. It was a sad good-bye. I love my dad very much.

I flew to Florida's panhandle; Naval Air Station Pensacola is on the beautiful Gulf of Mexico. I'd done some research on Pensacola and had learned it had the whitest sand in the world, its waters were crystal clear, and it could get hot as hell there. The navy base was the largest in the country. It was home for the Blue Angels, the navy's famous flight demonstration team. I was about to spend two years in one hell of a place—two years of shore duty before two years of sea duty. Sea duty is only as good as the ship you get stationed on.

I arrived on Monday, May 15, 1967. It felt like a hundred degrees. The last pieces of ice between my toes and up my nose melted. Boot camp had been cold. I swore I'd never go to Chicago again unless the weather was in the nineties and I could actually see a lake. Some of my buddies had gotten frostbite there after marching all hours of the day or night in frigid weather. It had to be the coldest place I've ever been to. You'd think having been born in warm, sunny San Diego and having global warming instilled in my body would have helped me stay warm in Chicago.

As it turned out, I spent almost eight years in Chicago when I was working for Merrill Lynch, and I'd fly into Chicago to catch flights to other places in the country as well. I believe I stayed in every hotel in the downtown area. My favorite was the Ambassador East on Goethe

Street, two blocks from Lake Michigan, which I swam in. I was there in the early '80s in the winter and experienced the three coldest day in my life. The wind chill factor pushed temps to minus 58 degrees. Even my eyes froze up. I had to turn my whole head to see where I was going. Makes me happy for global warming nowadays.

But down in Florida, each day was better than the previous. I was loving the heat waves there so much that I began to worship them. It got to the point that I couldn't stand opening a refrigerator and getting chilled. Unbeknown to me, I was getting primed for another heat wave two years later (and I'm not talking about the weather here) when I was sent to Vietnam and had to deal with rocket and mortars attacks that really raised the heat there.

Near the end of my two years, I requested thirty days' leave to go home. I didn't know where I was going next. It didn't matter as long as it wasn't Vietnam. Normally, one would get sea duty after two years of shore duty, but keep in mind I wrote "normally."

CHAPTER 33

M Y LEAVE REQUEST came back approved, so I called home to tell them the good news. For some weird reason, I didn't get my orders the usual way—in an envelope; instead, I received a Communications Notice from the Communications Office on the third floor of the building I was working in probably because of whom I was working for and more important, his rank.

I was to report to Almeida, California, to board a ship to fulfill my sea duty obligation for two years. I was happy to see no mention of Vietnam. I'd lucked out! I'd learn the name of the ship and time to report to it. I called home with that news and told my girlfriend, Angel, about it.

I received notice the next day that I'd be a member of the world-famous nuclear carrier CVN-67, the USS *Enterprise*. My dad had told me that aircraft carriers would be a good gig. I felt that I had it made in the shade; I'd be sailing the ocean blue instead of running through the jungles of Vietnam. My family passed along the good news to the rest of the family and to my close friends, but they weren't as happy as my beautiful and stunning girlfriend, Angel (who could have passed as Christina Aguilera's twin), whom I was about to ask to go with me to California and get married in San Diego as my parents had.

My time in Pensacola was about to end. I had what was called a skatin' job, but to me, it was a prestigious job. I was the personal driver for the chief of staff, a captain, a rear admiral, and even the admiral though he had a regular driver. I had hit it off well with the admiral and the captain. They reminded me of my dad; each had his quirks.

The captain and I bonded; I believe it was because I showed him more respect than had his previous driver. I bonded with the admiral maybe even more so than the captain probably because I happened to be seeing one of his daughters secretly at the bowling alley on base where we bowled or shot pool a few times a week. We never went off base, and I never introduced her to my buddies as the admiral's daughter.

That lasted two months until she went back to college. I began dating another girl, also very popular. She was well known in Pensacola; her sister was Dawn Cashwell, a Miss Florida and the first runner-up in the '67 Miss America pageant. I called Verla Lynn Cashwell Angel. She was much more beautiful than Dawn, and her dad was a retired navy commander.

A month prior to my getting the news about California, the admiral told me he wanted to go to Mobile. He wanted me to drive because he wanted to speak to me. I had no clue as to what he wanted to talk about unless he'd found out I was seeing his daughter. Outside the base, he cleared his throat and started talking. He said that he knew I was in a deep relationship with the girl I was dating, Angel. He said that we were a fine-looking couple and that if I wanted to stay in Pensacola for the next two years, he could have my orders changed. He told me he was going to Washington, DC, to head the navy's BUPERS (Bureau of Personnel). Rank does have its privileges. I told him that I was extremely happy to hear that but wanted to wait to see what my assignment was.

The day my orders arrived, I talked it over with my girlfriend. She said she'd love to go with me to California. She had no clue I'd ask her to marry me once we got out there. I told her I was planning on cutting my thirty days' leave at home to fifteen days. I wanted us to get married out there and find an apartment before I reported to my ship.

Three days before the admiral's change of command ceremony and my last day in Pensacola, I received a speed letter from the same Communications Office; I was to meet the *Enterprise* in Newport News, Virginia, as it was going to be dry-docked for a year. I figured I'd be spending another year of shore duty in Virginia.

Angel didn't mind going to Virginia, and my family was happy that I'd be even farther from Vietnam. I visualized Angel and me visiting her family in Florida and mine on Long Island back and forth. I told the admiral about the change in my orders. He asked me if I was happy with that, and of course I said yes.

Two days later, the change-of-command ceremony took place. The admiral surprised me by calling me up to the stage to help him give out the gold wings that the naval and marine aviators were to receive. That was an honor. Our new admiral took charge of the command, and the captain whom I'd been driving for a year was to remain as his chief of staff.

We all went back to the admiral's headquarters, where he asked me to do a small favor before he left. He wanted his two-star flag that was on the flagpole. His flag was always flown there when he was on base; it would come down when he was away. Our new admiral would have his own flag. I got it, folded it neatly, and handed it to him. He said, "Charlie my boy, I want you to have this. You did an excellent job here for me and for the two chiefs of staff. I especially liked the way you always brought smiles to people's faces when they came to our office."

I was surprised. He saluted me when he handed it off to me. I was very proud to have received it. We said our good-byes. I said good-bye to his wife and two daughters. The admiral asked me to drive him and his family to their plane for the flight to DC that evening. Again, I was honored to do so.

On the drive out there, the admiral has us laughing about some of the silly stuff that had occurred when I had driven him to some events or when I tried to play tennis or golf with him. Everyone was in tears laughing. He knew I'd been seeing his daughter at the bowling alley, but he said he'd trusted me. It was sweet sorrow to watch them board the plane after everyone gave me a hug good-bye. It was as if dear relatives were leaving. "Keep in touch!" the admiral said.

I waited until I saw them fly out over the base. The plane circled and dipped its wings directly over me as a way of saying farewell. I was crying so much on the way back to the barracks that I had to put the windshield wipers on.

I packed my stuff as I was leaving the next day. Some friends came to say good-bye. I had too much stuff to take. I figured I'd leave some of my civilian clothes, some records and a record player, and my guitar with Angel and we'd pick them up on a trip to Florida. I was also thinking of the right time to ask Angel to marry me, then or after my leave. I thought she might want to get married in Pensacola, where her friends and family were.

You're not gonna believe this. I got a call to report to headquarters. I went there and ran up to the second floor where I walked in and saw the admiral and a captain. It looked like they were about to have a friendly chat with me. They waved me over. The admiral asked me to tell him a little about myself, my family, and my girlfriend. After I did, he asked the captain to hand me a piece of paper on an end table. The words *new orders* punched me in the stomach. I wouldn't be reporting to the *Enterprise* in Newport News; civilians would be doing the work on the ship, not navy personnel.

A yeoman walked in with a pink paper. It looked like another speed letter. He gave it to the captain, who read it and handed it to the admiral. I got to read it next. "Charlie," the admiral said, "I know you heard of Murphy's law. Well, here's a perfect example. Hell, not more than two hours ago, Admiral Guinn departed the base and who comes and visits but Mr. Murphy!"

I couldn't decipher what I was reading even after my third attempt. It was all navy jargon I couldn't decipher. I asked the two of them to please tell me what it was trying to tell me about some kind of ship I was being assigned to named NavSupAct and where was it stationed.

My captain slowly told me I was not being assigned to a ship but to Naval Support Activity in Da Nang, Vietnam. I was going to be boots on the ground. I asked, "Is this some kind of joke? Are you two having fun with me?" I felt royally and totally fucked. All hell was breaking loose. My brain was breaking up.

My captain walked over to me, put his hands on my shoulders, and told me how sorry he was to hear this. The admiral told me how sorry he was too. All I could do was to stand up, salute them, shake their hands, say "It's been real," and leave.

As I left the building, I thought about going back and asking the admiral to call my former admiral with the news I needed to speak to him urgently. But I headed to the EM (enlisted men's) club for some beer, which I really needed right then.

Six beers later, I went back to my barracks and washed my face.

That's when I heard my name over the PA system. I was to report to the admiral's office. *I knew it! Someone made a big, fuckin' mistake and gave me the wrong orders!* I bet that the new admiral made a call to the old admiral to see what the hell had gone wrong.

I called the admiral's office. The yeoman told me that another speed letter had arrived and that the admiral and the captain wanted to see me a.s.a.p. I got there. I was handed another speed letter that stated I was still reporting to Virginia but I had to be there in three days, not thirty. I was to attend some kind of school there, a cargo handling school in Cheatham Annex outside Virginia Beach. *Cargo handling?*

I called Angel with the news I wasn't leaving for another two days. I said nothing about having to go to Vietnam for I figured I'd wait till the morning in case something changed overnight by my friend, the admiral, in DC. I got up at seven the next morning, showered, dressed, and had breakfast. I went to headquarters to see if my admiral in DC had called. I wanted to ask him about staying in Pensacola. After all, he had asked me to stay in touch with him.

I got word sometime around 8:30 a.m. when two other captains I knew from the admiral's staff walked in. I was told that the admiral who had left had had a change in plans. He and his family were going to go home to Austin, Texas, for two weeks before heading to DC. I realized I was stuck with my newest orders. All I could do was call home and tell my family I was going to a school for five days and then take my thirty days' leave.

My admiral had found a spot for me on a DC-37 going to Virginia for this schooling. Rank does have its privileges. I gave it a lot of thought. I decided to wait till my last day of school to break the news to Angel that I was headed for Vietnam and that I would be in-country, not on a ship.

CHAPTER 34

T HE NEXT DAY, I left for Cheatham Annex and spent five days
learning how to operate forklifts and other heavy equipment. It
was truly a mind blower; I had to rush through this, rush through
that—it was a crash course on how to handle the equipment even in total
darkness. And then I was headed for hell. I mean Vietnam.

Some chief petty officer told me I'd find out if my thirty days' leave
would start after my last class. Mr. Murphy rode again. Eleven others
in my class and I found out our leaves were on hold. We were going to
another school across the road, this time to learn survival training. We
had an hour to pack up and get there. I gathered my stuff and walked to
this building with my sea bag over my shoulder. I found a comfortable
spot and waited. Within ten minutes, at least a hundred sailors were
milling around in the room waiting. No one had a clue about why we
were there or why we were attending this special training.

It got real quiet when three men walked in all in camouflaged
fatigues and black berets. One walked up to a mic and introduced
himself and his sidekicks as SEALs. We learned we were there for
some accelerated class in counterinsurgency, three weeks of specialized
training. It wouldn't start until we completed any calls we wanted to, but
we had only two minutes to talk. We were led to an adjoining room lined
with wall phones. We were told to say, "I'm here for more schooling."
(We weren't to mention special training.) "I'll be here for three weeks. I'll
get new orders then." Nothing else could be said. I was glad I still had my
thirty days' leave. I called my family and Angel with the canned speech.

The training we were going to have was called SERE—Survive,

Evade, Resist, Escape. I thought I had already passed the first two having survived and evaded by not having to go to 'Nam for my first two years of my enlistment, but my chances of successfully resisting and escaping this training for the next three weeks weren't looking that good since our trainers were the best of the best in-country, out of country, boots on the ground, heads in the air, or asses underwater.

We were told we were required to have this training because we'd be in a combat zone and would run the risk of being captured. We needed to learn what we could and couldn't do, and we needed weapons training. The last week would involve surviving five days in the countryside of Virginia in a game of cat and mouse. We were the mice and they were the cats. The training I was given was at the Naval Amphibious Base, home to the SEALs on the East Coast.

I believe what they taught us saved my ass in 'Nam.

We were constantly told that if we were found doing something really stupid like getting caught and telling the enemy more than we were allowed to, we'd be considered unworthy and not dependable enough to be sent to 'Nam. We would be considered traitors to our country and it would be noted in our navy jacket (personnel file).

Somehow, I developed the confidence that I'd show them (and myself) that they couldn't break me. I gave a hundred percent of myself to the training; I persevered. I carried on thinking I was Superman, invincible.

Week one was strictly classroom; we learned about the people, the country, the weather, what to expect, and what to look for. We learned all navy regulations we'd have to adhere to if we were ever taken prisoner. (Nothing was said about saying our prayers.)

Week two was all weapons. We learned how to load, fire, disassemble, clean, and reassemble .45 caliber pistols (did that with my eyes closed when it came to disassembly and assembly), an M-16, an M-14, and a .50 and a .60 caliber machine gun. I became pretty proficient at hitting my targets. I was also given a quick lesson on loading and firing an M-79 grenade launcher (which I had the opportunity to use twice over there).

I could write a whole book on just week three. It was the highlight of my training. I spent the week in the countryside in an area that remotely resembled a jungle in Vietnam. (Uncle Sam could have saved money by keeping me there.) I learned how to keep my mouth shut during my interrogations. The SEALs played the VC; they dressed like them, spoke Vietnamese, and were quite good at scaring the shit out of me.

The instructors were determined to find out if we had listened to what we'd been taught in class and had paid strict attention to every detail as to what had been said about being captured and tortured to make us talk. Before I was finally caught, they would drill into us in their own special way that we hadn't paid attention in class when it came to concealing ourselves and evading them. This is where I had to sustain some of their pushing around to put us into the right frame of mind by not fucking up again and getting caught.

We were told that our objective was to get from point A to point B in two days. We'd have to travel by day and night and eat whatever we could catch—snakes, frogs, fish, or leftover burgers. The main thing was not to divulge any "classified" information because the enemy had ways to make us give it up. That is where our training became very intense. I found it surprising that I was given the actual baseball score of that first baseball game I went to with my family—Yankees 6, Baltimore 5. This was not to be given out under any circumstances. Even though they tried very hard to make me divulge this info, I kept my mouth shut and took their beatings, I mean, training, that one day of pure torture. Hell, I was shown various ways or methods that the enemy would use on us but at a lesser degree of torture. I did not enjoy this Spanish Inquisition the SEALs dealt out with smiles on their faces. I was stripped to my skivvies and dragged into this place that resembled a POW camp where I believe I had a serious face on me every second I was there. I never cracked a smile or a joke knowing I'd be punished for doing it. I mean questioned.

The SEALs were able to drum into me (sometimes with their fists, knees, or boots) to give up my classified info I'm sure they already knew. If I did, I wouldn't go to 'Nam. Whatever they did to me, I took it to prepare myself for the worst to come. And it got worse. My resilience was tested to the max, but I was able to complete the training. I say thanks to those SEALs for making me a better man. I was proud to serve my country and will always have the deepest respect for every SEAL. Wild horses couldn't pull me apart enough to make me spill my guts. (But I could be convinced to let a sexy blonde take part in my torture.)

The training taught me how to keep my mouth shut all the time (until I met some guys from DDC some forty-five years later). I was so gung-ho about my accomplishment. I was looking forward to my leave and partying my ass off.

But then, Mr. Murphy's sister showed up unexpectedly and fucked me up big-time.

CHAPTER 35

NEW ORDERS. No thirty-day leave. Somehow, my stint at the cargo handling school and SERE had eaten it up. I had five days left in the states before heading to 'Nam, where my Uncle Sam, whom I had never really met, wanted me. What kind of relative would have sent me to 'Nam considering my terror of anything green, particularly jungles?

I desperately needed someone to kick me in the ass for not taking the admiral up on his offer to assign me to Pensacola for the remainder of my enlistment. I would have thanked the kicker to no end.

I had five days to spend with my family but no time with Angel. I didn't know how to tell her I was to report in 'Nam in five days. My head was spinning. I packed my sea bag and went to the airport. My dad was going to pick me up at what's now JFK. Before he did, I called Angel to explain where I was, where I was going, and why I wouldn't see her for a year if I made it out of hell alive.

My dad was not a happy camper, I could tell, when he pulled up at the terminal. It wasn't until we merged onto the Cross Island Parkway that he asked, "You're going over there, aren't you?" He choked on his words. "So what ship will you be on?"

"Yes, Dad, I'm going there. I'm not assigned to any ship. I'm in-country. Boots on the ground."

Dead silence. A tear ran down his cheek. He choked up. "Okay. Do me a favor. Don't say a word to your mother or to your sisters or brother about this. Let's enjoy your thirty days home and make the best of it. Try not to give off any signs or show any emotions that you're going over there. You can break the news to them on the morning you have to leave. Do it while I'm making breakfast for everyone, got that?"

"Dad, I got it." I waited till the air cleared. He exited at Jamaica Avenue. I asked him to pull over so we could talk for a minute, which he did. I told him I'd be leaving in five days. He started to cry. "I'm sorry, Dad, but those are my orders. I'm scared. I don't want to go there! This whole thing sucks!" I didn't have the heart to tell him that the admiral I had worked for had given me an offer that I had turned down when I got the *Enterprise* order. I didn't see the need to bring it up just then.

"Hell! I didn't want to go there, but now I'm going!" Before we drove off, he told me to wipe my eyes. He didn't want others to see I'd been crying. That drive home was the most intensive ride I've ever taken. I was emotionally drained. He parked down the block from our house. He wanted us to chill out before we got home. He stared at me in silence, but then he told me about being on the USS *Satterlee*, DD-626, a destroyer. It and two other destroyers, being the closest to Omaha Beach, were letting loose at German bunkers along the top and ridge of Pointe du Huc. He was responsible for all the big guns onboard, giving the command to fire at the German bunkers so about 200 army rangers could scale the cliffs. My dad said he'd seen the horrors of war even though he had never stepped one foot on that beachhead. He said he didn't have to. He saw the bodies of his comrades floating next to his ship in a sea of red. He said that he told himself that if he ever had sons, he would never want them to see what war was like. He said he had demons in him due to what he had seen there when he was twenty-three.

There I was, twenty-one and scared shitless. It was July 4, 1969, our country's birthday, but I had no desire to celebrate. I didn't want to see or hear any fireworks. It would have reminded me of the training I'd just been through. I wanted my independence. I didn't want to go. But I wiped my tears after hearing my dad's story. I told him I was headed for Da Nang knowing it had been all over the news for the past few days as a place that had been getting rocketed and mortared. I told him not to worry. I told him I'd keep my mouth shut about this to the rest of the family.

On the morning I was to leave, my dad made eggs, bacon, and toast. He gave me the nod. I told my family the bad news. We were at the same table where we'd talked about Vietnam about two years earlier. My family's floodgates opened. My mom was taking it badly. I ate my eggs and bacon, stuffed two slices of toast in my mouth, and tried to wash it all down with a tall glass of milk. I peered over the top of the glass to look at my mom and got this massive lump in my throat. I started making the rounds of the table to say my good-byes to my brother and sisters, giving them each a big hug and kiss, which they returned. They held on to me for dear life. I took a knee by my mom. "Mom, I'll be okay. I'll be back here next July to celebrate your birthday on July 19, promise. You won't get another year older until I help you blow out your candles." I hugged her.

She held me so tight. She kissed me. "I love you, my son."

I think that was the first time I had made her cry. I grabbed my sea bag and started toward the door. "Mom, thanks for bringing me into this world." I had this horrible feeling as I walked to the car, where my dad was waiting. The previous four days had gone by so fast.

On our way to the airport, we talked about old times, mostly about when I'd been scared and when my life could have ended. At the airport, I could tell my dad was trying to be strong, but tears were running down his cheeks. I gave him a hug. "After what you told me a few days ago about what you did on D-Day, I realized you were my new hero. Superman's number two." I was seeing my dad in a whole new light. I asked him, "You know how much I fear roller-coasters, right? You remember my first ride? That's how I feel at this very moment. I'd ride the biggest, scariest roller-coaster for a year rather than go to Vietnam."

He laughed. His reply was golden. "Even at a time like this, you still find a way to humor me. Listen, son, I love you. Take care of yourself. See you next year."

"Love you too, Dad. See you!"

I smiled and gave him a wave. I gave him a salute.

CHAPTER 36

"**O**H ... WHEN I look back now that summer seemed to last forever ... back in the summer of ... '69. Those were the best years of my life."

Yes, the summer of '69 was one of the best times of my life. During that year, starting on July 10, I was in the number-two hot spot in Vietnam, the city of Da Nang on the coast of the South China Sea. The rest of the country was the number-one hot spot. I got there by flying from New York to LA, taking a bus for about an hour to San Bernardino, and boarding a flight to Honolulu. We went on and picked up some guys in Guam. We flew through that typhoon between Guam and Vietnam I mentioned earlier that gave me my first grey hairs.

We landed in Vietnam about 10:30 p.m. The captain informed us that the airport had been rocketed and they had to leave the area quickly. We grabbed whatever stuff we had in the overhead bins and got off as quickly as we could. We were told to board two yellow school buses. The rest of our stuff would catch up with us. I'd been to cargo handling school and had survived survival training. I had to board a school bus in a war zone.

At camp, we had to yell out, "Present" when we heard our names. We had about a twenty-minute ride through villages before we entered this makeshift archway that read Camp Tien Sha, my new home. We were told not to wander off. It was pretty dark. We couldn't see for shit. I heard someone call out my name. I had to head over to this barracks with the outside light on, go inside, and be checked in. I heard we were west of downtown Da Nang in a camp that housed navy personnel and marines. I was in what they referred to as the transient barracks. All I could see was a faint lightbulb glowing in the fucking dark. I went inside. I was told to find an empty bunk and wait till my name was called.

I checked to see if I still had my sealed brown envelope ready to be turned in. It contained my navy personnel file. I took the first empty bunk I came to, threw my sea bag on it, and closed my tired eyes. I waited to be told I was there to fight this fucking war of ours. After less than two minutes of shut-eye, I heard the loudest siren I'd ever heard. Some officer yelled, "Get the hell out! Get into the bunker! Take cover! Rocket attack!"

Bunker? Where the hell is there a bunker?

All the lights went out in the camp. I figured I might as well follow the sound in front of me hoping it would lead me to the bunker. Two guys behind me were hearing two different voices saying the same things I was thinking. The three of us walked into a barracks wall. We went the opposite direction and stopped when we hear this loud explosion to the left. It was so fucking loud that we thought it had been pretty close. A second explosion happened in the same location. It triggered multiple explosions that kept getting louder. We had front-row seats for a huge ball of fire billowing up. We had no idea it was billowing out and toward us. I witnessed the brightest reds, yellows, and oranges inside a humungous black cloud. The shockwave blew the three of us off our feet. My first taste of war without using my mouth.

The three of us ended up hitting the sandbagged bunker we were looking for. I happened to hit it smack square with my chest that stopped me in my travels as I was completely knocked out. I guess someone dragged me and the other two guys who had also been knocked out into the bunker. The guys in the bunker were shaking us to see if we were dead or alive. When we came to, someone asked if we were okay and if we could sit up.

I heard another siren, but it turned out to be the signal for "all clear." I felt like shit. Someone checked to see if I could walk on my own. Someone said, "We got your back." I'd experienced my first rocket attack within an hour of being in-country. I considered myself very lucky that

I had not been harmed much more than I already was from slamming into those sandbags.

I learned later that the three of us had been hit by a mass of air caused by the last explosion. At least two rockets hit the South Vietnamese Army (ARVN) major ammo dump about a hundred yards away. My welcome to 'Nam had come airmail. A simple basket would have done just fine. Back at the barracks, I vented a little. "God almighty, is this the kind of reception I get coming here? Who's responsible for this? This place sucks! Anyone have a cold beer? Anyone know when the next train is leaving?" I tried making light of another near-death experience. The navy had made a mistake by sending Charlie to fight charlie.

"Nice job," someone said. "Love your sense of humor. It was far better than your tryout as a stunt man out there. I mean, you did give quite a performance. I'm giving you a score of 7. Next time, don't flail your arms, for they really stand out with those bright colors behind you."

My sense of humor was as good as his. "Go fuck yourself. I'm taking the first train out of here in the morning. I don't care about the score you gave me. All I want to hear you tell me is which train, the local or the express, has a lounge car. Care to join me?"

We laughed. He told me he had dragged me into the bunker. His name was Dave, and he was a seabee (Construction Battalion) like me. Funny, I'd never been told I was a seabee. That's where I met Fredrick W. Douglass, a fellow DDC worker forty years later at Ground Zero. That's one of my amazing coincidences. He was departing for home the day I arrived in-country and had endured a rocket attack. Ground Zero years later was another war zone for us. We became the best of friends.

CHAPTER 37

I N THE BARRACKS, someone called out my name, but my ears were slightly muffled from the explosions. I got up and made my way over to the table where two lieutenant junior grades were. "You Kaczorowski?" I stopped rubbing my chest, which had taken the full brunt of the force when I hit the sandbags. I nonchalantly reached under my shirt and pulled out my sealed envelope. I handed it over so they could see it was still sealed.

"Are you that person?" one asked. "If so, what's wrong?"

I was taking my time with those low-ranking officers; I'd been dealing with commanders, captains, and a rear admiral for the past two years. "Yes, I am that person" I said without adding "sir" as I should have. I told them what I'd been through outside. I got this look from one officer while the other was giving him a weird facial expression, something that looked like a sigh of relief but with a smile. He opened the envelope and removed the file on me. He looked at his watch and stamped each paper. The other officer signed and dated them and put them back in the folder. He gave everything back to me. "Welcome to Vietnam, Ski!"

They called out to someone, who approached me with a stern look. "You belong to me, mister! You've been assigned to Seabees Construction Unit, CBM-1. You're here to support the 3rd Marine Division here in I Corps for now here in Da Nang. Please to meet you, Ski!"

I don't recall his name. I thanked the two JGs but muttered under my breath, "Go fuck yourself and the horses you rode in on." They hadn't asked me how I was doing or feeling; they couldn't have given a rat's ass about that.

This new guy told me to get my sea bag and head to a barracks right behind the one we were in. I was to pick out a bunk of my choice as long as it was in the rear of the barracks on the first floor. I was told to get some rest and be out in front of the barracks at 0600 to board a deuce and a half (a two-and-a-half-ton truck) that would take me to my assigned work. "Once you get there, report to the lieutenant. Bring your personnel folder in that brown envelope. You'll be assigned to this place called Bridge Ramp."

I picked up my bag and walked to my home away from home for my next 364 days. I found a bunk, set my alarm for 5:00 a.m. after noting it was 12:45 a.m. already, and stretched out using my sea bag as a pillow. I was looking forward to sleeping and waking up without chest pains. But some dude came over and kicked my bunk. "You should get your ass out of bed by four to get enough to eat at breakfast. It'll have to hold you over until dinner at seven. Chow hall is a fifteen-minute walk away. You don't want to miss your truck at 0600. You'll pay for it dearly if you do. Good night."

I said thanks but I don't think he heard me. I reset my alarm for four thirty.

I didn't need the alarm. I was rudely awakened by this very loud clapping sound at 4:12 a.m. I thought someone was giving me another Welcome to 'Nam reception. The clapping sound got louder and louder and closer and closer. I felt sand pouring all over me as if I were at a beach during a windstorm. Sand was coming through some screens. I covered my head and face the best I could with my shirt and let out a few choice curse words. I got so mad that I threw my trusty alarm clock at the wall. Somehow, that stopped the clapping. All I could hear was *fump fump fump.*

The next thing I heard were jet engines whining down. I got up, brushed the sand off me, and headed to a screen door. I stepped outside and saw three helicopters with their rotor blades slowing down. Some guys jumped out of the choppers carrying boxes and a few bags over to a building. I guessed they were delivering the mail. I'd been assigned to a barracks right next to the camps' landing zone for helicopters. *Why didn't that asshole tell me about this?*

I went in to soak my head and wash my face. It was four forty-five. I decided to head to the mess hall. I was thinking of writing to my good buddy, the admiral, a complaint about the three of them who were here in 'Nam busting my balls.

I loaded my tray at the mess hall with six eggs, four slices of toast, three sausages, three pieces of bacon, a box of Frosted Flakes, a banana, and a cup of fruit salad and a bowl. I put three pancakes covered with butter and syrup right over my eggs. I chugged one glass of milk and got two more before I found a seat and started to scarf this stuff down. I didn't want to talk to anyone. I began to hate the entire place and think of remaining days that I had to be here.

I finished my meal and got a cup of coffee and a donut and came back. I looked at the hundred or so guys there. The place could have held 500. On my way out, I washed whatever was going down into my stomach with another glass of cold milk. I grabbed two bananas, two oranges, and a plum for a snack later.

On my way back toward my barracks, I gave the sandbagged bunker a kiss. I was in front of my barracks before six. I saw this truck pull up. I climbed onboard and told the driver my name. He said, "Check. You ready to fight this war of ours?" Of course I said yes. Under my breath, I said "And any other fucker who ever pisses me off from here on in!"

I took a seat near three marines in full battle gear, flak jackets, helmets, and loaded to the hilt with clips for their M-16s. One said, "Oh, oh, we got a cherry here! Run for cover!" *How the fuck did he know?* War zones can get you cursing more so than normally.

This other marine asked me, "Where yuh from, and where yuh headed?" I told him originally from San Diego but lately Long Island and I was headed to Bridge Ramp. The three of them gave me this look. One said, "Listen here, cherry, take my advice. As soon as you get there, bend over and kiss your ass good-bye. Get someone to do it if necessary. You won't be there too long!" The three laughed laughing.

The driver yelled out, "We're picking up two more sightseers. Make room!" Two more sailors climbed onboard. The marine told me, "No matter where you go or work or how you fight this fuckin' war, always remember your sorry ass is always in danger. The VC here can get your ass with their rockets, mortars, ground fire, their women, or even some small kid with a satchel bag who comes up running asking for candy. Your ass is out there, and they're everywhere! You mentioned Bridge Ramp. Your sorry ass is definitely fucked big-time. You'll find out soon enough."

That was comforting news. I was feeling so much more at ease hearing this shit about my lovely ass, but what about me? Our conversation made my second day in-country so much more invigorating. I figured I might as well enjoy all this good shit I was hearing. I pulled out a banana and started eating it like a crazed monkey. I stopped halfway and asked the marine next to me, "Could you do me a big favor and stick the rest of this banana where the sun don't shine without me dropping my pants? You must be a pro by now!"

"You making a monkey out of me?"

"No I'm not, but feel free to stick it up your own ass. This Charlie here doesn't give a rat's ass what the fucking VC does here!" I laughed in his face and told him to leave me the fuck alone.

His response was right on the money. "Gee, I bet you have about three hundred and sixty-three days left to go in this fuckin' country. Am I right? So go fuck yourself and enjoy the rest of this fucking war getting someone to kiss your ass good-bye!"

I said nothing. I got up to see what my camp looked like from the road. I nonchalantly placed my hand over my ass and was waving my finger at that marine. I gazed up to look out toward these weird mountains that sat behind my barracks. One sailor told me, "That's Monkey Mountain. Do not go up that mountain for any reason. If you do, you'll know in less than five minutes why I'm telling you this." I figured I'd stay off it. That mountain was too fuckin' green anyway.

It was July 11, 1969, and I was halfway around the world thinking I'd rather have to deal with a huge chunk of kryptonite than any of this bullshit. I could have been surfing my ass off on Long Beach rather than hearing how I was going to lose it in 'Nam. One of Bryan Adams's songs says, "Ain't no use in complaining when you got a job to do." I realized I had to be ready if I wanted to survive in this war zone that was worse than hell.

The driver told us to look to the left to see where the rockets had landed the previous night. He pointed out where this huge ammo dump used to be. It was smoldering. Traffic was at a crawl. Three Vietnamese army guys on scooters were sitting there gazing at the mess. A vehicle went by with some animals on it, and then some kind of wagon filled with people. Kids on bicycles and plenty of small trucks loaded with people were trying to cut ahead of us. The driver kept blowing the horn and yelling at them to get out of his fucking way.

The road clutter was incredible. We came to a full stop. I heard a commotion coming from the rear of the truck. I walked back there and saw about fifteen or so kids dressed in shirts and pants or shorts that looked like they were parts of our uniforms; they were begging for candy or food. I looked at two boys about eight or nine and said, "No have! No candy!" They kept on begging. "I have none. Maybe later!" That was a huge mistake. Who knew they understood the queen's English? They shouted, "You number ten!" I quickly found out what he meant by that. He had a slingshot and hit me just below the eye with a piece of twig. I imagined him toting a rifle in a few years and being a better shot with it.

I cursed him with the same words I had cursed the helo pilots the night before. The truck started to move. The driver was blowing his horn. He wanted out of the area. I started cussing out the country, the people, those kids, the color green, and everything else I could think of that came to mind. What made me think of M&Ms I'll never know. I shouted at them, "Remember this face! Don't even think about fucking with me again because this Charlie's gonna whip your ass! And why the hell aren't you in school?"

I sat and gave the marines a big smile. One said, "That's it! You just found a way of ending this war for us. Nice going, Charlie! I guess they'll be sending me home early!"

It got real quiet. They were smirking. I said, "Fuck it and fuck you!"

Twenty minutes later, the driver shouted, "Bridge Ramp! One prematurely wounded navy cherry getting off!" Great. Another fuckin' comedian. I made a mental note to keep my other eye out for those kids, those three marines, and the driver.

CHAPTER 38

A s I was climbing off the back of the truck, the guy riding shotgun
said, "Hey, Cherry Charlie, I just want you to know something
about this place. It's known as the place not to be at because it's constantly
on high alert. See all those LSTs, landing crafts, and barges to the right
and all that ammo to your left? That ammo's is used by the 3rd Marine
Division here in I Corps, and the rest goes over to the Da Nang airbase,
twenty minutes away. You're next to downtown, which is always getting
hit with rockets and mortar fire, and don't overlook those two huge
gasoline tanks to your south."

I saw military equipment such as tanks, APCs, and jeeps, building
material, and ammo everywhere I looked. Guys were moving things by
forklift onto flatbeds or into huge, open storage areas. It made me think
of the ammo dump the night before and gave me a grey hair.

"It's not safe here, buddy. Good luck, take care, and God be with you.
And remember, serpentine!" He made the sign of the cross in front of
my face. I had no idea what he meant by serpentine unless it was part
of the last rites he'd just given me. He yelled at the driver, "Let's get the
fuck out of here pronto Tonto!"

Gee, more comforting words.

The trucks' tires kicked up some dirt and sand on me. The wiseass
marine who first spoke to me was mooning me over the side of the truck.
"You could have kissed my ass good-bye before you got off, sailor boy!
You're gonna wish you were going with me!" He fired a round from his
M-16 up to the sky and threw me kisses. *That's one crazy fuck.*

A petty officer 2nd class walked up and asked me my name. He said he was Bill Gager but wanted me to call him Gage. After I told him my name, he told me to follow him to Lieutenant Bill Greiner. He told me the lieutenant would probably tell me what my role there was. I didn't want to break Gage's or the lieutenant's bubbles, but I'd already gotten the lowdown from whoever that was riding shotgun.

Gage said, "I'll be your immediate supervisor here. There are twenty-five other seabees here. We all have each other's back. That's the only thing that matters."

As we were walking to the lieutenant's hootch (what they refer to as a small building), I saw two Vietnamese women in black pajamas sweeping out the hootch with some half-assed brooms. I told Gage how to pronounce my name. He said, "The loot won't be calling you by your name. We all have nicknames in my squad. Do you mind if we call you Ski? You already have a nickname?"

I thought, *Surfer Boy. Yeah!*

The loot gave me the lowdown and showed me where to pick up my gear after Gage gave me the grand tour. "God be with you while you're here, and we don't salute here," the loot said. Comforting news for a change. "You're gonna want to have at your side the gear and weapons we give you. Make sure your weapon is cleaned and the safety is on." We shook hands. "While you're here, just call me loot."

More comforting news. He reminded me of my old admiral or captain, whom I saluted only the first thing in the morning and the last thing at night.

Gage and I walked onto this huge roadway as wide as a football field. He pointed out this tower that stood about thirty feet high. I saw two armed marines and two ARVN soldiers there. I was told they kept a sharp eye on whatever was going on in all directions around this extremely busy facility. The roadway was a mixture of dirt, pebbles, sand, oil, and gasoline and diesel fuel. There were many flatbeds being loaded with ammo by navy personnel driving huge forklifts. Gage called them RTs, rough terrain vehicles.

He said that 99 percent of what I'd be doing there was driving a forklift. He yelled over the sound of the RTs, "Black powder. Extremely lethal! No smoking on the ramp, got it? Welcome to your new home, Ski. You're in the bull's-eye of the enemy's dartboard that also covers downtown, where we're constantly sitting ducks for the VC every minute of the day and night where charlie rules. Everything you see here in any direction makes us that more of a major target because of what we do here, what we have here, and who gets to use it. As you know, the enemy usually wears black pajamas and carries AK-47s. Well, they are also walking among us even as we speak especially those who sympathize with the VC."

I want to go home so bad. What the fuck is he talking about? I looked around and saw about 99 percent of the Vietnamese on and outside the ramp were in black pajamas. I was tempted to ask, "Would the real enemy please stand up and be counted for?"

I looked out of the corner of the eye I had almost lost thanks to that kid with the slingshot and saw some guys walking toward us doing some sort of dance. They were staring me down and calling me all kinds of names similar to what I'd been called in my SERE training. They began hissing like snakes. "Listen up, you pussies," Gage said. "This is our new team member, Ski, or you could call him Surfer Boy."

We shook hands and embraced each other. They told me their names and then their nicknames. "I got your back, now you got mine," they all said. I told them the same, and I said, "Let's get this over with. Which one of you wants to kiss my ass good-bye before I shove this banana up there?" showing them the banana. I told them what had occurred on the truck ride over. They laughed. "We finally got someone with a fuckin' sense of humor."

I said, "Let's go. I'll eat this banana now or afterward, but I won't be taking any of your shit while I'm here!" They started to laugh so hard that they begged me to stop. Gage said, "You just made their day!" They calmed down and were patting me on the back. They said they'd have to remember not to call me charlie while I was there. If they did, I should let one of my rounds from my .45 caliber travel toward their asses and they'd have to buy me a beer at the EM club in camp.

Gage told me he was our fearless team leader who would be evaluating how good of a job I was doing there. He told me that if I ever fucked up royally, he'd probably take no action because I would be dead. It would be good-bye Charlie, meaning me. I told them they had nothing to worry about. I told them what I'd been doing for the past two years.

All I heard was, "Well, what the fuck are you doing here? Did you fuck the admiral's daughter or the captain's wife? Come on, we won't tell. Your secret's safe here!"

Gage told me there were five other teams or squads each made up of five personnel that I'd get to know. "Ski, don't forget any of the stuff I'm about to tell you. Try to picture yourself in a very large box about the size of a football field. Look to your right. That's downtown Da Nang, our neighbor who is constantly a target for the VC. It's strictly off limits. Don't ever go there. In that direction, there's this ten-foot-high chain link fence you can't see right now because of all that dust and sand being kicked up over there. But behind that dust and sand is a five-foot-wide, three-foot-deep ditch right in front of that chain link fence that provides an additional obstruction in keeping anyone from hitting or plowing into those two huge fuel tanks you see. They sit out there for all the world to see. They're owned by Shell. They're extremely dangerous and extremely close to us, and charlie knows it. Never ever run to the south toward them if we're ever under rocket or mortar fire."

Wow. What was next? We'd covered only two directions of this imaginary box. I was thinking about the advice that marine gave me about my ass. I made a strong mental note that south was where Shell was and that if I dropped the *S*, that would leave me with *hell* to pay. All good as long as I could remember where south was.

"Over there to your left is The Han River that you came over to get here. Every so often, we'll get some crazy VC swimmers who like to try to blow up the bridge or a boat or a barge for the fun of it with projectiles or black powder. That usually occurs between seven at night and five in the morning." *So charlie liked swimming?* "We have marines constantly looking for swimmers on both sides of the bridge for our safety. We're here on twelve-hour shifts, one month days and one month nights, and one day off a week."

Twelve-hour shifts? Ouch. I was tempted to ask Gage if I'd heard him correctly about that, but all the guys were nodding their heads.

"Now as to our Camp Tien Sha, we're smack up to the base of that mountain you see over there in the distance. That's Monkey Mountain, and it's the only thing you want to see when you leave Bridge Ramp each day or night." After what had happened the night before, I thought I'd like to work days only. Gage asked me if I had any idea why they called it Monkey Mountain. "Is it because it has a lot of monkeys?" "Fuck no!" he said. "It's because of all the fucking monkeys! There are more of them there than anywhere else in the area!" I'd never heard of the species *fucking monkeys*. I was becoming well informed in such a short period. I envisioned myself monkeying around and swimming in the river if it got hotter than hell.

"Ski, getting back to that bridge. It's so important to the 3rd Marine Division and to us. They use it to get their supplies, vehicles, and ammo they shove up charlie's ass, and we use it to get our asses back in camp. Ski, one last item."

I was hoping it was about the swimming hours for the Hun River. He pointed north at a large rice paddy and this huge rock behind it that was more like a mountain. "See that small village beyond that rice paddy? More important, that massive, solid rock? That's Marble Mountain. That hunk of rock doesn't have one fuckin' marble on it, in it, or around it, but what comes out of there will make you lose your marbles. It stands out like a fuckin' sore thumb." (I was tempted to ask him why they didn't just call it Sore Thumb Mountain.)

"That place is on constant watch by some very keen observers close by. There's an area inside with lovely trees, waterfalls, flowers, and their shrines and temples. Our marines are constantly walking around out there hoping to catch the VC who keep on launching rockets and mortars at us, into downtown, and anywhere else they choose to hit. For some strange reason, they love to do it when they know we have lots of ammo here at Bridge Ramp, which is about 90 percent of the time. If we're not the target, then it's the bridge, or downtown. If charlie really wants to ruin our fuckin' day, he lets loose a rocket onto those two damn Shell fuel storage tanks. We'd be fini with 'Nam for good. Ski, I hate to say this, but they placed your sorry ass in one of the hottest, most fucked-up places in this entire country."

How did I get so fuckin' lucky? I said, "Oh well, I could always leave my sorry ass here and spend my time doing something useful like surfing. How close is the beach? I hear the enemy hasn't hit that yet." The guys laughed. "Happy to oblige with my humor anytime."

Gage gave me a quick smile. "I hope we can all laugh at this when we get the fuck out of here."

CHAPTER 39

W E'VE ALL HEARD someone say, "This is where I lost my youth."
I lost mine on the night of September 22, 1969, and note the
month. It was the night of my first major rocket and mortar attack; I
had no sandbagged bunker to slam into when the VC rained rockets
and mortars directly onto the ramp and an area of downtown. We were
extremely lucky that none of their rockets hit the area where we had just
stored a huge supply of napalm that was scheduled to be picked up at
dawn's early light for the airbase. We got clobbered big-time.

The night started out pretty quiet. We were doing our thing—off-
loading an LST and three landing crafts—when all hell broke loose as
VC rockets and mortars started hitting us. The first two rockets hit two
moored landing crafts that had volatile ammo onboard, which set off
multiple secondary explosions from the two crafts. There was debris
flying all over the ramp that brought total chaos, insanity, and bedlam to
everyone working there. Besides going fucking crazy and doing the best
we could to keep our cool and concentrate on our objectives, I learned
the art of serpentining—maneuvering my R/T in a snakelike move to
avoid colliding with another R/T driver who was transporting some
serious ammo onto a flatbed and the driver was anxiously awaiting to
take his load and get the fuck off the ramp.

I was extremely lucky that no harm came to me or any of my team
members as the VC had their fun with us. They stopped for a short lull
and then sent a barrage of mortars at us that continued for another hour.
We could have gone and taken cover in some beat-up, old, retrograde
tanks that were left in certain areas on the ramp if the going got really

bad. It took a while before we started seeing choppers flying toward the area of Marble Mountain and leashing a barrage of red tracer rounds on where they thought the rockets were being launched from.

We did some pretty heroic moves with our R/Ts moving ammo from bays onto flatbeds. At times, I found myself saying, "Eenee, meenie, minee, mo, where the fuck does this ammo go?" I could be humorous even while knocking on heaven's door.

Our lookout tower had taken a rocket; two marines and on ARVN soldier were killed. The metal walls that divided the bays for various ammo had melted from the heat, but the ammo there had been picked up there earlier that morning.

Around 0400, we heard that two more landing crafts full of ammo were due by sunrise. It was anybody's guess whether it would be easy come easy go with these landing crafts. We felt like dead men working but wouldn't admit to that. Anyone else would have called us crazy fucking assholes moving ammo during an attack.

That night, I got a taste of war like nothing I'd ever tasted. I was sick of the whole shebang. My gut didn't want to take any more of this shit. It wanted me to say "I shall return" as MacArthur had and go home for a few months. There were other nights like that one, but none were as bad as that one. Those fucking demons made themselves at home in me. I believe they'll be with me forever because of the way us 'Nam vets are looked upon as baby killers.

But my time at Bridge Ramp taught me how to serpentine. Don't laugh. I think that made me feel I was a little invincible. It made me a better dancer too based on the compliments I got on my dancing after I returned home. It's come in handy with my dealings with contractors as well and working under a different type of fire that involved deadlines, contracts, budgets, and the shit contractors would give me.

One time, I was with the team waiting for an LST (landing ship tank) to come into our assigned slip that was said to be loaded to the gills with projectiles. Gage asked for one volunteer from each of the five teams to transport supplies to three Marine base camps. We would go up by truck, and the volunteers would be riding shotgun. Yes, I do mean shotgun, not something you yell out today when you want to sit in the passenger seat. This was with a loaded shotgun and about a hundred rounds to keep things safe. We'd go north to Hue, Quang Tri, and Dong Ha.

I have no recollection of raising my hand. I think one of my squad members did it for me while I was daydreaming. I was there on my day off to take some photos of where I worked and what we did. I had every Sunday off. I'd take photos at Bridge Ramp or go to China Beach, our in-country R&R resort. After that, I made damn sure that when they asked for volunteers my hands were deep in my pockets holding onto the lining. I didn't like volunteering my life. We took five truckloads of different types of good old American beer to the marines. I kid you not.

I know what you're thinking: *Okay, what drug was he on? Yeah, sure, he surfed there! Right!* Well, honestly and seriously, I surfed there. Yes, we had boards over there. I'd ride wave after wave from sunrise to sundown even though they were only two or three feet high. It was a bit of sanity for me in a combat zone; I pretended there was no war going on. I never used any kind of drug of any sort; I never had the desire to even when some of my buddies taunted me there to try some. "There's no harm!" "Great! Then you take it." I had a tough time swallowing aspirin.

I'd have to psych myself up when I went back to war-torn Da Nang and saw military vehicles coming and going up and down the beach, guys manning their M-16s or .50 caliber machine guns or when the choppers would go flying by. Even today, if I'm on a beach and I hear a chopper, I'm right back in 'Nam.

CHAPTER 40

I FEEL OBLIGATED to tell you about my surfing. I've surfed some of the hottest surfing venues around the world, but the majority of them were along the West Coast. I've surfed Half Moon Bay (a little south of San Fran), Santa Barbara, Manhattan Beach near LAX, Redondo Beach, Huntington Beach, Newport Beach, Calabasas, and Windansea and Ocean Beach in San Diego, where I was born.

There was a time I did a one-two quick take (no, not a drug, asshole) on a beach outside this little town south of the border in Ensenada, Mexico, when I went there for a sightseeing visit and a few drinks at Hussong's Cantina. I offered a kid $10 to try his board. I took my three rides.

I've also surfed in Corpus Christi, Pensacola, Panama City, Virginia Beach, and Long Beach. I've surfed in Hawaii, where I tried my luck on the most famous beach of all, Waimea, though the waves weren't big the day I was there.

My ultimate surfing dream was to get my ass to Sydney and surf Bondi Beach and Coogee Beach. You're not gonna believe this, but I was able to get my ass out of Dodge when my request for seven days of R&R was approved. I got word from Gage that I'd be going to Sydney in early April 1970 mainly to surf and maybe meet someone who looked like a wholesome female with round eyes who would get my juices flowing if you know what I mean string bean jelly bean!

I packed some of the civilian clothes I'd brought to 'Nam for my seven-day, all-expenses-paid (by yours truly) excursion to the land down under. I'd saved up almost $450 for this getaway. I had to sign an agreement that I wouldn't go AWOL. I took a commercial airline for the five hours' flight to the northern city of Darwin and then another five hours to Sydney. I had a good time listening to some guys trying to entertain these gorgeous flight attendants with their amazing war stories. I still had another three months to go before I left for home and would probably do the same when I got there.

I went through an oral and anal check to make sure I wasn't importing any drugs. I took a bus to the three hotels we were allowed to stay in that were in an area known as Kings Cross. I decided to stay at the Hotel St. Charles naturally. I prayed the Lord would show me the way to the promised land in a saintly manner down under (if you get my drift) before I went back to the land to be forgotten.

I checked in, paid for my one-week stay, read the hotel rules that were handed to all servicemen from 'Nam, bought a soda, and took the elevator to the seventh floor. I entered my room, put my bag down, and splashed myself with cologne. It was a comfortable place that I hoped I'd mess up before the night was over with an Australian woman.

The flight attendants had told me of one place to go where I'd likely be approached by every woman in the place. They said I'd be fuckin' lucky being that I was the best-looking guy on the flight and they were sorry they couldn't have a night with me. One of the flight attendants told me that she wished she could stay in Sydney even for one night just to spend time with me and soar to some other places together.

Hearing such words coming from a good-looking, round-eyed woman made me feel extremely wanted. I told myself I believed I was due what was coming to me after having spent nine fucking months in the devil's backyard. I also believed I'd be halfway to heaven as soon as I got to this place where they said I'd be lucky.

CHAPTER 41

T HE PLACE THE flight attendants told me to go was the Cheetah
Lounge, the most popular nightclub in the Kings Cross area. I
walked in and casually strolled up to the bar without looking to see who
was there. I asked the bartender for their best beer. I wanted it cold. I'd
had enough of warm beer. I took a slow look around this huge room and
saw people dancing, laughing, and drinking, things I hadn't heard for
a long time. I figured that even if I didn't get lucky, I could drink to my
heart's content because my hotel was only a few blocks away. I wasn't
in a combat zone, but I figured I might have to fight off some of the
delicious-looking woman in the place or break up their fights over me.
I was fully prepared. I saw one luscious woman after another. I thought
that I might be awarded the Purple Heart for injuries sustained in bed
or for having a broken heart if I didn't get lucky.

I chugged my first beer and asked for a refill. I put a twenty on the
bar. I sensed someone standing close behind me; I could feel breath on
my neck and was poked on my back in two places and not by fingers.
I turned and faced a gift from God—the most outstanding shape and
form of a woman God could ever create. She was wearing a see-through
blouse. She wasn't wearing a bra. Certain parts of her breasts had done
the poking. I drooled as I tried to say, "Hello, and what brings the three
of you here?"

She laughed. "Are you always that direct with a woman without
knowing her name?"

"Yes, especially when she's being so direct with me!"

"My name's Zsuzsa. I'm known here as Tiger, but if you want, you can call me Susan." She gave me a huge smile. Wow, I had the choice of two women, a big pussy cat, and I hadn't had my second beer yet! I was about to tell her that my name was Charlie, known elsewhere as Ski, but that she could call me anything she wanted as long as her thighs were over my ears. But I decided not to. I'm a gentleman. She was a lady. A stunning, beautiful, well-endowed lady. Her accent sounded Hungarian. I got more and more hungry each time she pressed her firm nipples against my chest. She slowly leaned in wanting to get as close as possible without getting behind me (a small joke of mine) without having to move my feet or spread my legs to accommodate her. (Dreams do come true if you truly wish hard enough and long enough.)

I was right. She told me she was Hungarian, but it didn't matter if she was part gypsy, couldn't play a mean tambourine or a piano (but maybe an organ—mine), or didn't know how to make goulash the way I liked it, which was in bed. A quick look beyond her breasts convinced me that she was indeed perfect. I figured she was my age. She was about my height (maybe a little shorter than me if lying down), had beautiful, raven hair, lovely brown eyes, creamy soft skin, and more than likely a great pair of legs to wrap around my back. *Quick! Somebody pinch me and tell me I'm not dreaming!*

She told me she was called Tiger for the way she danced—like a cat. Whatever that meant. Do you think I cared what kind of animal she danced like? She started to look completely different to me as I imagine her nails going across my back. I didn't care if she had stripes under her clothes. I was ready to tell her that I'd be her catnip, that she could eat me alive. Hell, I hadn't even bought her a drink and I already had the whole night planned out.

She came in real close. She saw my smile. "What's your name? Did you just arrive here from Vietnam? Do you like to dance? Would you like to have breakfast with me?" I tried looking her in her eyes but was distracted by the constant pressure of her luscious body. *What did I do to deserve this? Am I lucky or what? My time in the land down under is going to be outstanding!*

"Charlie ... Yes ... Affirmative! ... and breakfast? Sure. Why not? I guess it's normal here to think about a meal for tomorrow being on the other side of the international dateline. And being below the equator,

I'm wondering if you had dinner first then lunch and the last being breakfast. It's muddling my mind to the point where I'm not sure if today is already tomorrow."

Her giggle jiggled her breasts. Oh, you should have been there. It had me thinking how long it had been since I've seen a woman's breast in an atmosphere much more pleasant compared to how I'd seen some Vietnamese women drop their pants and squat to the bathroom right next to you on the roadside. "How do you like your eggs, Zsuzsa? Sunnyside up, scrambled, or hard boiled?" My ten-hour flight had let me shed all those sick and disgusting things I'd seen in 'Nam. I wanted to give this lovely woman my fullest attention.

Australia is larger than the United States, and one of the country's outstanding, prominent, and well-developed monuments was standing in front of me. I wanted her to scramble my eggs. We talked some more, had a few drinks, and danced a couple of dances. She said, "Charlie, I love your sense of humor and how you've been treating me since we met. You're an absolute gentleman. Would it be okay if we go back to your hotel room and gather up your stuff and go to my place? I'd love to spend some time with you but only if you want to."

"I like you, Tiger, and I wouldn't wish for anything else right now unless you have a magic wand hidden somewhere."

"I'd love to prepare a home-cooked meal for you unless you'd rather go out for dinner."

"That's a great idea!" I said. "I'll buy whatever you need including beer and wine." I paid my tab. We went to my hotel for my bag and checked out just in case things went well and I got my eggs scrambled. The hotel was nice enough to return my deposit after seeing I hadn't disturbed my room one bit. I said, "I think going to your place is a wise choice because there was no stove in my room for you to do anything to my eggs."

She giggled again. "Are you always this funny?"

"Only when I'm around a cute tiger who plans to scramble my eggs—and that could be our little yoke, I mean, joke—or wants to eat me alive!" The more she giggled, the harder I got.

I had four fun-filled days (use your imagination) of doing what I wanted to do and whatever she wanted to do to me. She even brought over her older sister one night to join in the fun in having the two of them make one hell of a feast for dinner. We shared wine, beer, and laughter until it was time for bed. Yes, I thought I was going to die and go to heaven, but her lovely sister left us two lovebirds.

Yes, I'm sure you want to know if I ever got the chance to surf there. I did. I surfed Bondi and Coogee Beaches in the company of a lovely woman. I had more fun at Coogee because Susan wanted me to teach her how to surf. I had my hands full trying to show her how to stand on the board as we stood on the shoreline trying out these moves before going into the surf. Her boobs kept falling out of her top. I was loving every minute of it.

We finally went out. She gave it a try, and she did pretty well on standing up, but once the wave started pushing her toward shore, off she went into the soup. When she got up in knee-deep water, she was advertising her golden globes to everyone as she went to retrieve her top that had washed ashore.

I surfed until I was near exhausted. I needed to save some strength for when we got back to her apartment. She asked me if I could move the furniture around; she was expecting a new sofa to be delivered. I spent every minute with Susan as if they were my last minutes on earth. I tried to forget about that fucking war in 'Nam I'd be heading back to too soon.

We spent the following day sightseeing. We went to the famous Sydney Opera House, which was under construction. We went to their fantastic zoo at Bennelong Point and visited a few bars and clubs for drinks. I found a nice restaurant for a romantic dinner with her. That was the only time we ate out; she loved to cook, and she was good at it. She loved to eat raw meat such as steak tartare, which brought out the real tiger in her. We enjoyed each other immensely over and over, just being together, if you know what I mean. I didn't want to waste my time sleeping. I could do that on my flight back to hell. Besides, do you know how hard it is to sleep when you're trying to stay up as long as possible?

Before I left 'Nam to go to Sydney, I was told that the U.S. government didn't allow any military driving automobiles while they were in Australia. Probably because they drove on the other side of the road. And it knew damn well that once we got here, we'd most likely get lucky (as I did) and end up with someone who would drive us crazy enough that there wouldn't be a need for a car. Our government is very smart; I knew it wouldn't have steered us wrong.

Susan's apartment had a great view of Sydney harbor. I asked her why the water in the sink, shower, et cetera spun down in the opposite direction from what I was used to. Were the plumbers all left-handed? She started to get the hang of my humor. "I'll let you know as long as you can keep my juices flowing!"

I'll not go any further as to what else we did. That's a bit more personal! I won't tell you everything I did over there; this isn't that kind of book. I already told you more than I should have. Use your imagination. Multiply your thoughts by a factor of two and you'll be halfway there. Now you're thinking right.

I knew my time with her was coming to an end when I realized I could no longer walk. Yeah, go ahead and laugh. I pleaded (oh did I plead) if she could find a way of letting me have at least six hours of shut-eye to give my body a rest. When the six hours were up, she could wake me up in any way she pleased and do whatever she pleased as long it had nothing to do with making love to one another.

She agreed to my request and let me sleep for six straight hours. I awoke in a way I'll never forget. The time we had spent together had endeared us to one another. She begged me to go AWOL—not absent without official leave but for another week of lust, which would have killed me, but better there than in 'Nam.

During day six, I started thinking about my buddies in 'Nam. I hoped no harm had come their way. I was just trying to survive action with Susan. I asked myself if I was falling for her. But I might have been thinking more about her body and lovemaking than what things would have been like for us in normal times, not on leave, when I'd be thinking more with my mind than with my wild heart.

She surprised me about going for a drive and visiting her mom. I didn't mind the two-hour drive into the countryside in her small, blue Volkswagen. I had a chance to rest a little more. Her mom was happy to meet me. We had lunch, and I somehow got wrangled into this heart-to-heart talk with her mom. I was told that Tiger adored me, that I was the perfect gentleman for her, that I made her laugh, and that I would make a good husband so would I please marry her. I was asked numerous times if I loved her and if so, why I wouldn't marry her. That was the ultimate statement; it got me thinking more clearly. I thanked her for talking to me, but I told them both I had to go back to where I was needed the most. They didn't understand that.

I could tell Susan's mind was elsewhere on the drive back to Sydney. It must have been hard for her to concentrate on driving; she couldn't figure out why I wouldn't stay with her and forget about going back to my buddies and that horrible war. I told her I was truly sorry if I had hurt her feelings; all I wanted to do at that moment was hold her.

My remaining time in this paradise was about to end. I was pained knowing how much I must have been breaking her heart. She said, "I'm falling in love with you, Charlie. You're an amazing person. The days we've spent together have been some of the happiest in my life. I don't want to see them come to an end. Not like this."

So we spent the rest of the evening after she made a marvelous dinner christening her new sofa by making love there, then on the carpeted floor, and then her bed in total bliss until the early morning hours.

We got out of bed, showered together, and had breakfast. I gathered up my stuff, and we jumped into a cab to go back to my hotel to where I was to meet my bus back to the airport. She wanted to get on the bus with me. She was having her way with me right there in front of the hotel, kissing me like it was our last day on earth together. She kept on thanking me for giving her such a wonderful time and sweet memories. Her hugs and kisses were getting to me where I think I might have said, "Fuck it, I'm staying here with you. I'm going AWOL."

But I didn't. She didn't care who was watching as she showed her affection and kept telling me she wanted to marry me and that she would never find anyone like me. She even yelled out, "I want to have your baby!" The bus doors opened. She said again that I was the most perfect gentleman she had ever met, the funniest person she had ever met, and more than anything, someone who had a heart of gold. She said she would pray that I make it out of 'Nam alive. "If you want to come back to me, just pick up the phone and call me. You have my number. I left it on the back of the gift I gave you of the Polaroid photo we took on Bondi Beach."

She was making it so hard for me to leave. The bus driver was cursing me out, losing his patience, and blowing the horn. "We got to leave, now!"

I yelled, "Fuck the war, and fuck 'Nam! I must be fucking crazy leaving this amazing woman!"

He started to close the door and slowly began to move where I saw Susan giggling again about my comments. That was my chance to run for the door. She grabbed me by the arm before the driver closed the door. "I'll always love you, Charlie!" I looked into her beautiful brown eyes. She read my thoughts. I stepped up and threw my bag on a seat, sat down, and didn't look back. Those seven days with Zsuzsa had really gotten to me. What would you have done if you'd been in my situation?

I had plenty of time to dwell on how I had spent the past seven days with this amazing woman on my way back. I've never forgotten Zsuzsa. Whenever I hear the slightest word about the land down under, she always comes to mind. She was one of my "You're not gonna believe this" stories. She changed me. She changed my heart and my brain when it came to the way I treated women. I have become more of a gentleman and less of a sex-starved guy.

On April 13, 1970, I left my heart in Sydney. I had a strange coincidence on that same date some thirty-one years later. I was there for another good buddy of mine who had his life in a somewhat dangerous situation that involved a fight the whole world would have seen if the TV cameras were around the corner from where they were in full view of what took place that unforgettable night at Ground Zero. For some crazy reason, I believe I was supposed to be there for my buddy; that may have been the reason I'd been destined to be there and had had to say no to Zsuzsa. I found the whole matter very strange.

CHAPTER 42

O N MY BUS ride back to Camp Tien Sha from the Da Nang airbase, I wondered how my buddies had fared. I got in around twelve thirty in the morning and was surprised to see some guys I knew were out walking in the street (no sidewalks in camp). I figured they were heading back to the barracks after seeing a movie at the camp theater. I stuck my head out the window. "Hey you pussies, why aren't you out there fighting? Haven't you heard there's a war going on!" I grabbed my bag and got off the bus. The guys and I shook hands and slapped backs. "So you survived R&R! Did you go surfing over there, or did you spend all your time getting your monkey smacked?"

It felt good to be back home. One guy told me my team was off-loading numerous LSTs of their cargo, pro-jos (projectiles), 155 mm cannon rounds. I was surprised to hear that my team leader, Gage, had left for R&R unexpectedly. That is when I noticed odd facial expressions come over their faces. "Ski, this should be coming from one of your team members, but since you're here and we're seeing you first, we're gonna enjoy telling you we think you're going home. There's been an important-looking envelope on your bunk since the day you left for R&R. It looks like orders!"

"I'm going home? Can't be. I still have three months left in-country. I can't be that lucky, not after what I've just been through in Sydney." They had no idea what I was talking about. I picked up my bag and took off running toward my barracks. I thought Gage or one of my team members was playing a joke on me. Two of them were running alongside me. They wanted me to explain what I'd said about my time in

Sydney, but I raced to my barracks and to my bunk, which was covered with a shitload of sand. I cursed the choppers silently because some people were sleeping. I saw an envelope of the type that was big enough to contain orders and all my records. It read, Open Upon Your Return From R&R above my name.

I could feel another envelope inside, so I didn't know what to expect. The outside envelope did look official with a wax seal, but I still thought it could be a prank. Someone patted me on the back and said, "Hey, it was nice knowing you!"

Wow! I'm really going! I couldn't believe it. Maybe my admiral had gotten me an early out; I'd written him about what I'd been going through. But never jump to conclusions especially when your ass is in 'Nam. I opened the envelope. Yep, I was leaving Da Nang, but nothing about going home. I was to be ready to depart 1600 hours on April 14, 1970 for my departure over to Deep Water Piers, a place I would pass going to Bridge Ramp. I'd get my official orders when I checked in there. I figured I was going on a ship, the only things that docks at Deep Water Piers handled, ships. Somebody came up wanting to know about Sydney; he was thinking about going there rather than Bangkok. "Shit!" I said. "You want to know about Sydney? I just found out I should've stayed in fuckin' Sydney. Here I thought I was going home, but instead, I find out I'm going on some ship. Not in the mood to talk about to you about this. Maybe later. Sorry, partner."

He said, "Shit, well, wherever they're sending you, it can't be worse than Bridge Ramp! This place is worse than hell!"

The second page told me I was to take my weapons, helmet, and flak jacket and be out in front of my barracks at 1300, about twelve hours from then. No time to sleep. Too much to do.

Deep Water Piers was another ramp facility on the Han River that usually catered to civilian freighters or naval transport ships, things that would never dock at Bridge Ramp. Pow! That's when it hit me. My admiral had received my letter and had felt sorry for me. He probably had had me transferred out of here for the remainder of my sea duty. I wanted to scream for joy, but I wondered why I'd been told to take all my shit. It wasn't making a bit of sense. I tried to figure out what the hell was going on. My head was getting cloudy. I started to envision myself being on one of those transport ships so far out that I wouldn't be able to see the coast of this godforsaken place.

A sudden chill went down my back that made me snap out of my thoughts about Zsusza. Someone was holding a cold can of beer to the back of my head. I saw seven guys (gone seven days and then looking at seven guys?) all holding cold cans of beer in their hands, some dressed, some half-dressed, and two in the skivvies who came over to wish me farewell. A few of them were already feeling good if you know what I mean. We went outside to not disturb the sleepers. We raised our cans to the heavens. Someone raised a bottle of vodka (which I love dearly), and another one raised a bag of potato chips. We toasted each other with a "Fuckin' a!"

Word spread pretty fast in the barracks. Other guys came out to my 2:00 a.m. going-away party. I didn't exactly know where I was going, but it didn't matter—we had plenty of beer, a bottle of vodka, a bag of chips, and each other. We drank and talked till the sun came up. I thanked everyone for sharing some time with me. I needed a shower and a shave and to get back into my green fatigues and get breakfast. After I showered, I walked back to my sand-covered bunkbed and whom do I see come strolling in but everyone on my team except Gage. I called out their names, and they heard me and came running. "You fuckin' survived R&R? And here you are washing all those love juices off your body that you probably wanted to keep on until you left this fucking place. So how many different women did you fuck? You going back to marry one? Just look at that shit- eatin' grin on his face. We want to hear all about it!"

I started to tell them briefly what I did but quickly changed the subject by letting them know I was leaving. Their attitude quickly changed. They knew about the envelope on my bunk. I asked them "Where did Gage go on his R&R?" They said about 2300 the previous night. Rank does have its privileges, but all he had was a three-day, in-country pass. He had to take his Vietnamese wife (I had been his best man at their wedding) down to Saigon to see her family because her mom was very sick; she wanted to see her before she went with him to the states when his time was up the next month.

I began to wonder if he'd known about this before I left and didn't want to be here when I got back. I do recall him telling me, "It's time to get out of Dodge, Ski, so have yourself a fucking good time in Sydney. I mean it! It may be your last!" Was that just his way of joking with me, or was he giving me some good advice because he'd heard something from someone he knew who worked in headquarters, known here as the White Elephant?

They were wiped out. They just wanted to sleep. I said my good-byes and went to eat. When I came back, I got the quartermaster to open the property room for my M-16, my three bandoliers each containing six twenty-round clips, my .45 and holster and three boxes of rounds, my helmet, and my flak jacket. I brought everything over to my bunk and went through my footlocker that contained twelve reel-to-reel tapes filled with '60s songs, my tape recorder, headphones, and all the letters I'd received from home, my friends, and especially my Angel. I poured some sand that was on my bunk into an empty beer can for show-and-tell back home. I stuffed the clothes I'd worn in Sydney into my sea bag; they still had Susan's scent on them. I left some clothes in my footlocker for whomever needed them.

I went to the PX for some film for my camera. I figured I still had time to go to the EM club to say good-bye to the guys and Vietnamese women who worked there. It was bittersweet knowing my time there was coming to an end. I wanted to go to the ramp to say good-bye to my lieutenant and let him know he'd been a great CO of the facility. I wanted to tell him that I'd written to his younger sister and that we had a date planned for mid-August near Boston. He had written to her and told her I was a stand-up guy. I considered myself lucky to have been assigned to this place; I'd learned a hell of a lot about survival and how to serpentine. But my time was running out; getting to and from the ramp might make me late for my 1300 pickup, so I gave up on that idea.

I stayed in the EM club till I heard the Doors' "Light My Fire." Just as I was about to leave, I saw a bunch of marines I knew and bought them beers (10¢ each) and told them I was leaving to where who the fuck knew. I told them about my time in Sydney and how hard it had been to say good-bye to a girl who wanted to marry me. I took another look at their faces; I wanted to remember every one of them being with the 3rd Marine Division who had protected my ass at the ramp. It was a sad good-bye for us all. I wished them well, left the club, and headed to my barracks. I sat out back where the choppers landed. I wanted to see one arrive one last time knowing I didn't have to deal with their shit ever again.

Someone came up. "Are you Kaczorowski? I was told you might be sitting back here. Gage told me you'd be back from your R&R. He was holding all your mail. Here it is!"

I'd totally forgotten about my mail in all the chaos. I thanked him and quickly looked through it to see who had written. It was mostly letters from Angel, about twenty of them, a few from my family, and one letter from Washington, DC, from the admiral. He wrote that he had been sorry to hear what I'd been going through in Da Nang, a VC hot spot. I started to get this pain in my stomach and a bigger one in my heart for there was no mention of where I was going. Maybe the orders I was given had been done locally based on what the needed. I had no idea if it would be better or worse than here.

A deuce and a half came up to the barracks. The driver blew the horn. Someone jumped out of the truck and yelled my name. I looked at my watch. It was only 1250. I ran over and asked him if he was my ride to Deep Water Piers A gung-ho navy CPO, a lifer, yelled, "Are you Kaczorowski? Why aren't you out front with all your gear? Go! Get it! Put it up in the back of the truck and get the fuck in. We're late!" I wanted to tell the stupid lifer he was ten minutes early, but I didn't. I also was tempted to ask him, "You a seabee? If not, shut the fuck up!" but I didn't.

I started carrying my stuff to the rear of the truck. The chief asked with a smile, "What do you have inside that makes your footlocker look so heavy?" I replied, "My tape recorder, a bunch of tapes, my headphones, letters from home, my .45, ammo, and my flak jacket." "Great! I hope you heard all your tapes and you got them locked in your fuckin' memory bank because they aren't going with you and neither is the tape player. Keep your letters! You can take the footlocker. And you might need those headphones to help you sleep." He came out with this big, hearty laugh. "You're gonna be fighting a war where you're going a little different from here. You'll be on full alert every second you're there. Your sea bag is okay with whatever you got in it, and your helmet,

M-16, and your ammo is a definite go, but everything else, give it to your girlfriends over there who look like they're going to miss you dearly. Your drawings and photos and pictures on your footlocker look damn good. Do you surf?" Before I could answer, he said, "Get your sweet ass on my truck. Move it, surfer boy!"

The guys in front of the barracks had heard the ruckus this chief was raising. I called them over and told them I couldn't take my recorder or tapes. "Merry Christmas. You've been wonderful girlfriends since I've been here. Enjoy my tapes, and I hope you think of me when you listen to them!" They were in stiches. I smiled and threw kisses to them. "I promise I won't mention any of you to my girl back home." The chief knew I was making fun of him, but I didn't give a fuck. What could he have done for insubordination, send me to 'Nam?

I got onboard and yelled to the chief, "Good to go. Oh by the way, chief, all my girlfriends think you're cute. They'd love to see you after you drop me off. They'll miss me, but I told them they might get lucky because they know I've been a lousy fuck!"

The truck jerked. We started to move. I walked over to the cab area and asked the driver very quietly if he could make a stop at the mess hall so I could run inside for a quick glass of milk and two cookies since we'd be going right by it and that they'd been ten minutes early. Either I said that too loud or that chief lifer had 20/20 hearing because he came out with, "Fuckin' a. No sweat! While you're in there, get the same for me and two scoops of chocolate ice cream with chocolate syrup for the driver!"

We went by the mess hall without stopping and headed for Deep Water Piers. I had no idea what to expect other than I'd be on full alert every second I was there. *But where? Does he have a clue about where I'm going, or was he just busting my balls?*

We arrived at the piers, and I saw this landing craft in one of the slips. There had never been a landing craft docked there as far as I knew; it had always been freighters and transport ships. The landing craft had about forty or so guys standing around onboard. I could have been wrong, but it could have been waiting for me. That picture began to suck. *Where am I going on a landing craft?*

I saw a lieutenant waving us over. "Let's go. Get over here with your gear and orders. We're running late!"

Shit! What was the big rush? Was the war coming to an end? I grabbed my footlocker and sea bag and hustled over. The CPO yelled, "He's a real wiseass, Lieutenant. Have him swab the deck or clean the heads!" He gave me this shit-eating smile as the driver turned. I gave him the finger sign that told him he was number one, but I think I held up the wrong finger. "Be gentle with my girlfriends!"

The loot had no idea what had transpired between the chief and me but gave me this seething look. "You fuckin' seabees think you're something else over here, don't you?" All I could say in reply was, "Fuckin' a, Lieutenant, we are!" What could he have done to me just as we were about to take a cruise to nowhere?.

Two guys yelled at me about my memo. I handed it to them. They asked about my brown envelope. I lifted my shirt to show them it was stuck in my waistband. "Okay, Ski. Get onboard. Good luck to you! You're gonna need it in this one hell of a fucking place you're going to." *Now what the hell did he mean by that? Why should I board this landing craft after hearing this? Is he jerking me around or what?* I made my way to the ramp that led to the ship and could have sworn I heard someone mention the DMZ. *What the fuck am I going to the DMZ for?*

I put my footlocker down and repositioned my flak jacket and M-16 as I was hastily being called over by this petty officer 1st class wearing camouflaged fatigues and a black beret. I thought he was a SEAL until I saw his seabees' insignia—a bumblebee wearing a white sailor hat and holding a machine gun. *But why the black beret and camouflage fatigues?*

He had me sign some papers and gave me a carbon copy I was told to give it to the seabee I'd meet at my destination who would be dressed like him. He'd see to it that I got the same uniform so everyone would know I was a seabee. I was told to yell out, "Is there an asshole named Raymond Gordon onboard? If so, show me your ass!"

157

CHAPTER 43

SOMEONE YELLED, "You can kiss my fucking ass, but you first have to call me Flash!" Flash Gordon, of course, and there I was, a Superman wannabe, a match made in hell. I mean 'Nam. He was pointing at his ass. "Here you go!" I gave him a smile. We shook hands. I told him my name and said, "I'd like to be called Surfer Boy, but Ski will be fine. Just don't call me Charlie."

We laughed. I stacked my stuff next to his. We shared a little about ourselves. Turned out we were both avid surfers. He told my his nickname was Flash because he was quick on a board, and I told him that I'd been called Ski since I didn't ski and they couldn't call me Charlie. Flash thought that was hilarious. He said he was from Ft. Lauderdale. I said I was originally from San Diego but lately from Long Island. It was odd that we almost looked like twins.

We decided to walk around onboard and find out where the fuck we were going. I told Flash I didn't want to hear any bullshit about going up to the DMZ, three letters I'd removed from my fuckin' alphabet the minute I arrived in-country.

We were told to assemble in the middle of the craft nuts to butts— that meant real close—to hear the (good) news. I think I heard Flash say he'd ask if we could be excused to get some beer to salute our new friendship. His sense of humor scared the hell out of me; he seemed to be just as funny as I was.

A commander said, "Okay, listen up! In a few minutes, you'll be shoving off. Your location has been kept classified up until now. You'll be heading north for about nineteen hours about a mile or two off the coast."

Interesting. It was all "you," not "we." I can't imagine my very first ocean cruise would be classified.

"Your final destination will be your last duty station for whatever time you have remaining in-country. Your new home will be this small base camp. You're going up to Cua Viet."

Flash and I heard, "Oh shit!" "Oh oh." "You gotta be fuckin' kidding!" It got quiet on deck. We were leaving hell, I mean Da Nang, for someplace north where, instead of being colder, it would be hotter. And I'm not talking about the temperature. And why were they sending army, marines, and two seabees to a place that caused people to say, "Oh shit!" and "Oh oh"? Such comments gave Flash and me the most uncomfortable feeling in our guts. We both thought of asking to be excused, but it was too late.

We shoved off at 1730 hours (5:30 p.m.). The Beatles' song with the words "O blah di, o blah da, life goes on" were going through my head as we made our way into the South China Sea and headed north hugging the coast. We heard some guys talking about our wonderful destination. We didn't know if it was true, but one guy called it a real hole in the wall, not much of a camp, a place with just a military code name that had something to do with water.

That sounded good to me and Flash; we loved water especially if we could surf in it. I'm sure Flash thought of Clearwater, Florida, before I did; he was from Florida. We had wonderful visions dancing in our heads of a beautiful beach and surfboards like there were at China Beach in Da Nang. Flash and I gave each other big smiles and decided to hold off on the winks to each other till we got off the craft at Camp Oh Shit and see how exciting the kind of place we had with fuckin' a water!

Flash and I got to talking about surfing, and we stood at the same time and pretended we were riding the ship like a surfboard. Some guys were smoking weed, but Flash and I were getting high on our pretend surfing and watching the sun set. Flash told me he wanted to travel to all the great places along the West Coast from Oregon to Baja California. I told him about my surfing in Australia. "You surfed Bondi and Coogee Beach? Amazing!" He pulled out a cassette player and said that he had the first two albums on cassette of Led Zeppelin and quickly said "I'm dedicating this to you."

How unfuckin' real was it that he was a Zeppelin fan too? A match made in heaven. Maybe in hell, where we were. We simultaneously and spontaneously started playing air guitar on our M-16s. I knew then that we were crazy in the same way and that our senses of humor matched perfectly. We stopped for a second or two, and as if we'd rehearsed the move, we checked to make sure we didn't have rounds in the chambers and that our safeties were on. We were in our own perfect little world listening to the Zeppelin's "Good Times, Bad Times."

I told Flash that I'd had to leave my tapes and recorder with my girlfriends back in the barracks thanks to a certain CPO. Flash gave me this jealous look. "Don't worry, babe. Those girlfriends of yours don't mean a thing to me. We'll start off fresh. I'll forget all of mine as well."

We laughed uproariously. The guys around us must have thought we'd lost our marbles, or were high on something, or had something going on between us. Flash and I noticed some of the looks we were getting. He said, "I got just the song for you, sugar!" He hit the stop button and looked to find this other song and started playing it, "Your Time Is Gonna Come" as loud as he could. We went back to playing our air guitars with our eyes shut and standing as if we were surfing. We hit some swells that made us feel we were riding a big one toward shore. That ride should have gone down in surfing history as being the only five-foot-high wave ridden along the coast of South Vietnam going up to the DMZ.

Flash looked at his cassette and said that the batteries were running low. A few guys were yelling, "Turn up the fuckin' volume!" I wondered if they would mutiny over the matter of not being able to hear Plant and Page. The skipper heard the ruckus and told Flash to bring him his cassette player and cassettes. I think Flash cursed him out under his breath as I was doing as we headed up to the pilot house. Flash asked me, "Do you think he's going to throw them off for disturbing the other passengers onboard or hold us for ransom?" I gave him this blank look. "Most definitely on the ransom."

When we arrived at the pilot house, the skipper said, "Thank you, ladies. Be on your way." As we walked away, Flash grabbed my arm and asked, "Tell me you didn't date him too?" I said, "Fuckin' a, but he promised me he wasn't the kiss-and-tell type."

By the time we got back to where we'd been, our eyes were filled with tears from laughing so hard. Someone asked us, "What the fuck kind of shit drug are you two on? You two haven't stopped since we shoved off."

I had a hunch Flash was ready to come out with something, so I covered his mouth and said, "You're not gonna believe this, but we've been inhaling each other's farts so when it's time to kiss each other's ass good-bye when the end is near, we'll be used to the smell."

When I dropped my hand from Flash's mouth, he said, "I just let out another fart. Did you catch a whiff?"

Just then, we heard the Zeppelin's "Ramble On." The skipper had hooked up Flash's cassette player to the ship's loudspeakers. You're not gonna believe this, but that got everyone up and playing air guitar. Everyone was getting totally stoked. The skipper played all the other tapes Flash had given him about two or three times.

The music eventually stopped. The only thing we could hear was the landing craft plowing through turbulent waters. Flash and I were enjoying the waves. "You sure there's a war going on over here?" Flash asked.

I said, "Maybe if we fall asleep and wake up in the morning, we just might hear that the war is over, that the VC cried uncle after hearing Zeppelin's 'Dazed and Confused' so many times."

Some guy nearby said, "You two guys did some outstanding wave riding and have some great music. Thanks for taking my mind off this fuckin' war."

Flash and I got some food rations and some slightly cold beer that was still plentiful on the craft. We enjoyed the rest of our cruise. The sound of the craft skimming through the water lulled us to sleep. I dreamed about surfing, girls, and a car I wanted to get when I got home—a Camaro—and my family. I woke up for a short spell and thought about Flash and me making it out of there alive.

We woke up around 6:00 a.m. (What are you doing? How come you didn't say anything to me about the time? You don't say six a.m. in the military, you say oh six hundred!) We were wondering why everyone was standing on deck just looking to port. We got up saying good morning to one another but got shushed by the others. We looked where everyone else was looking and saw Cua Viet in the near distance. It looked beautiful. Some great-looking waves were breaking just off the shore. We looked at each other and probably had the same thought— *Heaven on earth!*

Before we could get a better look at our new heaven, we tried to figure out what the hell was going on. We saw two guys in this little inflatable doing something very quietly and wearing only their green military-issue bathing suits. One stayed at the stern handling a short paddle while the other had his head in the water. He was wearing a face mask and was fanning the water around. The landing craft engines shut down. Dead silence. No one was moving, talking, or even whispering. The two headed straight for the shore toward a concrete ramp sloping down into the water. Someone there was ready and waiting to guide us in. Someone whispered to me that we weren't going to the dock due to a potential problem we might have in front of us. That is why the two guys were doing their thing out there.

We watched one of the swimmers come up for air and push the water away from him as if he were searching for a lost contact lens. Some of us onboard were losing it just watching him go through the motions in silence. He gave a signal for the guy in the inflatable to stop paddling. He was studying the water and kept the inflatable perfectly still.

It was so quiet that I heard a fly sneeze in my ear. The skipper explained the guy was searching for any mines charlie may have left behind for fun. Our lives were in the hands of this brave swimmer. He went underwater and surfaced about twenty feet away. He stood up in waist-deep water and said, "All clear!" We whooped for joy. We said "Thank God!" and "Nice going!" instead of the old "Oh oh."

Our landing craft took the swimmer's path in. The skipper lowered the front ramp on the beach. The sand was pure white and the water was crystal clear where I was. My dad had described the sand and water on Omaha as being blood-soaked red. Flash gave me a shove in my back that snapped me out of my thoughts. He pointed at the waves breaking to the north. I said, "I think it's gonna be those North Vietnamese women in black, come out onto the beach and making themselves half-naked for us that may distract me from my surfing those beautiful waves."

Flash said, "They'll be really surprised when they meet us and are gonna want to party with us when I start calling you Charlie and end up dying laughing!" Of course, we both knew in our hearts that we would be fuckin' idiots to party with a bunch of half-naked North Vietnamese women when we had such excellent waves to surf.

Flash asked, "Did you pack a board in that sea bag of yours?"

"Yes," I said, "but I had to pack it in pieces. You have any glue?" That's when we heard those famous words, "Lock and load. Move out!" *Yeah, there is a war going on. What's wrong with us?*

Lock and load is what we did when we were about to do what we had to do with the bad guys. Flash and I put our flak jackets and helmets on, put clips into our M-16s, and checked to see that our safeties were on. I slapped on my .45 and holster and placed my sea bag over my shoulder. Flash helped me carry my footlocker. We hustled off the craft and were told to assemble by this CPO 2nd class who was wearing a black beret and camouflage fatigues. He blurted out living assignments over a bullhorn for everyone except Flash and me. He acted as if we weren't even there probably because he'd heard Flash say something about using a bullhorn to give us bullshit. Or maybe our pearly white teeth, long blond hair, and blue eyes had caught his eye and he wanted us all for himself.

He finally asked us, "You two—what are your names? Come forward with your gear!"

I nudged Flash and pointed out three Quonset huts to the far left. "You two brothers by any chance?" We shook our heads no. I think Flash and I were ready to tell him we were going steady and wanted to be left alone. He asked, "How does one of those three huts over there look to you?"

I thought this guy had just read my mind and I was totally fucked. We both said "Great."

He said, "Good. Go over and say hello to your new home. Be back here in twenty minutes!"

Flash and I checked our watches, grabbed our stuff, and headed to our new home. We looked around for any boards. We figured they must have been stored away as was the case at China Beach, but this place didn't look exactly like an in-country R&R place.

CHAPTER 44

FLASH AND I agreed that if we found any boards, we'd ask whomever owned them if we could keep them in our hut seeing as we were so close to the beach. An excellent arrangement.

We found out that the cute Quonset hut Flash and I had chosen from the distance was a big fucking mistake. We went from one to the other to pick out the best of the three and settled on one that had a wooden sign nailed above the door that read, Home Sweet Home. The other two were horrible beyond our wildest imaginations; this one was a hundred times better except for the smell. It wasn't exactly a *House & Garden* magazine place.

We saw a strange object that turned out to be a pile of shit a dog or a monkey had forgotten to clean up. Flash said he'd call down to the front desk and ask the bellhop to show us another hut. "This one hasn't been made up yet."

I chimed in, "We'll gladly double his tip."

We saw various other debris scattered around the room. It didn't compare to my luxury accommodations in Da Nang even factoring in all the dust and sand that would blow in. Flash was bitching about everything he was seeing. We saw four beds rather than bunks. "Did some stupid fuck who wanted his privacy shit here instead of using the latrine?"

We made about faces and saw another sign painted on a green sandbag: "Before you leave here, kiss your sweet ass good-bye. You may not get another chance!" Comforting advice. Flash and I gave each other weird looks, shook our heads, and spat on the floor. We said, "No way

Jose!" We put our gear in a shit-free, garbage-free spot and decided our home would eventually need a good cleaning. We were sure we'd been hoodwinked by the petty officer 2nd class.

I said, "Maybe later today or tomorrow, I'll ask one of the neighbors to kiss our asses. I know for a fact you won't be kissing my ass because I don't like the way your lip curls up when you give me a smug look. Come to think of it, I might have told a few people since I arrived in-country who had a similar condition to stay away from my ass for that very reason! So what do we do? Do we go back in there and clean up all that shit? Even though we met only yesterday and you're my new fuckin' buddy, I know there's no way in hell you'd be taking or giving me any shit while we're here unless it's just for the fun of it. Am I right?"

Flash laughed so hard he ended up rolling in the sand. Gee, I hadn't been trying to be funny; I'd been trying to be honest with him. By then, I was convinced he and I were being singled out as loony bins for playing air guitar on our M-16s and acting as if we'd been surfing so close to North Vietnam and thinking that because we were seabees, we could handle anything that came our way.

I asked Flash, "By any chance did you see any dogs or even a monkey since we've been here?"

He said, "No, but when I do find that mutha-fuckin' monkey who let his dog shit in our home, I'm gonna kick the living shit out of him. I'll do it while you're surfing because I know you can't stand any kind of cruelty toward animals unless some broad with big tits goes apeshit over you!"

It was my turn to laugh my ass off, but I didn't roll around in the sand because I had no idea what was under it.

When I stopped laughing, we noticed it had gotten extremely quiet—very odd for a war zone. We saw something we hadn't noticed earlier—some sort of decorative metal between two similar concrete structures. It looked like some kind of Asian symbol and was about ten feet high. It was about fifty feet away, but as we got closer, we could see these bright-gold letters that spelled out ATSB Clearwater. I said to Flash, "You're not gonna believe this, but I think we're in luck. This is what I thought about your beach in Clearwater, Florida and mine in San Diego, California. And here we are at "A Terrific Surfers' Beach." Boy was I wrong.

Someone behind us had overheard what I had said and was cracking up. He was walking toward us with this big stride and blurted out, "You stupid fucking assholes, those letters stand for Attack Tactical Support Base!"

Shit. Flash and I hadn't heard him coming up on us because the soft sand muffled noises. He didn't introduce himself. He was just a guy like us in green fatigues. They weren't camouflaged, but he definitely wasn't navy. He had some sort of unit patch and was sporting a stupid smirk. "This is the fucking last base camp or whatever you want to fuckin' call it. It's *the* number-one hellhole up here. We're at the end of the line in northern South Vietnam. So before you two assholes decide to wander off to do whatever you want to do or think of doing, just remember that you're just two miles from North Vietnam, got it?"

I figured that since he was being so nice and informative to us, he was probably thinking he was talking to some of his asshole friends. I said, "Great info! Thanks, buddy! So where do they keep the surfboards?"

He looked at us as if we had two heads each. Mr. Shit-for-Brains asked, "Why? You two girlfriends pussy surfers?"

I think Flash wanted to rip into him, but he calmly stated, "Fuckin' a. We've been going steady ever since we fell into the same foxhole one night back in Da Nang. We stayed there for several hours just to talk. We never exchanged rings, but Ski here did give me some sweet kisses to my ass. He was nice enough to clean the dirt out from under my nails that I got from scratching at the sides of the foxhole when he blew a puff of hot air up my ass. Who knows, I may return the favor to him tonight. Unless you want to?"

That time, I was the one who ripped out a loud laugh, but this guy just gave us a shit-eating grin and said, "Funny thing. Charlie snuck in here late last night. No one heard them come through the wire. We woke up this morning. No one had been killed, but they'd stolen our only two surfboards. Go figure."

I have to give credit where it's due here to my good buddy Flash who said long before Robert Duvall said it in *Apocalypse Now*, "Oh yeah? Well, charlie don't surf!" He added, "But my girlfriend Charlene and I do!" Flash kissed my hand, and I kissed his cheek. I said, "No surfboards? We'll just have to wax each other's legs then so we'll look nice for you this Saturday night. Don't worry. We won't let the other guys know about the three of us. Who knows, maybe one of your girlfriends here will tell me before Saturday if your balls hang low or high. I don't want them in Flash's way when he kisses your ass."

He gave us the sign with his finger that he was number one in camp as he walked away. Flash said, "We'd better go, sweetie. We don't want to be late for Little Big Horn." We were getting the evil eye from the master of the bullhorn knowing we were five minutes late and he waited for us. I told Flash softly, "Honey, after what you just said about us to that guy, you can kiss my ass later on and as long as you want any time any day!" I don't think I ever laughed that hard at myself since I'd been in-country. Flash yelled at the top of his lungs, "I'm gonna kiss your fuckin' ass like it was your last day on earth!"

That happened to come out at the same time our den mother asked the group, "Anyone here care to share a hut with me?" Flash's comment didn't exactly go over too well when we saw this petty officer 1st class dressed the same as our den mother looking at the two of us. He muttered something to our den mother. I saw Flash being motioned to come toward the petty officer and walk off with him. I was hoping Flash would ask him about surfboards considering the bullshit answer we'd gotten earlier.

Flash came back two minutes later and told me he'd been invited to go on the next three patrols here by having the pleasure in accompanying a small unit in camp, the army's Americal Division that Mr. Shit-for-Brains belonged to when they went into the bush. That did not sit well with us. Flash said he'd seen the perimeter of this camp or whatever they called it, and it didn't look good to him. He realized why this place had been referred to as a big "Oh no," and they told him not to say anything about it to me.

CHAPTER 45

W E WERE ABOUT to find out more about where we were and why we were there when the petty officer 2nd class and a petty officer 1st class introduced themselves followed by a young lieutenant, the CO of the place. He said, "My main job here is to see that you go home when your time is up and not in a box. You're here to do what you were sent here to do until it's time for you to leave."

Flash and I gave him a quick look-over. He appeared to be three or four years older than us. He said that over the next four days, he'd have a chance to speak with each one us to get to know us.

The PO 2nd class told everyone to gather around. He said, "We have two new seabees here who I understand are crazy fucks with a weird sense of humor. They'll be joining the other eighteen seabees here. I'll be speaking to our new ladies after I'm finished. Whether you're a seabee or not, I want the respect of all of you here for you'll find out soon enough I'm crazier than the two who just arrived having been here and having dealt with the enemy up here whether the VC or the NVA. You're going to learn soon enough how to deal with these assholes out there."

Flash and I looked at each other and figured that maybe that dude had told us the truth about the surfboards. *Shit! Now we can't surf here.*

"You're gonna have to deal with a few things up here that are probably way different from what you've dealt with at your last location such as Phu Bai, Hue, Quang Tri and Danang. Here, we have a lot of rats that have a tendency to run amok with or without the snakes that go after them. They mostly come out at night, so learn how to sleep with one eye open."

Flash and I realized that maybe it was rat shit in our hut. Maybe the snakes had eaten all the monkeys and dogs.

"The next thing you're gonna have to deal with is that other pain in the ass, that friendly, light-guided missile cruiser of ours over there. Ms. Noisy gets very temperamental around 2300 to about 0200, when she has a habit of letting you know she's out there even though she's sitting pretty quiet right now. But when she starts firing her salvos in that direction, you'll be cursing her out like there was no tomorrow. It's gonna take a while to get used to." His bullhorn let out a loud, ear-piercing squelch. "Like I said, this usually lasts throughout the night."

Flash asked me, "What? The squelch or the salvos?"

"And this is when you start dealing with the rats and snakes." I think he paused for a few seconds in order for us to comprehend what he was telling us or better still to get our hearing back. "We've been told by the South Vietnamese people over there in that hamlet behind us that the rats and snakes don't like that noise coming from the ship. It makes them angry. That's why they end up scurrying all over the place through our camp and into your Quonset huts. Do not shoot them. Use your bayonet or kick them. Brush them away, not onto anyone. A little bit of advice. Try to sleep with your bayonet in your hand or have it nearby." He took a five-second breather. "Then last but not least, every so often, you'll have the extreme pleasure of having our friendly pilots whether navy, marine, or air force, charm the pants off you by flying ever so low over our camp in their ever-popular F4-Bs, F4-Fs, and F4-Es, Phantoms. They usually fly directly over us to let us know that they know we're here as they go across the Cua Viet River and head north to do their thing.

"Then when we get two of these F-4s come screeching overhead and take off like bats out of hell, it's them telling us that our lovely B-52s will be flying well above our heads. About fifteen minutes later, you'll probably feel the ground shaking a little bit. All that's from the carpet bombing the B-52s are doing a little farther north."

The last thing he said to us was something along the lines of, "There's a saying up here that when I die, I'm sure to go to heaven because I spent my time in hell. Whoever said that must've been talking about this fucking place!"

I turned to Flash. "Gee, I always thought that Da Nang was hell. No way this could be hell too. It's way too beautiful. I'm outta here. Check please!"

The last thing he said was, "Meal time here is 0600 to 0800, 1200 to 1300, and 1800 to 1930. Movies at 2100." Flash and I headed back in silence to clean our place. Our visions of surfing the beautiful waves breaking past our hut were dying in our heads and hearts.

As for my time there, well, I worked long, hard hours in the blistering, hundred-plus-degree temperatures during the daytime and if need be in the freezing seventy degrees at night. We were there to build long, concrete-block houses for the Vietnamese in the nearby hamlets. We could see them outside our perimeter wire where every so often charlie would have fun with us by taking target practice on a new one-story building we'd finished just outside our perimeter. It was a non-classroom course entitled Construction vs. Demolition 101.

The war there was far more intense than what I had dealt with in Da Nang. I'd been under constant rocket and mortar attacks at Bridge Ramp for nine months, but it was ten times worse up at Cua Viet. I lost count on the number of rats and snakes I saw come into and through our hut and the number of times Ms. Noisy had kept me awake. And my good buddy Flash was picked five times, not three times, to go out with the Americal Unit for he was kinda liking being on special detail with this unit. The PO 2nd class told him never to talk about whatever he saw and did with them, to forget it and this place too.

One bad night, another seabee burst into our Quonset hut foaming at the mouth. He said he'd taken some kind of liquid drug from one of the villagers, drank it, and began to trip out. He had come back into camp holding his hands over his mouth and using his shirt to help him as he stumbled past the guys doing security. I had him sit on my bed. He tried to explain the different ways he was thinking of having me help him steal a boat so he could get home and see his wife and kid. He said he couldn't take being there anymore. He'd been there for almost his entire tour, and he had only two weeks to go.

I turned from the sight of the foam coming out of his mouth. He grabbed my hands in a vice grip. His eyes were bulging out of his head. I couldn't alert Flash to go for help because he was down by the shore drinking to his heart's content. When he came in, the sight of the foam sobered him up. He staggered out to get help. Four guys came, wrapped our patient in a blanket, and took him away. They tied him up so he couldn't use his hands or feet. He was medevacked out. We got word about an hour later that he had died in the chopper.

Cua Viet was not one of my fondest places to talk about back then. I never really said anything in my letters home or to Angel for I didn't want to go into any details about what took place up there, what I did, and what I saw except for what I just revealed to you in this book. But Cua Viet/DMZ had a lasting effect on me though I've tried to bury it deep in my mind in the hopes it would stay there.

Before I knew it, it was July 6, 1970. I had four days left in-country. My one-year tour of duty would soon be over. My CO was worried about my existence until he came to give me that spanking good news early that morning when he woke me up by tapping my head with his .45. I was leaving 'Nam four days shy of my 365 days. Only one thing bothered me—having to say good-bye to my best buddy, Flash. I knew I'd miss him and all the friends we'd made. I'm talking about the rats and snakes who'd visit us. We never had the heart to kill them. We just brushed them around with brooms.

When I eventually told Flash the news at breakfast, he understood and knew that I had to make my good-bye short and sweet. We knew we had a bond that would live forever. I gathered my stuff and gave him a hug. There weren't any landing crafts or choppers due for another week to take me back to Da Nang, so I was taking a deuce and a half that was taking supplies south to Dong Ha and then to Hue. Once I got to Hue (if I got there), I was to transfer to another supply truck and continue south to Da Nang. I loaded my stuff into a deuce and a half for the last time.

It was a very memorable ride. I was able to take some awesome shots—let me rephrase that—some awesome photos of the countryside as I sat on top of the supplies in the back of the truck. I didn't worry about being shot; I'd just survived three months at ATSB Clearwater. If I'd survived that hole in the wall, anything after that in 'Nam would be a walk in the park. I sat there proudly wearing my black beret with the base camp insignia on it and my camouflage fatigues, which made it real easy for the marines and the army personnel up there at the base camp know I was a fuckin' seabee.

I arrived at the Da Nang airbase and picked up my orders at the operations center. I was taking the Freedom Bird—what we called any airliner that was taking us home. I checked in my footlocker and my sea bag but learned I couldn't take my M-16 or my .45 home. They said I could take the last round out of each of them as a souvenir.

I handed over my flak jacket and helmet and thought of Flash, who had a few months to go. I knew I'd miss him. I felt extremely lucky to have had someone like him who was almost like me in every way. I thank the Lord above that he and I hadn't sustained any major injuries over there except for a few sprains here and there and a touch of food poisoning once or twice. Flash was going to call me when he got home so we could get together for old time's sake.

My most memorable night in 'Nam was Christmas Eve. It was the most horrible night. I'd love to forget it for twenty good reasons. If I were to tell you about it, I'd start off with, "You're not gonna believe this" because it's a story all to itself. I revealed it for the first time to my best buddies at DDC, Mike Kenny and Ron Vega, at the beach on Long Beach Island, New Jersey, in 2003. It was one hell of a fucking event in my life. It involved a young marine back at Camp Tien Sha and a fully loaded M-16. I'll leave it at that. On my most memorable day in 'Nam, I rode a fantastic, beautiful, glassy wave about five feet high for the length of China Beach in mid-September 1969.

I honestly say that I never did drugs in 'Nam in spite of the fact they were so easy to come by. That's maybe the reason I'll never be able to forget the events there. I think it was also because of what happened to my buddy in Cua Viet with whatever he had taken. I can still see his face whenever I see someone trying to get high on drugs.

I guess the only real injury I can talk about is what has gone unnoticed, hidden from the human eye—my scars of war. I'd get flashbacks that would hit me out of nowhere brought on by something I'd see or smell or touch about what I had experienced at the ripe old age of twenty-two in December '69 and what I went through up at the DMZ. All I was hoping for when I got home was peace of mind, happiness, and most of all not having to see any more death and devastation that were way too plentiful in Southeast Asia. I was preparing myself to be able to deal with the good times bad times for the rest of my life (having this survivor's instinct) where I would tell myself, *There's nothing out there that could be worse than 'Nam.* Boy was I wrong.

CHAPTER 46

I REMEMBER MY dad trying to explain to me and my brother, Mike, when I was ten and Mike was eight that we should be prepared for whatever came our way. That may have been his main reason for wanting us to join Cub Scouts, which we did.

Our first troop meeting took place in a community hall four blocks from where we lived. My dad told us we'd be learning many different things that were normally not taught in school such as how to get your leg unstuck between two branches in a tree or how to apply first aid if you got a severe cut on your arm. (I'd lost my footing climbing down a tree two weeks earlier and needed my dad's help with the matter. He told me on our walk home, "With all the clowning around you do, one of these days, it might not turn out to be so funny. Think before you do something foolish. You'll have the other boys take notice of what you do.") I did enjoy cracking up my friends, but I didn't want to get myself stuck in a tree just to achieve that. I got my dad's point.

A week later, there I was joining the Cub Scouts hoping to learn different ways of getting out of trees if my legs ever got caught in them again and not having to call my dad. After that first meeting, my dad said he would go over the rules with me and my brother when we get home so we should introduce ourselves to some of the boys.

We received manuals and learned where we could buy the cool uniforms of navy blue and bright yellow, my favorite colors. Even though I was in my street clothes, I walked up to these four boys in uniform and said, "I'm joining your troop. I'm such a well-tuned machine that I had to drink A-1 oil before I came here. If you need a hand with anything, let me know." My dad was right. They thought I was pretty funny and were already looking up to me.

The boys had patches on—lion heads, bear heads, wolf heads, and gold-and-silver arrowheads. Even their caps looked cool. I enjoyed earning badges and went into Boy Scouts. Michael was about to complete all his required stuff in the Cub Scouts and follow my footsteps. He followed them too closely one time and tripped over the rock I'd kicked. He ended up on the ground. "Don't you remember Dad telling us we had to be prepared for anything?" After that, he kept a distance from me in whatever we did including taking long vacations with his friends because I'd ask him, "Wouldn't you rather take a short trip instead?" (Come on! That's my humor cutting in again. Maybe *you* need a vacation.)

After being a Boy Scout for almost a year, I was being looked up to more than before by some of my fellow scouts and their dads. My dad became the scoutmaster for our troop. I had no idea he'd even applied for the position, but I was proud he was the man in charge. In Troop 124, I was out to get as many merit badges as possible and become an Eagle Scout. My dad was a great scoutmaster who came up with new ideas and planned hiking trips in the woods and excursions to the beach. On those trips, I earned badges for cooking, canoeing, archery, and many others having to do with nature.

I became proficient with a compass and learned how to find my way at night by using the stars so I'd never get lost. Actually, my first merit badge was in astronomy. I'd joke about getting lost during the daylight hours and having to use the compass. I asked my fellow scouts out in the woods, "What if that red arrow on top falls off? Then what do we do? Do we look for someone who can point out north? Maybe a hermit? I don't think so, so don't get lost!"

I'd go on and on with my questions even while I was walking with them and getting ourselves lost intentionally just for the sheer pleasure of trying to find our way back and in doing so seeing new places and meeting others in the woods. I had so much fun doing this that I even continued the game of mine when I started traveling for Merrill Lynch. I enjoyed getting lost. On one of my lost adventures, I stumbled across the best chili place in Wichita, Kansas, way off the beaten path.

I had a blast getting other scouts lost and showing them how to get back by a different route. I always noted where the sun was before we started out. My dad encouraged me to go for Eagle Scout, so I worked on my badges and helped others get theirs. I made Star Scout in no time and wanted to make Life Scout and then Eagle Scout to make my dad proud.

Guidance, preparedness, and lots of work got me there, but it seems I was not totally prepared. Something was coming that I didn't see coming. Shame on me.

CHAPTER 47

S AD TO SAY, I never made Life Scout. I was two badges short when my thoughts of going on in scouting went spiraling downward. My drive died out. Today, I consider it a stupid mistake not having made Eagle Scout. I wish I had the chance to tell my dad before he passed away how deeply sorry I was for giving up so quickly on becoming an Eagle Scout.

You're not gonna believe this, but I dropped out because I'd just graduated from high school in '65 and wanted to get out there and make some money in the real world. I didn't tell my dad I'd dropped out of the troop on a night he wasn't able to attend because he had to work late.

I was consumed with thoughts about earning money and buying my own clothes and a car and dating more girls than I could handle. I wanted to spread my wings like an eagle and enjoy the happiness in seeing them in my nest (the backseat) to then spread their— You know what I mean. I couldn't or wouldn't spend any more of my spare time chasing the remaining two merit badges to make Life Scout and then going for Eagle Scout.

At the time, I had no desire to go to college. I thought I already had the smarts, and I'd have the best of both worlds—living at home and not having to buy food or gas. And with my own car, I could go wherever I wanted. I was only seventeen. I thought I had it made in the shade. I was convinced that I'd end up working for somebody important and famous and that it would rub off on me and money and fame would come my way. I didn't see a problem with that.

I wanted a job in the exciting world of architecture. I loved to draw, and I had a keen eye for design. I'd draw houses I wanted to live in. I thought once I found a job in the field, I'd take some college classes at night. I'd quickly end up set for life, I was sure. I could taste it.

I'd completed three years of architectural drafting and building construction at Sewanhaka High School, a well-known vocational and technical high school on Long Island. My teacher told me I had potential. I also took art there; I was always doodling in my spare time drawing whatever came to mind. My talents made be believe I wouldn't have a hard time finding a good job. Even if it turned out not to be my ultimate dream, I figured I could work and go to college at night. With all that in mind, I gave up scouting.

The second reason I stopped going for Eagle Scout was that I indeed did find a great job! It was my first step toward the good life. I felt luck was really on my side as to how I even got this job. But I had to tell my dad. When I did, he was infuriated with me. We had our first father-to-son talk on that topic. He wanted me to find a job I loved, something that didn't seem like work and made me not worry about what I was getting paid. I more or less told him I didn't need scouting anymore because I was on cloud nine. We ended up having somewhat of a heated discussion. I knew I was hurting his feelings. I told him I had no intentions of going to college just then.

After that talk, I'd never mention anything important when I was going out; I knew he'd follow after me and explain that dropping out of scouts was the biggest mistake I'd ever made. Look, I never gave my dad any lip, never talked back at him, never cursed or raised my voice to him because I had the highest respect for him, but I didn't have to agree with him as I had to do when I was younger.

After getting a good tongue lashing about quitting the scouts, I was told something that quickly changed my attitude; he told me I'd have to contribute toward the expenses and especially for the car if I wanted to continue using it. "Sure, Dad, how much?"

Let me tell you how I got that job. On a Saturday evening a day or two after I graduated, he said, "Your best bet if you want to find a good-paying job is to go into Manhattan first thing Monday morning and make your first stop the New York State Employment Office. We'll go out on Sunday. I'll buy you a suit, shirt, tie, and dress shoes so you'll look good when you fill out the application. Try to speak to someone, anyone, and let them know about your strong desire to work in the field of architecture and hopefully with a prominent architectural firm that will recognize your talent. It would be a step in the right direction since you already decided to drop out of scouting and not go to college. You better prepare yourself for whatever comes your way." I took his advice. Feeling totally confident in myself, I went out into the world on that Monday morning and did exactly what he said.

You're not gonna believe this. The next day, my mom took a call. I came home from surfing and learned I had an interview the next day at an architectural firm in Manhattan. She was so excited and happy for me that she made my day way better than any of the waves I'd ridden that day or the girls I'd met there.

I was psyched. I was ready for my interview. I got lucky. After long interviews with the personnel director and a supervisor, I was told on the spot I was hired! My supervisor had a sense of humor similar to mine, so I thought he was joking when he asked me if I could start work the next day or Thursday. They needed to replace someone who had had to leave suddenly. Of course I said yes. I felt like Mickey Mantle hitting his 500th homerun. My dream of working in New York and making lots money were coming true. When I was told what my starting salary would be, "Ooh fa!" I was beside myself. I had a great job with a very prominent architectural office; I'd be working in a very busy plan room—it was totally unreal.

But within two weeks, I was ready to call it quits. Why? Because I was getting lost. And that time, I wasn't having that much fun getting lost. I had to deliver or pick up drawings just about every day in the vast concrete jungle of Midtown and Downtown Manhattan. I didn't have my trusty compass. I had no clue about the avenues and streets in that vast city. Getting lost there was totally nerve-racking. I started to hate the traveling part of my job; I'd know I'd get lost every time I went down to the subway.

My firm, Harrison & Abramowitz Architects, took up the whole fifth floor of a well-known building at 630 Fifth Avenue in Midtown. It was in the International Building of the Rockefeller Center complex, where my good buddy Charlie Atlas stood out front with the world on his shoulders. I felt I was doing the same.

Wallace Harrison and Max Abramowitz ruled the roost. Each morning before I entered the building, I'd greet Charlie Atlas with, "Good morning, Charlie. How's your day so far?" I'd go through the revolving doors and say, "Okay, Charlie, I'll take it from here!" even though I knew I'd get lost somehow, somewhere that day. When I'd leave for home, I'd give him a quick wink to let him know the world was back on his shoulders.

To get home, I'd take the subway, and then a city bus from Jamaica to the Queens/Nassau borderline by the Cross Island Parkway in Bellerose. It was something I had to do every day to work in the big city. (Here it is some fifty years later and I'm still doing the same commute but from a different town a little farther east and south but only ten minutes away.)

Besides getting lost, I also had to work in the plan room filing away these huge drawings and ordering blueprints from a printer when they were too big to handle in-house with the printer they taught me how to use. I really was ready to call it quits after just two weeks.

One night, I came home, and my dad saw me looking kind of grumpy. "How's the job going?"

I said, "I'm ready to quit, Dad!"

"Charlie, life isn't all peaches and cream. There'll be times when you just want to chuck it all, but that's when you want to sit and think about your options before making that final decision. You deal with the problem or the situation or walk away hoping to find something better. Just remember, the grass is not always greener on the other side of the hill. You're giving up too soon!"

I gave it another try. I wanted to get over that hurdle and carry on. Sure enough, my dad was right. I received additional responsibilities besides working in the plan room and making trips to deliver or pick up drawings. I was told I'd be handling some of Mr. Harrison's personal requests such as going to his Fifth Avenue apartment at 65th Street across from Central Park near the Children's Zoo. I'd take things to his home or pick things up there for him related to the work or projects he was involved in at the time. One of them was with Governor Nelson Rockefeller, his brother-in-law. His apartment had a beautiful view of the park. I waited there for some time one day waiting for a special delivery of a small crate that I was told contained four small paintings given to him by Marc Chagall.

I called his secretary when the crate arrived. Mr. Harrison came over, and we opened the crate. You're not gonna believe this, but Mr. Harrison actually offered one to me, but I turned it down for I was never into Chagall's paintings nor did I think it was right to take a gift that had been given to my first boss. But who knows what that would have been worth today?

CHAPTER 48

D O YOU RECALL where I mentioned that I believe I was driven to write this book? You can blame it on this strange event that took place on a Sunday morning a week after what had taken place on the prior Saturday on Long Beach Island, New Jersey, where I experienced some amazing and unbelievable surprising coincidences.

Early one Sunday morning, I was driving along the south shore of Long Island on Ocean Parkway. I could see the sky and the ocean meet on any day, but that day, I was seeing the horizon in a whole new light. I think it was the first time I didn't see a single ship, plane, or even seagull. Maybe it was because I was still tossing around in my head what I'd experienced the week before and wasn't looking closely. I was taking the ride to clear my mind before my daughter woke up and would need her car, which I was in.

I drove to Jones Beach, one of prettiest on the entire East Coast, about fifteen minutes away. I watched the sun come up. I was listening to one of my favorite CDs I'd brought along. When Led Zeppelin's "Kashmir" came on, I cranked up the volume. That song got me thinking about writing a short story about what had happened last Saturday but I had no idea where and how to start it. The music was a soothing accompaniment to my thoughts about what had happened.

I somehow veered off the road and past the shoulder onto the grass, but the parkway was empty. I got back on the road. As I passed them, I gazed at Tobay Beach and Gilgo Beach, the two hottest spots back in the day (and still are today) where I use to surf. If they were ever too crowded, I'd head back to Long Beach, which was just as good if not better than those two.

I imagined being back out there on my surfboard waiting for the right wave. I had this Con surfboard, an eight-foot-six-inch that was probably referred to as a big board. It was bright yellow with a beautiful red butterfly at the nose and one variable skeg (fin, also red) under the tail. Back then, we didn't have leashes that hooked us up to the board. We'd have to chase them if we got knocked off.

My board was a way-brighter yellow than even my '67 Chevy Camaro SS with black interior, hidden headlights, four-speed transmission, dual exhausts with chrome tips, and a 350/350 mean engine that sounded positively beautiful when I revved it and took off at a light. It definitely turned heads just as I did with my shoulder length, bleached-blond, surfer hair. I'd hang my head out the window to blow my hair back, radio blasting. I'd downshift, rev the engine, and leave a patch of rubber. Those were my golden years even though I was just in my late teens.

Let me get you back to where we were. I went through all four gears as I listened to Led Zeppelin and entertained thoughts about writing that short story. Somehow, everything got all mixed up in my brain, and an odd feeling came over me. I felt like I'd been smacked by a massive wave that took my mind off my driving. I saw that I was doing seventy. Behind me and ahead of me, there wasn't a soul in sight. I was doing eighty. All the pressure on my brain had leaked down into my right foot. (I have to ask my mechanic about that abnormality.) I tapped the brakes and downshifted. I eventually came to a stop right on the parkway.

The horizon looked very strange. I tapped my steering wheel and waited to hear what song would come on the radio instead of the CD since the song had ended. I think I made a big mistake doing that. I couldn't believe my ears. I was hearing "Low Rider" by War, a song that was very popular in the mid-seventies. It was a good open-road tune that always gave me a high similar to what I got when I surfed. (I'll say it again—I'm proud to say I never got high on any type of drug because I hated the thought of doing any kind of drug.)

But this song had a constant rhythmic guitar sound along with a drum beat that carried me away and made me feel super great being behind the wheel (and I do mean the steering wheel) and being the only person on the road, which hardly ever occurs unless you're in Montana around four in the morning.

I turned up the volume and the bass. I wanted to really feel the music. The beat began to turn every little thought in my head into a video about everything that had taken place that Saturday. I don't know why I decided to put the windows down; it was as if someone or something wanted me to hear the roar of the ocean waves crashing onshore. I heard, "Take a little trip, take a little trip, take a little trip … with me!" The words blaring out of all six speakers made me look at myself in the rearview mirror and ask, *Am I getting some kind of message here?* I thought I might have been transported to a strange new world where I was seeing my life in a whole new light having these amazing, surprising coincidences occur to me as they had that Saturday; those had been the most powerful ones of all. *Why me and why now?*

My dear readers, why aren't you answering me? Can't you see I'm looking for an answer? If you have it, please call me. My number's listed toward the back. And while you're at it, could you please tell me why everyone sings "Take Me Out to the Ballgame" when they're already there? Makes no sense.

But there I was sitting in the car. The song came to an end. I wanted to hear more waves and more music, but soothing music. I switched stations and punched the button to open the sunroof. I turned off the engine. The sun's rays calmed me as did the salty air. I felt a powerful presence in the car with me. The rays were drawing me to them. I felt as if I were soaring out the sunroof and heading to the heavens. I felt warm. I was floating on a cloud. I believe I was there for more than a minute. I descended into the car behind the steering wheel. I was sure my old heart had just been replaced with a new, wild heart that had me feeling more alive than I'd felt in a long time.

I started up the car and took off like a bat out of hell. This sense of thrill ran through me. I gave off a deep sigh, checked all my mirrors for any traffic, hit the gas, and watched the needle head toward 120 mph. I owned the highway. I slowed down, but I thought, *Yes, I'm invincible!* I felt this really warm rush. No, the heater wasn't on. The feeling reminded me of the tingles I'd gotten that Saturday morning when I had those amazing, surprising coincidences and before I had that strange occurrence on the 59th Street Bridge on 9/11.

I think a new spark was ignited in my heart and soul that began to assure me that I ought to start writing that short story and talk only about what had occurred that Saturday morning and what I had experienced that day being that they were related to one another and 9/11. I wondered if *Reader's Digest* readers would like it.

If you've found what I've just told you to be moving, buckle up. You're in for a humdinger of a ride. Take a little trip … take a little trip … with me.

CHAPTER 49

CHANGED FOREVER—THAT DESCRIBES a majority of the people who experienced September 11, 2001, at the WTC. It probably also relates to those who saw it unfold on TV and in the newspapers. These people were saying that their personal lives and relationships were no longer the same.

I noticed a change in my life when I went across the 59th Street Bridge later that afternoon on 9/11. Then again, maybe my life began to change the minute I saw the upper floors of the two towers up in smoke and flames and witnessed fourteen people jump to their deaths from the North Tower as I stood across the street about fifty yards from the North Tower on Church Street.

I'd arrived at the last E train subway stop, the WTC, at six after nine that morning. I heard from people coming down into the subway area—something you'd see more so in the evening rush hour—that two planes had hit the towers. I was thinking a Cessna or a Piper Cub. An airliner never entered my mind. I was pissed off at the subway; I was already half an hour late due to two delays I had in Queens for an important meeting I had scheduled for eight thirty with an architect to talk and walk through two floors in a building a block away at 100 Church Street. I had a nine thirty meeting every Tuesday with a client, the City of New York Human Resources Administration at 250 Church Street, only three or four blocks north.

The delays I'd had in Queens maybe saved my life. I'd never have imagined seeing the North and South Towers filled with smoke and flames and seeing people clutching the sides of ripped-out windows.

I witnessed people jumping to their deaths. I saw white office paper standing out against the black smoke and the orange-red flames. I'm sorry for some of these details, but trust me—it was a thousand times worse seeing it than describing it.

This continued for fifty-five minutes. I stood in shock watching hundreds of people trying to evacuate onto the plaza from both buildings at street level and avoid being struck by falling debris. The smoke and flames got worse.

At that next moment, 9:59am, I reentered a dark period in my life. I heard an explosion that reminded me of those I'd heard in Vietnam. I went into combat mode. I beat feet automatically from that eerie sound; I headed north up Church Street. I had no intention of looking at what was occurring behind me though I had a pretty good idea what was taking place.

As I was running, I wondered if Margie had heard me say I was looking forward to being back at the WTC for my meetings. I went for cover to a building about three blocks away. I was simply trying to survive. You have no idea what it's like unless you've been in a similar situation.

CHAPTER 50

I HAD AN unusual amount of surprising coincidences occur to me on Memorial Day in 2009, a quiet day compared to the previous three days. I was on Long Beach Island, New Jersey, at the beach house where we held our Festivus celebrations in September. But on that Memorial Day, I was remembering our fallen heroes in the company of a comrade of mine from Vietnam with whom I'd had some but not much contact. Maybe it wasn't meant for me to meet and talk with him before that special occasion.

We had agreed to meet at this cozy beach house that was next door to the one where I was staying. I could usually hear the waves crashing, but the sea was quiet that day. The silence was sending a slight chill up my back; it was way too quiet for me. I believe I actually heard one or two hairs on my head grow out or fall out. I didn't hear any birds chirping or dogs barking or flies buzzing. I felt a presence. *Okay, Charlie, shrug this off. Nothing's going on. Go back to sleep for an hour.*

I forgot all about the stillness was just thankful for another beautiful day. I was still exhausted from all the fishing I'd done the past two days. I planned to go to the convenience store for a large, freshly brewed French Vanilla coffee, a good wake me up along with a buttered roll to help me with some serious thinking I needed prior to my 9:00 a.m. meeting with my friend.

I used my watch alarm to wake me up on time, not the clock next to my bed; I didn't want to disturb the other sleepyheads in the beach house, my family. I didn't want to rattle things in the kitchen by making coffee (that would have given Margie "grounds" for divorce). Noelle was there, as was Margie's sister, Mary Ann, and her daughter, Kara Ann.

After I got my coffee and roll, I walked to the beach and tried to figure out why things were so quiet. Maybe so it was I could think while the sun worshiper in me soaked in some early rays. I wanted to do some more surfcasting. I've had a ritual for twenty-five years of yelling out before casting a line, "This is for thee, Charlie Tuna! I'm coming to get you. I'm not joking. Be prepared. I'm the best!" It doesn't matter if this works. At least I give myself a good laugh.

I made my way down to the dunes and sipped my coffee. I passed the picnic bench that had been there forever. I wanted to get to the shore and do my thinking there. I hoped to see something along the horizon to help me focus. The still ocean got me thinking about how I should start my conversation with this guy named Chuck. I didn't want our talk to end up going all over the place. My mind has a habit of going so fast that my mouth starts going fast too, and I sound like I have a bunch of marbles in it. (Some people have thought I was losing my marbles at times like that.) I wanted a clear head for our conversation, one as calm as the mirror-like ocean I was facing. I saw my face's reflection in the water. It looked filled with deep emotion and anticipation of my conversation with Chuck. Those feelings had been building up for years ever since I had first seen him.

I splashed a bit of my coffee into the ocean as a toast; I wanted to fish in it later.

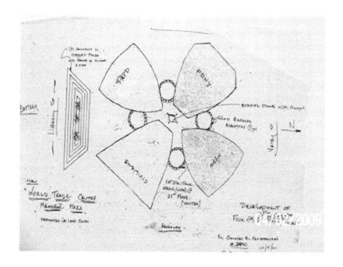

My original first design for the redevelopment
for the World Trade Center

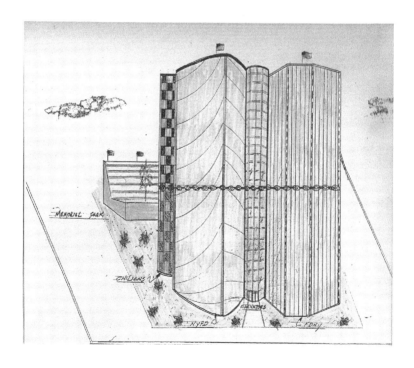

Elevation Rendering of my first design

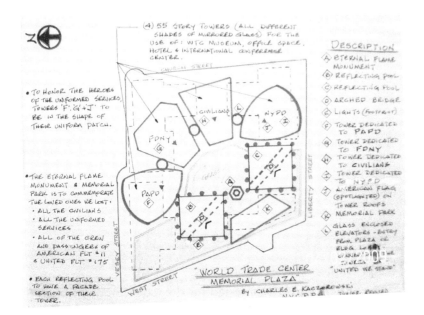

Revision: Design spread over 16 acres

Plan view rendering of 16 acres

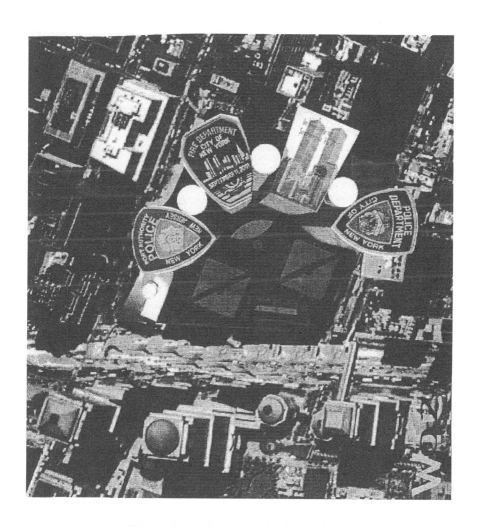

View of site plan at night from above

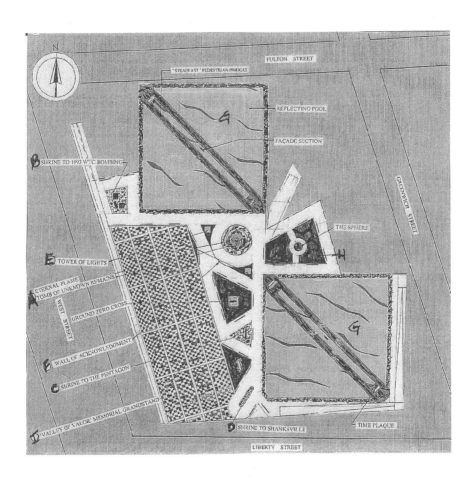

911 Memorial Design

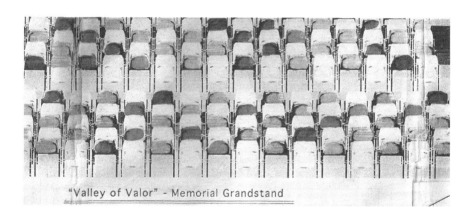

"Valley of Valor" - Memorial Grandstand

"Valley of Valor"

Living memorial design

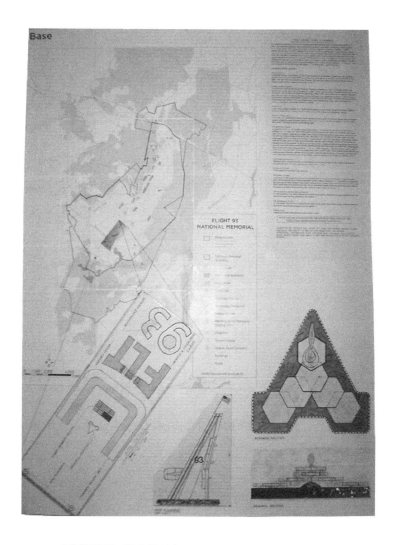

UNITED FLIGHT 93 MEMORIAL DESIGN

MY AWARD WINNING PHOTO FOR ENR
MAGAZINE (TAKEN AT GROUND ZERO)

MY STREET SIGNS AT THE "FESTIVUS"

DDC GUYS AT THE "FESTIRVUS"

GROUP
PHOTO AT THE "FESTIVUS"

04/19/2009

My extended family in Oklahoma City

CHAPTER 51

I WANT TO tell you how Chuck and I met, but before I do, I'll tell you something about that day itself. It was on a beautiful quiet Friday morning in September 2004 on Long Beach Island. I'd arrived the previous day in preparation for that year's Festivus. I went out to the convenience store for a few things.

I walked past Susan's house and saw this guy working on his beach house. My mind was still a little cloudy from having too good of a time with five of my buddies who were still asleep in the house after a long evening of drinking, eating, more drinking, and laughs along with quiet moments as we pondered our time at Ground Zero. Lucky for me, the convenience store was in walking distance. I could let those sleeping dogs lie and not bother any for a ride.

Every year since our first gathering there, our attendance has increased by a few people whether we knew them or not. Just joking. Every yearly Festivus was more memorable than the previous. One time, some people I didn't know stopped in to inquire about the humorous signs I'd put out front offering drinks and burgers to all-comers.

Anyway, getting back to that morning, I saw my neighbor stepping off his ladder. "Good morning! How you doing?" I asked. I enjoy small talk with people on the island. This stranger wasn't aware he was in for a real treat.

"Good morning to you! What's your name?"

"Charlie K. What's yours?"

"Chuck J."

I was sure his humorous side was just like mine. His reply reminded me of how those who worked recovery/cleanup at Ground Zero would greet each other. I said, "I'll stop by and see you on my return from the store." I made my way up the street. I think he may have said something to me; maybe he had said something to himself. Whatever it was faded away in the breeze.

I was on my way for newspapers and some donuts and rolls to go with the butter and jelly we had along with some coffee to hold us over until breakfast. Edmundo, Ed, would prepare our traditional breakfast. He'd rise and say, "Stay out of my way! Stay out of the kitchen! I'll be making my famous, one-of-a-kind blueberry pancakes!" He'd serve them on an aluminum tray and famously say, "Guys, as you know, I made these from scratch."

I hope and pray that you, Ed, with your unending desire to make them for us, used pancake mix. I hope making them from scratch didn't involve the number of times I've seen you scratch your butt with your right hand as you moved frantically about in the kitchen with a bowl of mix in your left hand. It's okay. No sweat! I'll tell my readers that you were wearing your famous PJs or some kind of shorts clean or not or turned inside out or not.

The guys with whom I worked with at DDC in the recovery/cleanup operations at Ground Zero met at this beach house every September. We did a great job there, we finished way ahead of schedule and way under budget. I was proud of our agency and the dedicated people I had worked with there. I mentioned that I met Susan, who owned this beach house, two years after I left Ground Zero, who was gracious enough to let us use it for our September get-togethers. She had told me about Chuck, her neighbor at the beach who was from Baltimore.

That year, '08, Susan said that Chuck had asked if I would be there for Memorial Day in '09. I considered that odd. I'd first seen Chuck in '04 but hadn't had any contact with him since then. Then I saw him on my walk that morning in September '08. I wondered what was occurring to me on this amazing island; I was wondering what kind of surprise I'd have next at a beach house that I considered my little piece of paradise.

CHAPTER 52

"GO AHEAD, CHARLIE, have a seat. If you'd like, you can start first. If not, I will." Chuck came out with this casual suggestion (but it sounded more like a military order to me) as he pointed to a patio chair across from him. I carefully stepped up onto the patio trying not to spill my coffee. I thanked him for the invitation and sat. I could tell our morning was off to a great start before I even got there. After my walk, I felt totally reassured that everything would go well. It was beginning to look like another warm, sunny day.

We toasted each other with our coffees. I said, "Okay, I'll go first."

Go get something to drink, readers, come back, and make yourselves comfortable. You're not gonna believe this. I told him I'd come out to the island mainly to see him. Chuck said he'd known I was coming with my wife and daughter. He said his wife had competed in a triathlon the day before on the mainland as she had done the year before. I figured I'd better tell him right away that I had only a few hours to talk with him. I wanted to cover as much as possible. I told him that I'd been coming to this beautiful island for the past six years and that I'd started writing a short story about what had occurred there in September with Helen next door.

My mission with Chuck was going to be very simple. I wanted to talk about the war, our war, a little bit about 9/11, and a few things about his life and mine. I also wanted to thank him for the use of his gas grill in September. If our grill had been there that day, this all would have been an "It is what it was" matter and this book wouldn't have been the result.

He and I talked about our time in 'Nam. We were taken aback by each other's story. We were involved in the war in different ways and at different times. I told him about the different times I'd encountered charlie at unannounced and unexpected times, nothing like a typical meeting in a conference room; my dealings with charlie had been more like dodgerocket or dodgemortar than dodgeball. My first game of that with them was more than enough for me. Their rocket and mortar attacks had me tasting hell on the tip of my tongue.

Chuck had a faraway look. He sipped his coffee and cleared his throat. "Well, Charlie, it was totally different for me over there." He had had countless meetings with charlie; they were on his agenda daily. He'd had the upper hand. At his meetings with them, he'd piss them off to the point that they shot missiles at him. I began to admire him. I was extremely proud of him. I was seeing him in a different light.

I told him I'd been there in '69. I said that whenever I heard that Bryan Adams song, it would take me back to when I landed in-country on July 10. I told him about being under rocket fire at Da Nang airbase and getting out of Dodge to Camp Tien Sha near Monkey Mountain to work at Bridge Ramp. I explained that I'd spent my last three months in the DMZ in Cua Viet, two miles south of North Vietnam, and I'd been without volunteering for it to a few other exotic places including Phu Bai, Hue, Quang Tri, Dong Ha, and Tam My. I told him I'd wanted to leave a.s.a.p.a., which stand for "as soon as possible asshole!"

Chuck said that he hadn't learned much of the language because his encounters with charlie had involved him with his head in the clouds (no, not with the help of any drugs). Some guys get all the luck. He was there in '71 and had been assigned to Da Nang Air Base. He'd been a captain in the air force who had flown F4-E Phantoms. "Two hundred and sixty-nine missions over South Vietnam with my head in the clouds," he said. I told him that was an incredible number of missions, but his look told me he had me in his sights.

"You know what, Charlie? When I was over there doing my thing, I never gave much thought to what it was like for you and the other guys on the ground dealing with all that shit up close and personal. It was like you and I fought two different wars in the same godforsaken place."

All I could do was nod. I had no comeback to that.

His mention of 269 missions over South Vietnam smacked my

memory bank, but I couldn't recall at the time where I had written that same number down many years ago. He told me he'd also flown nineteen hairy missions over North Vietnam.

"Excuse me, Chuck," I said. "I just want to call my mom and dad and ask them to check something for me really quick."

"Sure, go ahead."

I called my folks, said hi, and asked them to go to the sun parlor and look at the back of the photo I'd sent them from 'Nam. My dad did so. "Okay, son, what do you want to know?"

"Dad, what did I write on the back of the photo?"

He replied, "Dear Mom and Dad, I'm dee dee mow Da Nang! Day 269! I'm off to the DMZ! Don't worry! Love, hugs, and kisses, your son, Charles." (Dee dee mow is Vietnamese for "Go away," "Bye, bye," and "Get lost" in a nice way.) I thanked them and said good-bye. I gave Chuck a big smile.

"What did they say?" he asked. I told him. "Wow!" he said. "That's what I call a coincidence, Charlie! I find that a little odd."

We shook our heads and stared into the street. We got to the point that we both agreed to kick in the afterburners—leave our discussion on 'Nam and speed ahead some thirty-plus years to the present. I told him about my experiences on 9/11 and the time I had spent at Ground Zero. He said that Susan had mentioned I'd been there. I told him about some of the memorable moments that I had all in about thirty minutes. (Don't worry; you'll be reading about this later.)

Out of nowhere, I asked him on what date he'd married Ann. September 10 was his answer. Just hearing him say "September" gave me a chill. He told me he and Ann were glad it hadn't been September 11. I didn't think there was need to ask him in what year they'd married unless he was going to offer me a nice glass of Merlot or Chardonnay.

"Chuck, mine's September 29. My daughter Noelle's birthday is the same day. Do you remember last September when you let me use your gas grill? I think in some mystical way, your house and the house I stay at got connected for some strange reason and that's why these surprising coincidences are coming up."

He and I gave our minds a break.

CHAPTER 53

I SAT THERE with my eyes closed. Total silence for a while. Chuck spoke. "Charlie, didn't you just say a few minutes ago that you had ninety-two days left in-country when you got up to the DMZ?" I nodded. "And you said you were married on the twenty-ninth?" I nodded. "We just learned that the two of us got married in the ninth month and we have a two and a nine between us. Do you realize that it's taken six years for us to actually meet? If we put that six between the two and the nine, that's the number of missions I flew and the number of days you spent in Da Nang. Wouldn't you say that was also one hell of an amazing, surprising coincidence for you?"

"You can say that again!" I said, but he didn't. The hairs on my left arm were standing up again. Are you finding this somewhat unbelievable? Are you the slightest bit curious as to why or what the connection between Chuck and me was? If you don't, you probably have no clue whatsoever why they have alternate side of the street parking in Manhattan on certain days of the week even though not everyone drives into Manhattan on those days. Do you care? Wanna go back and read that sign again where you parked? I'll wait till you get back before I continue.

I looked at my watch. Chuck and I had been talking for almost two hours. I had no idea where the time had gone. I told him that it was time to call it a day, that Marge and Noelle were waiting for me to do some shopping before I went fishing.

I'm finding it troublesome having to use the same words over and over to describe some of my surprising coincidences such as *amazing, unbelievable,* or *remarkable,* so just remember that my surprising coincidences were fuckin' outstanding! There. I got that off my chest.

I got up, but the slant-backed Adirondack chair I had been sitting in had put some kinks in my back. "Look, Chuck, we got to do this again real soon, but not in these chairs. I'll bring my own. Maybe we can continue this coming September after the eleventh. I'll be here for our Festivus. Put it on your calendar. I'm inviting you, your wife, and your daughter. I insist! We might need your gas grill again!" We laughed. "Chuck, by the way, what day's your birthday?"

He smiled. "Why? You thinking of buying me a gift?"

"Yeah. It'll be my way of thanking you for the use of your grill!"

"It's passed. August seventeenth."

"You shitting me? That's my wife's birthday!"

We were again in disbelief. I asked, "Aren't you here with your wife and daughter like I am?"

"Wow! Simply amazing!" he said, and we chuckled.

My Blackberry vibrated and then jingled. I excused myself for a second to glance at the screen. It was a repeat of an earlier message that had been sent to me the night before. It was red-flagged Important. It was from the New York Blood Bank. I said, "They must really need me bad!" not realizing I was reading it aloud. "The city's blood bank was notifying me to please help. The blood supply's low, and they need me to donate."

I excused myself and replied that I couldn't donate until early July; I'd just had a cardiac catheterization procedure done and had been told I couldn't donate until two months had passed. What I should have done was call my buddy Bob Silver, DDC's safety officer and fellow 'Nam vet to ask him when the agency's next blood drive was before committing to donating on my own.

Chuck had a peculiar look on his face. He said, "Hey, Charlie, sorry to hear you had to have that procedure. Are you okay?" He paused. "By the way, how often do you give blood?"

"I'm doing fine. They thought I had some problem with my heart, but it turned out to be my lungs. As for giving blood, I try to donate at least two, three times a year, and if need be, I go when they call for help. I'm a universal donor, O negative."

Chuck beamed. "Charlie, you're not gonna believe this, but I have the same blood type!"

I was totally dumbfounded. (I'm not sure anyone could be only half dumbfounded. And I'm not fully convinced that half & half is really half milk and half cream.) We were experiencing another surprising coincidence. We just shook our heads. Then we shook hands. I knew I'd give him a respectable embrace knowing we'd been meant to meet. He gripped my hand and leaned in. "Charlie, you're not gonna believe this either, but there may be a day that I'll need you to save my life, and one day, you might need me to save yours. We're two of a kind. One for all and all for one!"

Our hearts and minds were the same and would be as long as we lived. We nodded, smiled, gave each other pats on the shoulders, and called it a day. I was in shock. *This is totally, unbelievable!* As I was making my way back to my beach house, I turned to look at a guy I hardly knew but for whom I had the deepest respect. We had so much in common besides being 'Nam vets. I'm pretty sure that both of us felt we'd just got shot out of nowhere by these amazing coincidences. Monday, May 25, 2009 was the most memorable Memorial Day for me.

I just needed to do one more thing. I assumed Chuck was ready to go in. I needed to say these two simple words and nothing more, but he beat me to the punch. What he said and did still baffles me today. You're not gonna believe this, but he gave me a short salute. We both said at the same time, "See ya!"

CHAPTER 54

D URING OUR CONVERSATION, my mind kept going back to the first day I saw Chuck in September 2004. I wish I'd gone back to talk to him then even if it had been for just five minutes; I might have found out a lot earlier than I did some of the stuff we talked about on Memorial Day. I would have treated him more like family than just a friend during the intervening years. I could have when I had come back from the convenience store, but then again, maybe I was supposed to wait.

I get this strange sensation in my wild heart whenever Chuck's name comes up or I hear someone mention an F-4 Phantom. I'm surprised this phenomenon I have going on in my heart has never been mentioned in any of the medical journals, or *House & Garden,* or *Reader's Digest* since this unknown phenomenon was already condensed. I guess that's why certain things happen when they do and why they do.

I don't recall seeing Chuck at his beach house on the number of times I'd been coming to stay at Susan's beach house usually for two to four days after Labor Day. But the island is pretty quiet then. The cable guy would stop by when we were there, but I think he was just trying to get himself invited to our Festivus festivities.

On that amazing weekend in 2008, the guys and I arrived and checked out Susan's place. We wanted to make sure the previous renters hadn't damaged anything inside or out. I wanted to check the grill to see if we had enough propane, and that's when I saw our famous grill wasn't there. The rest of us needed it for Festivus. *I'm screwed.* I was generally the grillmeister those weekends. I considered the missing grill a disaster.

Try to envision this if you can because I won't be using my hands. I'm

Polish. I was anticipating hungry guests at noon Saturday. Remember Pompeii? Can you picture the hot lava streaming down the streets of that Roman town after Mt. Vesuvius erupted? Can you imagine people running amuck, all kinds of bedlam as the soles of their feet were being grilled? I could very well have had similar consequences even though there was no volcano anywhere on Long Beach Island and there was no grill to burn anybody's feet. Didn't I just tell you a minute ago that our grill was gone? Haven't you been paying attention?

Anyway, we were expecting hundreds, some of whom would have traveled long distances. Wait a second. Did I just say hundreds? My apologies. I meant handfuls. But big handfuls. I knew they'd interrogate me about the missing grill. That by itself would have had me erupting in anger and spewing hot comments at them. After all, I was the fucking chef. I couldn't very well tell them, "No need to worry. Charlie K will serve you peanut butter, banana, and mayonnaise sandwiches." They would have run amuck. Just the words *peanut butter* can send certain people into panicked tailspins. You don't want to witness that unless you're wearing a metal cup to protect your balls. I've had countless nightmares about not having strapped one on.

Then again, I could serve crunchy peanut butter and forget about barbecuing chickpeas with baked beans and just add a few more bags of croutons in the salads until we figured out the grill thing. They'd have plenty to drink. Alternatively, I could tell them, "You can eat whatever we have in the house, or you can head back to your cars. Don't bother to say good-bye. Go to the Terrace Tavern on the main boulevard. Great food and drinks and always a live band! This weekend it's Chaos & Bedlam. I heard there was a small cover charge, but it's peanuts!" There I go with my humor again.

Well, there was never any chaos and bedlam because thank God I got to use Chuck's grill, and the only fleeing that ever came to light was those damn beach fleas that hung around in the backyard for what I don't know. Everything went off without a hitch. We had a fabulous Festivus that year.

CHAPTER 55

I REFER TO Long Beach Island as my little piece of paradise because I had experienced something powerful there nine months before Chuck and I had our talk. I met a woman whom I will always say magically appeared on the island during a Festivus. Our lives became intertwined. I believe meeting her was the cornerstone of my desire to write this book.

It was in September, of course, the month when so many of my "You're not gonna believe this" events occurred. Susan's house was right next to Chuck's, as I've mentioned. But I'd never heard of the island until I went there to attend a seminar. Otherwise, I could have lived the rest of my life not knowing about this beautiful place and not having had all the surprising coincidences I've had there.

I'm finding it hard to keep track of all the islands in my area. I lived on Long Island and worked on another island, Manhattan. At times, I'd run over to Roosevelt Island or Staten Island or even Randall's Island, and I'd been to others in the area including Gardiner's Island, Plum Island, Fire Island, Shelter Island, and Block Island, which were not as popular as Rhode Island or the Thousand Islands in upstate New York. But I don't see myself anytime in the near future going there unless I switch over to a different salad dressing altogether. (What this has to do with what I just said about Long Beach Island beats the hell out of me.)

Long Beach Island is a popular resort from late May to early October. I've met many tourists there who have told me that they'd heard about this place a long time ago, visited it once, and kept coming back since. There are year 'round residents on the island, but it really jumps during summers. The island comprises areas and communities with nautical names—Harvey

Cedars, Ship Bottom, Spray Beach, Surf City, and of course Beach Haven Terrace, where Susan's beach house is. The houses range from small and medium to big. Inexpensive to expensive. Quaint and otherwise. Old, renovated, and new. Long Beach Boulevard runs the length of the island. The bay is on the north side and the ocean is on the south side. There are plenty of shops, restaurants, bars, hotels, motels, and inns.

Those who live on the island and work in Manhattan have about a ninety-minute drive without traffic. There are no trains or buses I know of that go to the mainland. Getting to this island in the summer could take you a little longer especially from the Big Apple; you have to factor in the time of day, the speed at which you travel, and of course the weather and road conditions. Sometimes, the commute is as easy as apple pie. I love coming to this island no matter how long it takes to get there or to go home with or without the apple pie.

As I'd mentioned earlier, I'd been invited by Susan to use her beach house on the island for our Festivus celebrations. I met her in connection with our work at the WTC, and we became the best of friends and have been ever since; we've bonded just as I have with the others from DDC. But it was just four days after I met her that she offered us the use of her beach house. Who does something like that?

I didn't care what it looked like; it was a place by the beach on this beautiful island, and to have it for a weekend was unreal. Most of my surprising coincidences occurred there. I guess it's true what they say on the island: "What are neighbors for if they're not your friends?" I know you're thinking I should have said, "What are friends for if they're not your neighbors?" Well I didn't. If I'd meant that, I would have written it that way. Don't put words in my mouth. Besides, this book has already been printed, so there!

All the houses on the island have decent spaces between them even if some look closer to their neighbors than others do. You can still huff and puff at your neighbors from time to time knowing I won't be going around to spread the crazy myth about some big bad wolf lurking about the three little pigs' houses. What I'll tell you in the next chapter or two will blow you away, and it won't be by the hairs of my chinny chin chin either.

Take a break. Get a ham and cheese sandwich and grab a cold beer. I'll wait till you get back.

CHAPTER 56

Y OU'RE BACK? WELL, as I've said, I've been going to this beach island and staying at the same beach house for the past eight years for some very good reasons. First, it was offered to me by the owner, and second, the majority of my surprising coincidences occurred there.

Susan was holding a seminar on the island to help those who had worked at Ground Zero deal with trauma of their experiences whatever they were. My boss had asked me and three others in our office if we wanted to attend. We said yes. When he told us where it would be held, I believe all four of us had blank looks not knowing where this place was.

But we went and stayed at this lovely inn, which turned out to be a mile south of Susan's place as the crow flies, but I don't trust crows a bit. Seagulls, on the other hand, are hard working. But I digress. We all had our own rooms. Thank God I didn't have to share a room with someone who snored. I don't snore. I know it. I've never heard myself snore at all when I was sleeping. Our inn had a neat-looking, wrap-around porch with wicker chairs, sofas, and a swing, and inside were many interesting clocks all over the place.

My crew—Ron Vega, Mike Kenny, and Loan Dinh (who has married and is now Mrs. Murray)—learned so much about one another and the other fifteen attendees. During our four-day seminar, we shared our feelings about having worked at Ground Zero with each other openly. Everyone in the group had a different profession and had worked there in different capacities. Susan felt that we all were equals and all had stories to tell. The seminar was moving, inspirational, and interesting. At times, I relived times in 'Nam. I know I had no sort of trauma due to what I had witnessed on 9/11 or the 2,274 hours I spent at Ground Zero. I think my demons were the 8,664 hours I spent in 'Nam. Susan and her associates of her Sky Help organization picked up on that.

The island was beautiful. I was hooked line and sinker when I got to the beach. I remembered two beaches I'd spent some time on halfway around the world. I refer to one of them as one hell of a beach and the other one as a son of a beach. They were in 'Nam, two beaches I could never say I'd fallen in love with as I normally did with beaches because of where I happened to be and why I happened to be there.

On the last day of the seminar, I was with Ron Vega, Mike Kenny, and Loan Dinh when I happen to mention to Susan about our yearly bonding get-together. The rest is history.

During our time there, Susan casually mentioned that her neighbors at her beach house were friendly and outgoing. Maybe one of the reasons I never had conversations with them was because I hadn't told Susan I was probably the most outgoing person in the world or at least this side of the Mississippi. I could have said this side of the Hudson River, but New Jersey is still questionable because of the high tolls you have to pay to get there. And I'd spend a lot of time there surfcasting.

Susan, if you're reading this, I want you to know you have an outpouring heart filled with extreme kindness for letting someone like me stay at your beach house that became a major factor where my life intertwined with your neighbors in such an unbelievable way that at times I believe it was partly due to some kind of divine intervention and nothing else, except that you might be one of those wonderful angels I keep mentioning.

CHAPTER 57

I MENTIONED THAT Chuck had flown for the air force in 'Nam. And I mentioned that I had spent two years at Pensacola Naval Air Station driving officers around including Captain James Armstrong, the chief of staff, and Rear Admiral Dick. H. Guinn, the chief of Naval Air Basic Training who determined who had what it took to be a naval aviator and get high, shoot high, and fly high.

The base was home to our country's best navy and marine pilots and amazing jet fighters, bombers, assorted military aircraft, and helicopters. I had my four wheels on the ground—a '67 black-and-white, four-door Chevy Biscayne sedan with a three-speed transmission (on the column), hidden flashing red lights in the grill (for an emergency) and license plates that noted who was in the car, whether the captain or the admiral.

Captain Armstrong was a great guy. He was quiet spoken; he reminded me of my Uncle Stanley. The second captain I drove, Captain John C. Miller, had a sense of humor I truly enjoyed, and his wife, Jayne, was even funnier. His middle name was Charles, and Charles was his son's name; that was the case with my dad and me.

I was always in the company of captains, commanders, and other naval officers along with many enlisted and civilian personnel who all worked for the admiral's command. I probably drove the same amount of time for the rear admiral as I did for the two captains even though the admiral had a personal driver. At times, he asked for me to be his driver. Rank has its privileges, remember?

One day, I had to drive Admiral Guinn (you never said "Rear" when you addressed him even if you were walking behind him) and Captain Armstrong out to Forrest Sherman Field on the base. I had no idea why. Usually, the admiral's aide would give me a quick heads-up as to where I had to go and what I'd be doing prior to getting in the car, but it was all hush-hush that morning.

We arrived at the airfield. Some enlisted men pointed me to the fight operations tower. During my serpentine maneuvering, the admiral told the captain and me that we were in for a special treat. He said we were there to watch a spectacular flight demonstration between two types of aircraft that would perform some pretty radical maneuvers over us. We had front-row seating. Maybe I should say front-row standing. I felt a thrill going through my body. It was a sunny day—not a cloud in the sky. It was the first time I'd had them both in the car, and it was my first time seeing a flight demonstration.

When I pulled up at the tower, I was waved in closer by a crewmember of the Blue Angels in the team's familiar jumpsuit. He saluted the car and told me to drive behind the flight ops building; someone would direct me from there. As I drove around to the rear of the building, the admiral told me that I'd see a Grumman F11 F-1 Tiger, the jet fighter the Blue Angels were flying, and a brand-new McDonnell Douglas F-4J Phantom II, a possible replacement for the Tiger that the navy and the marines would be flying in Vietnam; it was the navy's newest toy. And oh what a toy it was.

We walked on the tarmac to where another member of the Blue Angels was standing around talking with someone I assumed was the flight instructor. The admiral saw the officer who was summoning us and said that he would be the man that morning to describe what we'd be seeing.

When we got close enough, they snapped to attention and saluted the admiral and the captain. I didn't salute. The admiral had told me I didn't need to salute an officer when I was with him or the captain unless the officer was of higher rank than a rear admiral. Again, rank has its privileges even when you're an enlisted man. I was pretty well known on base considering I wore a blue-and-gold braided lanyard over my left shoulder; I kinda stood out among the other enlisted men on base.

The flight instructor said, "Good morning, sir" to both of them. He gave me a look as he held his salute. The admiral said, "Carry on!" to him.

The instructor told us that in about a minute, an F-1 Tiger would approach from the south over the gulf followed by an F-4 with a fierce-looking nose that would be playing catch-up.

Within seconds, the first jet came screaming over our heads and shot up into the wild blue yonder at an unbelievable speed. Seeing that so close was unbelievable! We were told by the instructor to look to our right again to see this demon maneuvering toward us going through the motions and chasing the F-1. That alone was something I'll never forget. Once or twice during the demonstration, both pilots flew directly above us, doing a 360-degree roll in four quick moves, and took off like there was no tomorrow. Even the hairs on the back of my neck were standing at attention.

The admiral and the captain were enjoying the performance; they were probably imagining themselves in the cockpit behind the stick of the Phantom making those moves themselves. They were highly decorated naval aviators who had fought in World War II and had flown numerous missions off carrier decks in the Atlantic and Pacific theaters.

I pretended to be Superman staying right alongside the Phantom having my own personal high and loving every minute of it. I saw the Phantom quickly turn toward us flying upside down. I could see the pilot's helmet as he came by in a slow, low pass probably less than a hundred feet above our heads—not something you get to see other places. One again, the hairs on the back of my neck went vertical. I'd always thought that only a woman's touch could do that. Well, I was proven wrong.

The admiral and the captain were commenting on how the Phantom was a fierce-looking demon and an amazing jet fighter and that it had great potential well beyond the Tiger. They said it could be the aircraft to use for the Blue Angels to heighten their spectacular demonstrations to the public at air shows. That was a memorable day for me at Pensacola.

Another memorable time was when I picked up Lieutenant Roger Staubach, the star quarterback for the navy's football team, the Pensacola Goshawks. Roger and I became good friends before he left for a tour in

'Nam. He of course later played for the Dallas Cowboys as their star quarterback. Who knew?

The F-4 Phantom II became my favorite aircraft of all time. I saw it in action in the DMZ. We were having quite a few of them shot down. Some pilots were lucky to parachute to safety. Others were killed or captured. Meeting Chuck later was a real personal honor for me. He told me that his job had been to draw fire from enemy gun encampments; he'd relay the coordinates, and other aircraft would go after the guns. Chuck was the guinea pig. Whenever I see that black-and-white POW/MIA flag flying anywhere, my heart goes out to my fellow comrades who were captured and are still listed as missing in action. War is hell.

The surprising coincides I had with Chuck as to his rank and what he flew in 'Nam became very powerful for me being that it was only forty years we met and became blood brothers. I find that surprising.

CHAPTER 58

I F YOU THOUGHT my past chapters were pretty surprising, well, life is full of surprises, and I've had my share of them. I believe 90 percent of them have been fabulous and the other 10 percent were good, and for some weird reason, the IRS is still taking out taxes on them. Go figure.

I started with my surprising coincidences right after 9/11; they are responsible for my wild heart. I wonder if my cardiologist had ever seen it in any of my EKGs. It would make a good article for a medical journal. I'm still seeing him. I don't think he really knows what's in store for me except for Macy's and Sears; he and I love holiday sales, and Macy's has some sort of parade that makes me want to march right out there and talk about myself to as many people as possible about this book.

I love the marching bands, the floats, and the huge cartoon-character balloons. They remind me of how much stuff I still want to convey to you that has me connected to 'Nam, 9/11, my time at Ground Zero, some of the other events I took part in, and a few more of my amazing and totally unbelievable surprising coincidences that occurred to me especially like the one I had early one morning at the site that was so powerful and totally unbelievable that I'm still referring to it as another one of my many blessings. Oh, you wild heart. What have you done to me?

CHAPTER 59

T HIS IS PERHAPS the perfect chapter to talk about luck. I have at times considered myself lucky to have survived the majority of the events I have lived through. I had luck on my side, or it just wasn't my time to go, or my wonderful angels were with me then.

So many people have told me I had more lives than a cat, which I know I do. Ever since I left my work at Ground Zero, black cats stop and look at me. I'm not making this up. They stare at me, and I stare back; it's my way of saying, "I got you beat." They make complete turnarounds and go back whence they came knowing who rules.

I've been through hurricanes, blizzards, monsoons, typhoons, heat spells, frigid temperatures, tornados, fires, and earthquakes. Never a flash flood unless you want to count the flash floods of rockets and mortars in 'Nam I lived through and some other things that have come my way in ways you couldn't imagine.

I was in a truck accident in Da Nang. I was taking a deuce and a half off the upper deck of an LST; the marines were picking it up later that evening. As I was driving down the dirt road doing thirty to forty, a couple of things started to go wrong. First, the brakes gave out. Then the floor shift handle broke off at the floor mount. And the horn wasn't working, so I couldn't exactly get anyone's attention. I was heading directly to where these two huge Shell tanks—and I mean huge—were. They were about thirty feet high and sixty feet wide. I didn't want to tangle with them if I didn't have to. On both sides were broken-down equipment and vehicles that left no openings wide enough to get through. My first thought was driving into a ditch about five feet deep and five feet wide about ten feet in front of this ten-foot-high chain link fence meant to keep vehicles from crashing into the huge gasoline tanks and blowing the entire place to kingdom come. That's what the VC would try to do with their rockets.

I did a good job of hitting that ditch at the right time and place, but I went flying over the steering wheel, out the window (which luckily had no glass in it), onto the hood, and into the fence. My maneuvers knocked out two back teeth on my left side. Luckily, I was right-handed. And you can't see where the teeth were even if I smile.

Some guys ran over to see how I was. I had a bloody mouth and bruises to my arm, chest, and leg. Overall, I had nothing major to worry about, but I was still taken to the medical facility by the airbase. The doc told me that I had been very lucky but not lucky enough to be sent home.

Another time, my squad and I were having to off-load some kind of material that was on pallets on this barge. We didn't know what it was; we hadn't received a manifest as we normally would. We'd just been ordered by a navy lieutenant to take it off and get it onto these flatbed trucks that were coming onto the ramp. Whatever it was, it was going to the airbase. Each pallet held two fifty-five-gallon, black-metal drums that had three-inch-wide bright-orange stripes around them and were strapped to each other by a one-inch-wide metal band.

We were down to the last two pallets when one of my squad members lifted one off the barge with a forklift. He didn't notice that the band that had connected the barrels had snapped off. A drum fell off and started rolling down the ramp toward the drink alongside the barge. We still had half a load of the same material sitting on this landing craft to the right of it. We were using these 10,000 pound forklifts, RTs that we used to remove every other kind of ammo we were usually having to remove from LSTs, barges, landing crafts, and one or two other types of crafts.

Our squad member tried to pick it up by maneuvering the forks. He accidently pierced the drum. Liquid spewed out and mixed with the water. Four of us jumped off our RTs and went running into the drink to try to push it back onto the forks, get it upright, and stop the spillage. We were getting soaked with this liquid that mixed so easily with the ocean water of the South China Sea. We were up to our armpits doing our best to guide it to the truck. The loot in charge came up. "Get that fucking drum back onto the forklift and onto this flatbed so it can get to the airbase!"

We finally managed to get it onto the truck, but we were suddenly the ones going to the airbase in his jeep. He drove like a bat out of hell through the streets of Da Nang to the airbase and brought us directly to a truck-washing station. We were told to get out and scrub ourselves up and down with soap and water and brushes. We were actually rinsed off by guys with firehoses.

After that, he drove us back soaking wet and dropped us off. On leaving, he said, "Good luck. Take care of yourselves." He saluted us and left. We had no idea what he meant by that comment. But I think I got his drift ten years after the fact when his comment came back to haunt me. I had to leave work one morning for I had these massive headaches and I felt I was burning up. I went to my doctor, who drove me to the ER.

Over a course of three weeks of crushing headaches and 104-degree fever, I was told I had hepatitis. Then mono. Then some kind of viral infection. Five specialists in all poked and prodded me and asked me all kinds of questions. They wanted to do a biopsy on my liver. It turned out it was inflamed and enlarged to two and a half times the normal size of a liver. And it wasn't smothered in onions, the way I normally have liver. My doctor said that if I had done nothing about it when I first got those headaches and the fever, one glass of beer could have killed me. That was 1980. It got me thinking about those drums. I wrote to the navy and finally got an answer—Agent Orange had been in those drums.

So far, I've been lucky if you don't count a few close calls with death being in a couple of major car accidents, a couple of near heart attacks, some close calls with a few rocket and mortar attacks here and there in 'Nam. I refer to those as mini-events in my life. They include a few times flying around the country when I had some other close calls in the wild blue yonder that kept giving me grey hairs. But I'm still here to talk about them.

CHAPTER 60

As I've mentioned, my work for Merrill Lynch had me serpentining around the country on American and United. I've also taken helicopters, trains, and even a ferry ride. Then, I'd take rental cars all over. Traveling was a high back then, between '67 and '92, for me. I found myself at times completely off the map someplace I'd never heard of and would have to find my way back to where I wasn't lost quite as much. But in the process, I met many interesting people and consider myself lucky for having done so. Especially when I got lost.

I get a little lost when I start talking about my wonderful angels. You're not gonna believe this, but some of them I believe are real. I began to compare some of them to a few of the people I have met, know, and possibly are my closest friends who have decided (or were told to) join me on this amazing journey I've been on. I've actually taken short walks around to the back of some of them to see if they had wings. I wanted to inform the big guy upstairs that he was doing one "hell" of a job giving me a taste of "heaven" on "earth."

Do you think angels have voice mail? Who exactly calls them?

CHAPTER 61

B E HONEST NOW. Do you think it was mere chance or the hand of fate that led you to this book considering all the others you could have bought or checked out of your local library? Can you give me an honest answer? Would you know the answer? Did you understand the question? Can you give me your answer in the form of a question? If not, don't even think about getting on *Jeopardy*.

Some people refer to mere chance or the hand of fate as an unusual or strange occurrence or, if you wish, a surprising coincidence. Some skeptics think of such strange events as nothing more than synchronicity. Whatever name you wish to use is okay with me.

Speaking of whatever name you wish to use, let me tell you something about my name. No, not Charlie but Kaczorowski. It was tough growing up with a long last name. First, I had to learn all twenty-six letters in the alphabet. Then, I had to learn the eleven of them that made up my last name without the help of any alphabet song. After the fourth or fifth letter (with or without musical accompaniment), I'd be all over the place. What was I supposed to do with six letters remaining?

In his infinite wisdom, Dad did my brother, my sisters, and me a real big favor by skipping a possible jingle to learn how to spell our name and decided to take our last name, Kaczorowski, and rang out a new and shorter version proclaiming (I believe the proclamation even went to the local butcher) that his four children would all be known as Kaczor (*Kay*-zor) with two syllables, not four or five. Wow! Saying my last name became as easy as apple pie (my third favorite after coconut custard and blueberry).

When my dad's brother, Felix, heard about this sudden change in identity, he said, "All well and good for you and your family, but my daughters will be using the family name (royally speaking of course) till they are married." That made my dad come out with a second proclamation—the four of us would use the shortened version until we graduated from high school and not a day more. (He added, "God help you graduate.")

We all agreed to the two proclamations without knowing the definition of the word *proclamation* or looking at one another for consensus. We didn't worry if the butcher, who was Polish like us, did say that my dad had butchered the family name. I don't think he knew what *proclamation* meant either for that matter.

Anyway, from that moment on, I was known as Charles Kaczor. The family name, Kaczorowski (Kacha-*rouf*-ski), went to the family archives and tree right next to my dad's complete collection of (vinyl) records of John Phillip Sousa's marching band that boldly stood out next to his favorite chair in our living room. I guess it was left there as a reminder for my dad to give us our marching orders to graduate.

If you want to pronounce my family name of Polish nobility with an accent, you must (and I insist) pronounce it correctly by trying to sound more like a Russian. Put two teaspoons of butter, a touch of horseradish, and four heaping tablespoons of tarragon into two cups of sour cream. Trust me. It's one hell of a party dip.

I graduated high school in June '65, but I waited until I turned seventeen on December 8 to go back to using my full family name on my driver's license. Michael, who graduated two years later, did the same, but my sisters—Charnat, ten months older than me, and Marianne, two years younger than Michael—stuck with the shorter version. I guess they figured it would be cheaper on their wedding invitations to have fewer letters in their last names. (But then again, their last names would be changing anyway.)

Because of all this going on with our family name, the family tree that dates as far back as the early 1800s or the late 1790s (like after the bowling season), we had lines going every which way and branching off here and there to the point that Stephen, my landscaper, who had been asking to see my family tree for quite some time only because he's also Polish, said that he'd start charging more just for the pruning and removal of any new branches on my family tree. Where does it end? Who's next? My plumber as he tries to flush out some info on my background too?

Did you happen to notice that my name wasn't changed until after I had graduated from high school? You want to check on my graduation and grades? Best of luck. I won't be found because of the name I'm using now. "Listen up! There's never been a Charles Kaczorowski in attendance here! Quit calling us!" you'd hear. Maybe that's why I never got invited to a class reunion. I'm the Invisible Man. Read my mail. It's always addressed to "occupant" or "resident." I've had to go to town to check to make sure I wasn't paying additional taxes for those two guys.

Do me a favor. Take another look at my photo on the back. Do you trust that face? I know I would. Don't you think I already look like a well-known author or soon-to-be well-known author? Thank you.

Let's get back to my name. For more than a century— Oops. Wrong book. I meant, for more than thirty-six years, I've been known by so many different names and nicknames, more than anyone I know except for Mr. Alias, John Doe, or maybe one or two indecent names I was given while I was in survival training in the navy prior to going to 'Nam that are so totally unprintable here and may be the main reason why I'm not listed in *Who's Who in America* yet. I guess once they update their records on me (not like the Census Bureau, which gave up on me back in '84 after calling me and taking well over three hours to explain to them the total confusion regarding my name), it'll all straightened out before I die.

At my very first job back in '65, I was always called Charles, never Charlie, by everyone, which I didn't mind one bit because it was my name. Maybe I should have insisted that they should call me Charlie or Chuck as my mom did with my dad, but I didn't want to be fired for you know, name calling!

Anyway, that went on for two years until I left the business world and went to do my patriotic duty by enlisting in the navy (mainly because I didn't want to be drafted into the army and be sent to Vietnam). I signed up and was sworn in on February 27, 1967, my dad's forty-sixth birthday. At boot camp, I was called all kinds of names some of which were so unintelligible I can't spell them, so I can't print them here. They were simply downright fucking disgusting. I hadn't joined the navy for that. I wanted to see the world just as my dad had during World War II but didn't want to go any place where fighting was going on.

More than anything, I truly felt that the color green was very unbecoming on me because of my revulsion for kryptonite and because green definitely clashed with my sultry blue eyes. I didn't want anything upsetting the entire female population and having them complain that my eyes went from blue to hazel when I wore green. I couldn't have that. Blue is blue and knowing that everything over there in 'Nam was green, I wasn't in the right frame of mind to deal with that.

Let me jump back for a minute to boot camp. On my second day there, this petty officer 1st class called me Ski, which to me was way better than all the other names I was being called. (Hell, why didn't he bother to take the time to ask me first if I skied at all? I didn't. I surfed! I should have been called Surf. Oh, did I surf!) Actually, I was called Ski the entire time I spent in the navy till I left on July 10, 1970. Only my female friends and my three main bosses I had in Pensacola called me Charlie.

Then I went to 'Nam, not a place I wanted to be called charlie with a capital letter or not. When I came home, it took some time for me to convince myself it was time to get off my ass and look for work back in New York City. That was a jungle too albeit a concrete jungle. I was getting infatuated again with the fast pace of the city and looking forward to having a job that I could sink my teeth into and make some big bucks. I wanted something that would make me feel I wasn't working but was just enjoying myself.

It took some time pounding pavement and going to interview after interview before I was lucky to finally find a job. It was great for a while until I felt I needed something better than what I already had, something more satisfying where it didn't matter if I wore out the soles of my shoes. Guess what? I got a job working for a very popular shoe company in the South Bronx where I became their new and only designer for their shoe stores. The company was National Shoes; you remember their short jingle, "National Shoes, ring the bell" (Now that I think about it, maybe my dad should have gone to them for help on our last name.) They had stores all along the East Coast, but the majority of them were all over New York City—A. S. Beck, Joffrey, and of course National Shoes.

I stayed with them for one year by working in their headquarters and having to travel to the various malls in cities down south to check on the construction and alterations that were needed here and there. When I wasn't traveling, I worked at headquarters on drawings and made sure they were ready to go out with the afternoon mail.

Every so often, I'd be talking with the receptionist and the postal worker who brought us our mail and took my packages or rolls of drawings back to the post office. He worked out of the garage directly across the street from us. On the opposite side of our building was the Bronx House of Detention, and we parked in the Yankee Stadium parking lot on Gerard Avenue. Anyway, the postal worker who I would be conversing with and was so pleasant to talk to was David Berkowitz. I'm sure his name rings a bell; he was the Son of Sam, the .44 caliber shooter/killer who went around killing people sitting in their cars at night. I find that somewhat of a surprising coincidence for me only because I was designing and having to oversee construction by traveling to various cities to our company's shoe stores wearing out my shoes and getting holes in my soles while this schmuck, David, was handling and delivering my drawings and documents I needed as he traveled all over our city pumping some pretty big holes into people with his .44. I learned later on that David was eventually booted off to prison for his deadly acts.

There came a time later that year that the company advised everyone it was relocating and shuffling off to Boston to merge with another company. I decided I wouldn't be kicking up my heels to go with them, so there I was putting my best foot forward again and pounding the pavement once more looking for a job.

I found another job working on Long Island about ten minutes from where I lived, and then another in Clifton, New Jersey for a few months, and another on Long Island but in Queens, where everyone called me Charlie or Charles or Chuck. I answered to all of them. I was working for Atlantic & Pacific Tea Company, otherwise known as the A&P. I was designing their new supermarkets and preparing drawings so contractors could bid on them.

At lunch one day, I walked through the reception area of the building I was working in at the time in Queens and saw a *New York Times* on a table. I picked it up and skimmed through it. I came across an ad that seemed to have been written just for me. I called the number and was given a date and time for an interview. I went, and I was hired on the spot.

My new company was right across the street from the South Tower of the WTC. In September 1978, I started working; it was the best job I'd had in a long time. I was working for the biggest brokerage firm on Wall Street, Merrill Lynch, as its facilities project manager in its world headquarters at One Liberty Plaza. I was on the fiftieth floor of the fifty-five-story building. I had a fantastic view of the city looking north from my cubicle. I was working with other designers and project managers handling designs for any office across the country that required alteration, expansion, or relocation.

Even though I'd introduced myself as Charles Kaczorowski when I applied for the job, on the day I started, I was called Charlie Kaczorowski; I didn't have to convince anyone not to call me Charles. I'd always introduce myself with both names at this Fortune 500 company. I didn't see myself having to climb that so-called corporate ladder; I was already fifty floors up and even above the president and chairman of the board.

One day, my boss told me to hit the road. No, I hadn't been fired. He wanted me to take that seminar on real estate development at NYU I mentioned earlier, get a corporate credit card, and start traveling for my work. All my plane, hotel, and rental car arrangements would be made for me. I was thirty and could fly wherever I was needed like Superman. I flew to Ohio, Indiana, Michigan, Illinois, and Wisconsin once or twice a week and more if need be.

In the summer of '79, my boss told me I needed a fresh, new, bigger and better cape because I'd be flying to a few more states including Virginia, Florida, Georgia, Kansas, Missouri, and Texas. Somehow, word had gotten back from Merrill managers out in the field that I'd been doing a great job in the field. I became known as Charlie Kacz and had that new nickname for quite some time.

I'd present my own design for a certain brokerage office that I was to be involved in for a major renovation or some minor alterations and then see that the work was completed. I was then asked to become involved in this new program; I had a team of about a dozen or so in-house designers for the regional operations centers, those ROCs I'd mentioned that were 50,000-square-foot computer back office facilities that where the backbones for offices in the area.

I was involved in site selection, preliminary lease negotiation, and overall design layout. My team would produce the construction documents we'd put out to bid with major contractors in any one city. We'd set up time tables, and I'd go on site to handle problems as they cropped up and stay there until they were handled. I'd then move on to the next location. I worked closely with the company's internal and local communication companies and especially with our great interior design department making sure that all the right fabrics, paint, fixtures, carpeting, and furniture for the offices complemented any one building. I was told that I was doing such a great job that I was eventually covering all the lower forty-seven (I didn't handle Alaska, Hawaii, or Maine) while I was working at Merrill.

It was sometime in '82 that I met Michael Bloomberg, who is now our great mayor of New York (who I now work for if you went up the chain of command) at a major meeting back at Merrill's headquarters. Merrill got involved being the only company on Wall Street to be using Mike's new Bloomberg Financial Data System equipment for stock quotes. Eventually, it went into every new and existing office across the country before it went worldwide in all our offices. (Maybe I had something to do with Mike Bloomberg becoming a billionaire.)

It got to a point that I was traveling so much around the country almost every single week that I was on a first-name basis with the crews of the American and United Airlines flights I'd take wherever I saw them around the country. (It's ironic that American and United flights were hijacked by those fuckin' terrorists on 9/11.)

During this time, some executive in Detroit started calling my simply Kacz. He later became Merrill's chair, and we became good friends. It got to the point that I'd respond only to that name even when Margie would say, "'Charlie, dinner's ready!" Charlie just wasn't registering for a while, and I missed some meals for that reason; Margie said she got tired of calling me.

I was Kacz until my last day at Merrill in '89. Those were good days. I could actually write a book about where I went, where I stayed, and what famous people I had dinners and drinks with mostly in the LA area. I'll never forget any of those times for they were too good to be true.

CHAPTER 62

I HAPPENED TO pick up the copy of the *New York Times* on a subway seat and browsed the pages for a construction job on my way home from my last day at Merrill. I'd resigned. Let's just say there was some bad blood between me and those I had to report to; I wasn't a happy camper, so I left.

One ad caught my eye. I had the qualifications. I interviewed for the job and got it during the interview. It didn't require traveling, which was good. Margie and I were talking about starting a family. I became a construction project manager for Herbert Construction in Midtown Manhattan. I was told I'd be working on numerous projects involving build-outs for major retail companies on Fifth Avenue, but on my first day, I was taken off that list to oversee projects in New York City and was told to see the big boss.

I met with three executives; they told me because of my corporate background, I'd be the perfect candidate to replace a project manager who was working in LA. I'd be taking her place in overseeing the construction of any work needed in the Shearson-Lehman offices in its western region—fourteen states including Alaska and Hawaii. I'd be working out of an office on the 106th floor of the South Tower at the WTC and another office in the Luckman Building in Beverly Hills, which would be my primary office.

I was back to traveling again. I couldn't turn it down. I needed the job, and the salary was way better than what Merrill had been giving me. I traveled for a year and later went back to the main Herbert office to handle projects in the city. I became so stressed out due to the problems I was running into with the contractors given to me to work with that in the fourth month of doing that, I had my first near heart attack. It occurred the day before Margie's and my seventeenth wedding anniversary. I was rushed to a hospital, went home the following day, and was told to stay home and rest for at least two weeks.

I was sent to oversee the build-out of two floors at 85 Broadway, Goldman Sachs's new world headquarters. Once my two floors were completed, I was sent to oversee all the renovations for American Express in its new world Headquarters in the World Financial Center right across the street from the North Tower.

I stayed there for five years and enjoyed every minute except for when I was too close for comfort when a certain event occurred at the WTC on February 26, 1993. I had a two-year lapse looking for a job in the city. Due to a slowdown in the construction industry, I did something completely different until I found another job in construction. I sent my resume in for a job I saw and had two interviews in a building in Queens by the East River.

On February 26, 2001, I started working for the City of New York Department of Design & Construction, DDC. I told everyone there and in the field that I wanted to be called Charlie Kaczorowski—no nicknames. That lasted nine months. You'd think that anyone who had gone through so many variations of his or her name would have ended up with a split personality or worse; there were actually one or two times that I thought I was having an identity crisis. It got so bad that one time, I inadvertently called someone but didn't realize I'd dialed the wrong number. The person at the other end asked, "Who is this?" The voice did sound familiar. *I thought everyone knew me!*

When 9/11 occurred, I said, "Most definitely," when my boss, Assistant Commissioner Lou Mendes, asked me if I wanted to work at Ground Zero. It wasn't too long before another Charlie was doing something similar to what I was but for one of our main contractors. My boss wanted to differentiate between us, so I became Charlie K, and that name stuck with me for years. So many people far and wide across this great country of ours and even in a few foreign countries thought my name was Charlie Kay. I bet anyone who knew me at Ground Zero didn't know what that *K* stood for. I was an alias without being an alias. I still get mail addressed to Occupant or Resident and even Charlie Kay.

You're not gonna believe this, but numerous times, strangers would sit down next to me on a bus or the subway when I'd be trying to type this story on my laptop and overlook my screen. They'd want to know more about my surprising coincidences. I could have told them, but I'd say, "Good things come to those who are patient. You're gonna have to wait till my book comes out."

By the way, my name is, Bond … James Bond. But you can call me Charlie K.

CHAPTER 63

I NEVER KNEW the true meaning of the phrases *surprising coincidence, hand of fate,* or *mere chance* until I researched them. I was surprised to learn that they occur mostly for specific reasons. I got more involved in this subject that had started to play a big part in my life. It was getting to the point that I spent so much time on it that I felt I'd entered a fifth dimension. My research became so overbearing that I called it quits.

But something I'd read stuck in my wild heart. Elizabeth Kübler-Ross wrote "Is it true, there are no mistakes, no coincidences. All events are blessings given to us to learn from." Seeing the word *blessings* told me I was on the right track after all. I began to recall certain surprising coincidences that occurred to me one night at Ground Zero when I believe God talked to me in his whimsical way by blowing a gust of wind into the tent in which I was eating dinner at two in the morning. I asked God, "Were some of my surprising coincidences blessings and nothing else? Did some of the wonderful people I've met after 9/11 enter my life for specific reasons? And why have most of these surprising coincidences occurred in September?"

I wondered if they were products of synchronicity—two or more unconnected things happening at the same time—or divine intervention? I believe it is a small world. Or maybe I need a better pair of reading glasses that would also enhance my eyes.

One day back in grade school, Sister Lucy was discussing religion. She had a habit of getting her point across by walking past your desk and rapping her ruler on your desk. If you didn't move your hand away fast enough, that meant you were sleeping or daydreaming. That's what

I was doing one day—daydreaming, not sleeping. I was glancing back and forth at this big picture on the wall of God majestically standing in the vast universe with earth in the palm of his hand. Somehow, that picture has managed to stay locked in my mind in such a way that ever since these surprising coincidences started, I've been asking myself, *Why do I feel as if I'm already in heaven here on earth?*

Chapter 64

THE SURPRISING COINCIDENCE that occurred on a very hot Sunday in August 2009 was amazing. I was relaxing in my new, comfortable chaise lounge in my backyard and taking it all in. I was listening to classic rock on Q104.3 FM while drinking cold Coronas I was plucking from a very nearby cooler. All the bottle caps were off, so I had no need to grab the church key when I wanted another. I could reach down and get a beer with my eyes closed. I toasted the heat. *Bring it on*, I told the hot sun. I was soaked in sweat, just the way I liked it. I consider any temperature below fifty as freezing.

I'd been out there for more than an hour when out of nowhere, my eyes started to burn and I felt a tear or two stream down my face. I found that odd. It wasn't the sun's strong rays causing that. It was the announcements I was hearing about that year's 9/11 commemoration.

I'd attended them all. The DJ sounded sincere as he shared his feelings about the remembrance of that fateful day. He mentioned that if we could, we should all try to find the time to help someone in need, someone who may have been affected by 9/11 in the slightest way. The more he talked, the more my heart strings were being tugged. My heart raced a little faster, but I wasn't feeling it under all that heat and my beer drinking. I believe I began to convince myself that it was the combination of what I had witnessed that fateful day, my time at Ground Zero, and all those touching memories I had with the family members at every memorial ceremony over the previous few years. They'd become so powerful that I guess all my buried emotions started to come out and were hitting home.

The more this guy talked, the more the tears flowed down my cheeks. It felt that my heart was ready to bust out of my chest. I imagined 9/11 as a video of something that had occurred just the day before. I envisioned people I'd met since that day at Ground Zero and the faces of some of the family members I've been seeing at every memorial service. The faces of the lost loved ones had embedded themselves in my head. I saw the faces of my entire family who have shown deep concern for my well-being and state of mind due to what I'd gone through over the years. Especially my mom and dad, who are eighty-eight years young.

Yes, for those of you who are reading this right now and know that I'm talking about you, in one way or another, you've all struck chords in me, and I'm holding all of you responsible for making my eyes tear and burn. But my tears were due to joy rather than sadness. I began to feel a tightness in my chest. I told myself, *It's okay. The tightness is due to lying in the chaise lounge and having to stretch for more beers.* I changed my position. I was becoming deeply immersed in all my feelings for everyone I'd met from the day after 9/11; I was reliving it.

Out of all the songs out there, to come on at that very moment in time, was the song by U2, "It's a Beautiful Day." Perfect timing.

CHAPTER 65

As I mentioned, I'm not a great typist. I'm a great two-finger typist though. This flaw of mine started a long time ago. It was my fault for opening my mouth and asking a kid I was playing with if I could have a try at this new kids' game he was showing some other kids that was totally new to me—cat's cradle, that game with the long string tied in a loop that you have to weave into a pattern just by moving your fingers.

I was about eight. My attempts at making a cat's cradle frustrated me to the point that I wanted to break that damned string. Instead, I mashed it underfoot in front of the other kids. I'm sure the owner of the string is today a pediatric psychiatrist lecturing on kids who get frustrated easily when they discover they don't have super powers.

I never tried that stupid cat's cradle until much later when my cousins, who were married and had kids of their own, asked me to show them how it was done. I tried distracting them by showing them how to tie slipknots and excusing myself to go to the bathroom. Come to think of it, I never had a problem making any kind of knots or having to tie up things when I was in the Boy Scouts. Go figure.

But I do recall when I was in boot camp and got extremely nervous and worried when I was told I'd be attending parachute rigger school after boot camp. I lucked out; my orders got mixed up with those of another Charles K; he went and I didn't.

And years later, I tried to untangle a Rubik's Cube but just cramped my fingers badly. I no longer wanted any part of it. I gave it to my dad to try. Would you believe if I told you that my dad showed me in a few days how he could get the colors all lined up in minutes? He threw it back at me and said, "It's so damn easy. Now you give it another try!" I tossed it from one hand to the other and then into my bottom dresser drawer, where it still is.

Somewhere back around 1979, something strange happened. It was a Wednesday evening or a Thursday afternoon in September when I was with my wife at a Broadway play or maybe a concert. The person I was sitting next to was kind enough to point something out to me that she had noticed—whenever I was applauding, she said, my left hand looked as if it was moving much slower than my right hand. She said she was hearing just a half of a clap. I found that hard to believe, but I waited for the next opportunity to clap to see if what she was telling me was true. Lo and behold, I realized she was right. I excused myself to go to the men's room. I did. I watched myself clap in the mirror casually and then in a frenzy. That's when I noticed this physical deformity. I told myself that to save myself embarrassment, I'd start giving out loud whistles instead of applauding and messing up in public.

I believe all three of these afflictions resulted in my typing with just my two middle fingers. If you don't believe me, I'll give you the finger. It's God's honest truth about my using just those two fingers to type and my willingness to give one to unbelievers.

Every picture tells a story, doesn't it? That's why I included photos in this book. As far as every picture telling a story, picture this. One time, I was getting ready to leave for work. I'd made coffee, buttered a corn muffin, and grabbed the leash. I waited for Leah to come walking over; I was taking her out for her morning walk. She was our beautiful, loving, twelve-year-old beagle. I had to get a move on. As I was going out the door, I heard Margie call out probably about something she was seeing on TV, but I had to walk Leah. I figured I'd talk to Margie about it when I got back.

Ten minutes later, I came back and took a swig of coffee. "I'm back!"

She asked, "How was it for you at yesterday's ceremony?"

I hadn't gotten home till late the night before. She'd been asleep. I figured I could wait till the morning to tell her how my day had gone. But there I was not having time to talk to her. "Marge, I really got to get going. I'll call you at work later!"

She was curious about the ceremony because I'd participated in it and a lot had happened. Compared to the past five ceremonies, that one had been completely different for me. In the past, I had always stood as a member of the honor guard down in the Pit at Ground Zero, but that year, I had a different role—I was one of the readers who called out the names of lost loved ones. We called out the names rather than just read them. I called out twelve names. I'd listened to a CD of the names so I'd know how to pronounce them; it was a matter of respect for their families.

Usually, family members would read the names, but that year, those who had been involved in the rescue/recovery operations participated in that. I was highly motivated to take part in the service that way and was so pleased to have been asked by the mayor's office to do so. I didn't know who else from DDC would be there.

CHAPTER 66

I HADN'T MENTIONED to my wife that I'd received a phone call at work from the mayor's office about the invitation I was going to receive in the mail at home, so I figured I'd just let the mail come and let Margie enjoy the surprise as much as I did.

Of course, when I got the call, I had told the person in charge that I was deeply honored to have been asked to do this after having participated in the past ceremonies. So there I was getting a few last things to take with me to work. I stopped to hear this TV news reporter talking about the emotions of the previous day's ceremony. As I came walking out of the room, I heard a different view on the same subject from a reporter on the channel Marge was watching. We saw highlights of the ceremony and heard from reporters on the street around Ground Zero.

I could feel the emotions coming from the newscasters and from some of the people who were being interviewed as they touched on some special moments of the ceremony. There we were seven years later, but the emotions were still present in these people as if it had been yesterday. I'd been affected as well. I stopped in my tracks and took a deep breath. I had to release some of these emotions that were lingering in me. It was definitely one of the most emotional ceremonies that I had ever attended at the site. I was still overwhelmed. My emotions were raw. My nerves were on edge as they had been when I was on the podium the day before. I'd tried to camouflage my emotions waiting for my turn to call out my names.

I started coughing, which made my eyes tear up and made people think I had a cold coming on. I continued with this slight charade till it was time to go up to the stage. I had a bit of stage fright knowing well over 200 million eyes were watching me on TV and right in front of me. I was becoming very uncomfortable; it felt as if my blood were draining out of my body. I tried to compose myself to call out my names. But my heart was aching as I remembered what I had seen and done there at Ground Zero. The loss of so many was going through my mind as I read my names as respectfully and reverently as I could. It was an emotional time for me.

Well, as I turned around in my hallway and started toward the backdoor, Marge walked in and asked, "Charlie, where you going today?" I stopped, turned toward her, leaned in, gave a quick kiss to her lips, and simply said I was going to the 9th Precinct. (Ever since that fateful day, I always make an effort to go out of my way to inform Marge about where I'd be for the day.)

I was going to the NYPD 9th Precinct for a meeting with the elevator contractor to see what was causing the two new elevators to malfunction. The precinct was on the lower East Side of Manhattan at 321 E. 5th Street between 1st and 2nd Avenues. I was the project manager for the complete rebuilding of this famous precinct. It had been used for two popular TV shows, *Barney Miller* and *NYPD Blue* besides having an amazing history.

As I would walk away from the house, I'd casually give a wave without looking back whether she saw it or not; I was implying, *I'll see you later.* I did that when I'd leave for work at Ground Zero at seven thirty in the evening heading for the graveyard shift. Margie mentioned that after the first few nights I left for work there, something strange and touching occurred. My ritual was to kiss Marge goodnight and give Noelle, who was ten at the time, a big hug and tell her I loved her. I'd give her a kiss on the cheek and say goodnight to her and leave.

Marge said that as soon as I'd put her down, she'd run to the dining room window and watch me till I was out of sight. The last thing she always did was give me this casual wave good-bye. When I heard that, it brought tears to my eyes. So I started my next night into work doing the same as always, but I then had this little extra ritual; I knew exactly when to give this wave back to her without turning around. I knew she'd be watching me.

Marge was watching unbeknown to me as she stood behind Noelle. She said that Noelle would wave at the same time I did. Once, Marge told me, "Noelle just turned around, looked up at me, and said with that beautiful smile on her face, 'We'll see Daddy tomorrow. Goodnight, Mommy!'" That story brings a lump to my throat that gets bigger with each retelling. I just love telling it. It makes me teary-eyed. I could feel the love I had for them and what they had for me.

Let me get back to where I was—just about to leave for work that morning. I was making my way up Spruce Street to catch the bus and get to the subway in Jamaica, Queens. That part of my trip took about thirty to forty-five minutes. I could still feel that I had a few leftover feelings from yesterday. They'd been stirred up big-time by the morning news. Do they ever really go away?

Over the years, I've immersed myself in everything and anything related to 9/11. Being at the ceremony the day before felt like being at the first anniversary ceremony, a powerful and emotional day for me and everyone else there. I know I did everything right. I called out my twelve names perfectly. I felt this enormous weight roll off my shoulders. I left the podium with an unbelievable feeling. I looked back to memorize where I had stood on the podium and looked up to the sky. I think it was straight up into heaven. It was as if I were being summoned by one of my angel buddies. A wonderful feeling came over me that I hadn't felt for a very long time. It was comforting, oh so comforting.

CHAPTER 67

M Y WILD HEART was feeling calm ever since 9/11. I felt it was
a butterfly waiting to break out of its cocoon and take flight.
Maybe it was all the angels from the WTC and from American Airlines
flight 11 and United Airlines flight 175 who were all saying, "Thank you,
Charlie K—you did good!" I still wonder if there was a hidden meaning
in all this telling me that my time at Ground Zero was worth it.

I was reflecting on so many things that occurred there that I forgot
to check my way to make it across the busy turnpike. My bus quickly
approached the bus stop. The vibration from my cell phone on my pants
belt snapped me out of my thoughts. I didn't recognize the number, but
I took the call as I boarded the bus. "Hello, who is this? How can I help
you, or better still, how can you help me?" I didn't recognize the friendly
voice, a young woman's. "Hi, Charlie K, it's Allison!" *Allison who?* "I
hope you still remember me from St. Peter's Church! I came up there to
New York City with three other girls from here in Florida, and we all
volunteered there for three weeks back in January 2002."

I still couldn't place the voice or remember who it was. I'd met
so many volunteers who worked around the site. So I went for it. "Hi,
Allison. What did I do to deserve this phone call especially this early in
the morning?" I figured I'd just let her keep on talking hoping that my
illustrious mind would soon recall who she was.

"You were always so nice to me and to the rest of the girls. You
always found time to talk to us in the chapel about your role at the
site. I remember the night you told us how much it meant to you to be
there after what you'd seen that fateful morning a few minutes after

the second plane hit. We especially enjoyed when you came in, usually around the same time, one forty-five in the morning, to grab a cup of coffee and a donut. You always joked with us."

My brain was trying to zero in on a face to put with the voice.

"You always made us laugh when you joked and teased us, and you even asked us numerous questions as to why the coffee we gave you had so much water in it. You always added, 'This is grounds for divorce!' I've never forgotten that!"

Finally it clicked. "Wow! Allison, you've got some memory!"

"I don't think you know this, but whenever you left the chapel because someone was calling you on the radio, the other volunteers and I would ask each other, 'How does this guy come in, talk to us, get coffee and a donut, joke about the coffee, briefly tell us what's going on out there, and then say, "See you later!" and leave?' You acted as if there was nothing wrong with all that death and horror that you were seeing night after night. Like it didn't faze you in the least. We all thought that you were an amazing person then and more so today. We also found out from another volunteer in New York that we were right about you from the start. You're an amazing person!"

I had no idea what she was talking about.

"We were told that there was this beautiful memorial designed for all the survivors of 9/11 and that this designer was nice enough to include all of us volunteers. We couldn't believe it. When we looked into it further, we called another volunteer in New York, who said, 'You're not gonna believe this, but Charlie K was the designer!' You gave us recognition. We were happy that it was you. Thank you so much for thinking of us, for remembering us, and most of all for honoring us. I'm speaking for the other girls too. We're so proud we met you, and we send our love to you."

I figured I'd better cut into her emotional conversation before my cell phone battery died; it was chirping. "Thank you, Allison. So this is why I got this surprising call from you? Are you in town? Are you coming to town? You do know that this town has a lots and lots of water mostly in the coffee. It's my kind of town Chicago is!"

She laughed. "You still have your crazy sense of humor. That's good!"

I decided to give the girl a break. "I'm sorry, Allison. I got a little carried away. My emotions are on this roller-coaster ride from yesterday. It hasn't stopped or slowed down!"

There was a hush over the phone for a second or two. Her voice changed. "Charlie, the reason why I called you was that, and it's the craziest thing, but yesterday, as I was going through my closet that had some old clothes and a pile of handbags, I came across the wallet that I had with me when I was up there volunteering. I had the TV on, and I was watching bits and pieces of the 9/11 anniversary ceremony. Every so often, I'd look up at the TV to see if I knew any of the people who were reading the names. As I was rummaging through some papers, receipts, and what-have-you from the wallet, I happened to come across the business card that you'd given me. I don't know if you remember, but you gave your card to all of us and told us that if we were ever in New York to call.

"Well, Charlie K, just as I was ready to put it aside on the table, there you were on TV. I mean, I think it was you. You were standing next to this other guy who I believe was a Port Authority police officer. You were taking turns reading names. Do you have a beard now but kind of grey looking?"

I said, "Yes, that was me!"

"I thought it was strange that I happened to find your card after all these years and then like magic there you were on TV right in front of me!"

I replied, "I'd say it is! But how did you get this number? It's new."

"Very simple. I went on the web, looked up your agency, got the main number, and after a few times trying, I finally got a human being to talk to me. She was nice enough to transfer me to whom I believe was your secretary. She was so nice and happy enough to give me your new cell number. And here I am!"

I just barely heard her say "here I am" when my phone went dead. Of all the times! And I didn't have my charger with me. *Shoot!* I'd have to make a quick stop and get it charged up at my office in Long Island City. I felt bad that she might be thinking I was playing a joke on her by hanging up. That had happened before to me numerous times especially with Margie. I'd end up having to explain myself later with a big apology. I was hoping Allison's number was still on my phone. *I don't even know her last name or where in Florida she was calling from. Maybe she'll call me back later today. Then again, maybe she won't!* That had been the story of my life with every other woman before I met my wife.

When I got to work, I went straight to my cubicle skipping the usual greetings I'd give people there seeing as I was out in the field 90 percent of my time. I was like a farmer who was always outstanding in his field. My phone was blinking red—I had messages. I figured Allison had called that number, which was on my business card. The messages were from people calling to say they'd seen me on TV. They just wanted to say hi and see how I was doing. I thought that was nice, but none of the calls was from Allison. I jotted down the names and numbers so I could call them later, and I hoped Allison would call back too. I grabbed my spare charger to charge my phone when I got to the precinct.

I was heading for the 9th Precinct. I signed in the daily log book that I'd been there and where I'd be later so people there could track me down. I made my way back to the subway for a train to Manhattan's lower East Side. As I sat on the train, I looked at the names and numbers of those who had called me earlier. It gave me a great feeling. I was still amazed by what Allison had told me earlier about finding my business card almost five years after I'd last seen her. I must say that was a surprising coincidence.

I'd heard the voice messages from people I hadn't seen or heard from since they left Ground Zero. I found that also very surprising. I knew all the people I'd met there were wonderful and caring people, especially the volunteers. They had all touched my life in very special ways. I guess because of the surrounding circumstances, being there at Ground Zero, and the total unreality of the site made everyone and everything I came in contact with just a little bit more important in my life.

I think my life's path made a slight veer off the map in a very mystifying direction when Allison told me about finding my card. I had no idea I'd be surrounded by so many of these unexplainable surprising coincidences; I didn't understand the why and the why now. I knew that God worked in mysterious ways and that the wisdom and perseverance we gather along the way led us to more-virtuous lives. I don't recall ever having so many powerful, surprising coincidences in my life. Maybe they did occur to me, but I'd never given them a second thought. I think I would remember something as powerful as those I'll be telling you about.

I have had more than my share of these flashbacks (that were quite eventful) about my time in 'Nam, and one had happened during the July 4th holiday celebration in New York. Margie and I went to see the Macy's fireworks display, our first time for that. We were standing along the East River, and we smelled black powder and cordite that hung in the air above us; we were just opposite the barge from where the fireworks were being launched. All of it took me back to 1969, a hot and heavy time of rocket and mortar attacks for me.

I want to ask you some far-fetched questions. No, they're not about the war or the Macy's fireworks! Please think about your answer before you blurt it out; I know you have a habit of doing that. How many people do you think you've met in your life? Was your answer, "Hell, I don't know"? That's okay. You're doing really well. Okay, next question. How many times would you say you had surprising coincidences when you were conversing with any of them? Possibly one or two or more, right? Okay, now for your final question. Do you need to take a break? Go to the bathroom? Have a smoke? No. Okay. When you had a surprising coincidence, did you find yourself saying or hearing the other person say, "Wow! That's totally amazing! It really is a small world!" Most likely, it was said every time. Trust me. I know what I'm talking about.

CHAPTER 68

I T WAS A beautiful sunny Monday morning. It was also my last day at Ground Zero. It was July 1, 2002. The clear blue sky and temperature reminded me of that fateful morning ten months earlier. I just completed signing out for my final shift. I'd worked from midnight to eight in the morning. When I'd been asked, I worked the eight to four or the four to midnight shifts and sometimes both if another supervisor hadn't been able to make it. I didn't mind it one bit. I wanted to be there.

In some ways, that day felt like the day I left 'Nam; the place did look like a war zone. My feelings were bittersweet. Later that morning, I was to go back to DDC's headquarters in Long Island City to see my assistant commissioner and find out what project I'd be assigned to next. I had a hunch I'd be heading back to the three construction projects I had been doing in Brooklyn and East Harlem prior to getting deeply involved with Ground Zero. Those three projects felt like they were worlds away.

As I started to go around on the twenty-fifth floor of the American Express building (where DDC had its alternate headquarters to oversee and manage the site) to say my good-byes, I saw a few remaining DDC personnel and some people from other companies or agencies that also worked there. I saw a few who were getting ready to start their shifts plus a few of the contractors and consultants who also shared the floor with us. Someone called out, "Good luck to you, Charlie K. It was great working with you!" Some of them were still there since we had all had met ten months earlier at PS 89, farther north up West Street, DDC's first field office, that was set up on September 11.

Working at the site was very dangerous. The cleanup and the

removal of the debris from the devastation was a major, concerted effort by everyone who worked there. The men and woman of DDC who served there should have left there holding their heads high and to feel deeply proud of that massive undertaking. We completed this job as the whole world watched us.

I served as a site supervisor; I did my job to the fullest having the deepest respect and admiration for those I worked with; we were truly the best of the very best. We earned the respect of many of the first responders who were also there including other rescue workers, all the various construction trades, the volunteers, the military, and especially the Army Corps of Engineers.

As I left the building, I knew in my wild heart that I was taking along thousands of fond memories that would stay with me forever. It was sad to leave there; I knew I might not see or hear from anyone there again, and I had gotten close to them. I slowly walked up Vesey Street still within the perimeter's north boundary and headed toward the subway station, the E train, that was a little beyond the perimeter fence on the east side. It was the same station I'd arrived at on 9:06 a.m. of September 11, 2001. I casually gave a few quick glances around where the complex had once stood. Some workers yelled, "Good morning, Charlie K!" I replied, "Have a good day!" I didn't want to get into a conversation with anyone right then; it was my time to leave.

I went through the main gate past security and members of the Port Authority Police Department. I had to let them know I was leaving for the last time. I noticed the steeple on St. Paul's Chapel directly across the street; its rear doors were open. It gave off a presence as if it and the spirits in the old, historic cemetery were drawing me in. The historic chapel had been built in the late 1700s; George Washington had worshiped there. How the chapel had survived the destruction that had rained down was beyond me though I knew God worked in mysterious ways.

I thought someone must have written a sign above the doors that read, "Come on over, Charlie K, and make one final visit. We know you're leaving us." I crossed Church Street on an angle away from the subway steps and continued my way to Vesey Street and headed east toward Broadway to an entrance through the wrought-iron fence.

Everyone who worked at Ground Zero knew that whenever they entered here, they would always find a smiling face on any of the volunteers who worked there day and night. Those smiling faces brought on some very friendly conversations that made you forget what you were seeing and doing on the site; it was a home away from home. Workers would stop in even though their families were waiting for them at home. But that was the case with the families of the almost 3,000 loved ones who were never going home.

Barbara Horn volunteered there. She always had a smile on her face when she greeted you. Her sparkling blue eyes left you feeling you were floating on an ocean. Her aura was calming. She could do that with or without speaking or joking with you about anything. She truly cared about our well-being especially when we'd go there on breaks. It didn't matter if it was for coffee, or just to chat for a while about something unrelated to the site, or to have a meal—she had a way of bringing you back to reality. I'd try to get to her even if it was for only a few minutes instead of some of the other volunteers. (Sorry, ladies, RHIP!)

The chapel also provided space for one or two massage therapists, chiropractors, podiatrists, and if need be social workers for any counseling someone might need. (If someone needed a stand-up comedian, I was available on request.)

Some of the workers would take a few zzzzs in pews whether the chapel was noisy or quiet. I was one of them times when I'd get there an hour or two before my shift. I found that a warm, friendly smile before a few winks was much more comforting than a coffee. There were times when I'd stop in to see her and she was busy doing things, so I would give her a quick wink to let her know I was doing okay. A couple of times, I went to the chapel after having worked two shifts and I'd need an hour or so to get myself ready to make it home. I'd doze off even if workers in the pews around me were talking or laughing. At times, I'd tell a volunteer who I was, what I did, and when I'd like them to wake me.

I'd always sit in the same pew, fourth from the back on the right side. I seemed to have left my mark having scuffed up the off-white paint on the backrest either from my work boots or the walkie-talkie I carried. It's been said and quoted that Washington had slept there as well as at other historical sites throughout the state. I believe it's been said he even sat in the front pew of this chapel. Yeah, I think it was on a Tuesday evening just after Bingo as he counted his winnings, mostly quarters. So George Washington and Charlie K had something in common, a connection if you will; we sat and slept there. The only difference is that he ended up with his face on the $1 bill while I'm still trying to save face just trying to pay any one of my bills with any quarters I may have! I guess I can chalk that up as a historically or hysterically surprising coincidence.

I made my way to the chapel and my pew. I took it all in. I saw visitors and tourists making their way into the chapel to view all the memorabilia that had been placed in and outside the chapel. A lot of this stuff was left hanging and secured to the wrought-iron fence that enclosed the chapel and its cemetery; it had been started by family members, friends, and the people who lived and worked in the area. Most of the items left on the fence were filling up the walls on the first floor and up in the balcony. It resembled a special kind of small-town museum that displayed photos of their longtime residents who had passed away.

Over and around these photos were letters and posters asking for help and if anyone had seen these people. Every so often, I could hear some of the visitors asking numerous questions to the volunteers there about what had occurred at the chapel. I was taken aback by all that. The volunteers who worked in and around the site deserved special recognition especially from me because I was there for a very long time.

Ten years later, I say thank you to them for their dedication and devotion that was beyond reproach. Ladies, you're all absolute sweethearts, and you'll always be in my heart. I love you all dearly.

CHAPTER 69

O N THAT FATEFUL day when I finally arrived home to see Margie and my daughter, I nearly broke down and cried, but I didn't want Noelle to see me crying. I went into the bathroom and ran the water to cover my crying. I knew Margie was waiting for me to talk to her. She seemed very calm and collected when I walked in, but she was extremely quiet; she didn't ask a single question. She probably thought that I'd speak when I was ready to. I wasn't going to tell her any of the graphic details that were still weighing heavily on my mind.

Normally, I'd sit at the kitchen table if there was something important I wanted to tell her, but that time, all I said was that I'd eat something and go to bed. She gave me a 1,000-yard stare when I walked into the bedroom. I forgot about dinner. I got undressed and went under the sheets, curled up, and shut my eyes trying to shut out the entire world.

I took a quick peek around the room and saw only Leah, our beagle, staring at me just as Noelle had earlier but with deep, saddened eyes. *Does she sense something?* I gave her a wave to call her over. She walked up to the bed. I believe she wanted me to pet her or give her a kiss on the nose, so I did. I lay down and stared at the ceiling. I read somewhere that when a person experiences a very traumatic event firsthand, it's hard to shake it off or try to pretend it didn't happen. My mind was filled to the hilt. Scenes of what I had seen earlier that day played over and over. I closed my eyes and fell asleep.

I dreamed I was sitting in St. Paul's Chapel back in the day when I was working in the WTC complex. I was startled by someone nudging me on my back. I turned around and saw the two friendly, smiling faces of these middle-aged women who were looking at me with these beautiful, matching, questioning eyes. (You don't know what questioning eyes are? Haven't you ever been stopped by a cop where he walks up to you, doesn't say anything, and just looks at you? I'm sure you didn't care if his eyes were beautiful or not or if they even matched yours!)

One woman started to apologize for their nudging and startling me. They wanted to know the best way to get to the Plaza Hotel. One said, "My sister and I are from Battle Creek, Michigan. We've been here before for New Year's Eve about ten years ago with our families." I told them that Battle Creek was a great city, that I'd been there back in the mid-eighties and loved seeing Tony the Tiger at the Kellogg's cereal plant. I told them I'd been all over their lovely state mainly around the Detroit area. I also told them I'd never been in New York for the New Year's Eve celebration—too many people, too much noise, and too much cold to hang around waiting for a ball to drop symbolizing when it was the next year. I had a slew of calendars for that. They found that quite funny and laughed.

As I inched my way out of the pew, one asked, "How come you didn't ask us why we were going to the Plaza?" I realized maybe I should have. Were they thinking of taking me there for lunch or a drink because of what I'd said about their state? I'm very funny with strangers. I took out my wallet, grabbed a pen from my pocket, and wrote "Charlie Kacz" above my name on two business cards I handed them. They looked at them and smiled. I asked them if they've been to the top of the WTC. When they replied, "No!" I said, "Good … lets go. My treat!" I saw us walk across the street toward the South Tower. That's all I remember of that dream.

I get a lump in my throat when I remember Saturday, September 1, 2001, just ten days earlier. I had taken Margie, Noelle, and my niece Kara Ann into the city to do something completely different for a change. I suggested we check out the Empire State Building that had this special ride on one of the lower floors. There, they had you sit on this stadium-like seating on a concrete platform installed on some kind of mechanical system with springs and cables that made you feel you were on a helicopter as you watched a video of flying through and above the city. We all enjoyed it, and I love flying in choppers!

Then we went to the observation deck. I couldn't stop talking about the Twin Towers, which we could see in the distance. I suggested we try this boat ride on the Hudson River on the Beast, and after that go to the WTC. We headed to the West Side along the Hudson by the piers where the USS *Intrepid*, a World War II aircraft carrier, was permanently docked as a naval museum. There, this speedboat, the Beast (actually, there are two of them) waited for riders. It was a pretty good-sized speedboat that held forty or so people and raced up and down the Hudson as hard rock blasted from its speakers. The boat made quick moves left and right so the wake spray could soak you.

It first headed north then slowly turned around and headed south toward the Statue of Liberty. It slowed down and stopped off Lower Manhattan. They gave you about five minutes for photo taking and then quickly sped back up the river. It stopped at the George Washington Bridge, went back to Lady Liberty, and then headed for the dock. It was a thrill!

As the boat sat there off the tip of Lower Manhattan, people were taking pictures. I told Margie, Noelle, and Kara, "Next Saturday, I'll take you to the Top of the World! We'll go onto the roof of the WTC." I pointed toward the Twin Towers. "We'll look down at this same location. You'll be so amazed especially when you'll see some small airplanes actually flying below us and go past other buildings. It's truly something to see. You're going to thank me for taking you there!"

Margie thought we could go the next weekend if the weather was good. I wanted to so much. Noelle wanted to see this fantastic view of the harbor and toward the Verrazano Bridge, the same view I had in 1990, the year she was born. I told Noelle and Kara that at times, it rained below me; they found that very hard to believe.

It's hard to believe they never had the opportunity to go there. I'm sorry I hadn't taken them that Saturday.

Stand-up comedian Steven Wright once said, "Whenever I think of the past, it always brings back so many memories."

CHAPTER 70

I DEDICATE THIS chapter to my good buddy, Mike Kenny. It's one unimaginable chapter in his life and mine. It all started around two thirty in the afternoon a few days before April 13, 2002. I was at DDC when I saw Mike talking with some of the people in his unit. I heard him talking about his family. I excused myself. (No, I hadn't belched or farted.) "Mike, by any chance are you leaving soon to go down to the site?" He worked the four-to-midnight shift at Ground Zero.

"Yeah. Why?"

I replied, "Can I grab a lift with you if you're driving there? I have a meeting at 250 Church Street with HRA, your client, at four. As you know, they are only four blocks from the site."

He said, "Of course!"

I knew he'd say yes. Didn't I already tell you he was my good buddy? Is anyone paying attention besides me?

"Just give me five minutes," he said. It was actually eleven minutes, but who was counting?

As we were leaving DDC, he asked, "Aren't you working tonight at the site?"

I guessed he was wondering why I was going downtown so early way before my shift started. I replied, "Yeah, but I was called to a very important meeting with the client to address three big change orders that needs approval." I figured I'd go to the meeting, resolve any issues relating to the change orders, and go to St. Paul's for some shut-eye before my shift.

We took the Brooklyn Queens Expressway. As we were exiting it and taking the ramp to the bridge, Mike said, "You know what, Charlie K? All we have to do now at Ground Zero from this day forward since we only have a few more months to go with the recovery/cleanup is to keep doing what we've been doing, keep our noses clean, and make sure we don't have any major problems. After all is said and done, we can give ourselves a pat on the back for doing a great job. We're gonna shine! And years from now when I'm sitting in my rocking chair, I can tell my grandchildren with pride what you and I and everyone else did for the city."

He was proud of his proclamation. He was right except for the shine part that would come later.

The night of April 13, 2002, was the last night for the Tower of Lights to shine toward the heavens. Those beams should have been turned toward the ramp at Ground Zero a few hours earlier though they were scheduled to be turned off at sunrise on the morning of the fourteenth. This beautiful tribute, which could be seen for miles, was set to be gone for good.

Mike was working on the thirteenth but never finished his shift. He was the only DDC representative there supervising the operations. Usually, there would be at least three or four DDC project managers there for that shift, but that night, it just so happened that two didn't show up. Mike would be the only one there until I arrived.

I'd love to go into every detail of the events that night and the next two nights that affected Mike for months and months, but I'm not. That's a whole 'nother story. I'm cutting to the chase here. Officers of the Port Authority Police Department (PAPD) arrested Mike for something that happened about eleven fifteen that night. He was charged with assaulting PAPD officers (Ha!), resisting arrest (Ha!), disorderly conduct (Ha!), and obstruction of government administration and harassment (Ha ha ha!). He jumped into a scuffle trying to protect a laborer who was about to take a serious beating from the PAPD. Mike said he reacted "only because I was trying to stop one human being from getting the beating of his life from four other human beings." Instead, Mike got the beating of his life from the PAPD and faced the multiple charges I just listed.

He got more than just a beating. He thought he'd done the right thing. He intervened and ended up with a shiner not quite like the one he'd mentioned earlier. At the time, I down in the Pit about six hundred feet away. I hadn't seen what had led up to the incident, and I hadn't heard the commotion. There's so much to this story that I think it would be best if I just said, "I'm truly glad that I was there that night for my good buddy, Mike Kenny. I am also glad I truly feel my testimony at both of his trials, the criminal and the civil one, was found to be very helpful to his defense. I'll always be there for him again if needed." I just hope that if it ever happens again, it's with the NYPD, with which I've have a very good working relationship since 2003.

You're not gonna believe these coincidences. The first one has to do with the date of Mike's event, April 13, the same date thirty-two years earlier that I decided to go back to 'Nam to continue fighting that crazy war instead of going AWOL in Sydney when I was there for R&R. Maybe I was seeing some internal towers of light shining in my head at the time that blinded me to my choice of not going back.

The second one was when Mike was acquitted by a Manhattan jury of all criminal charges, which happened on September 29! As I've mentioned, most of my surprising coincidences happened in Septembers. What were the odds of that happening on that particular date? That morning, before the jury came back with its verdict, I told Mike that I wanted to see him a free man, that I wanted the jury to do the right thing. Mike wished me a happy wedding anniversary.

We both gave the other an early gift that day. (No, there was nothing from my wife.) That day was very memorable for me and more so for Mike; he became even more than a good buddy of mine. He became a dear and close friend. All good things come to those who wait. Believe me, he waited, and so did I. I'm just wondering how could it be that I was there for Mike to get to the top of the ramp not knowing the incident involved him but also because of what had taken place on April 13, 1970. Coincidence or what?

It was somewhere in 2010 when I casually mentioned to my dad what I was writing about in my book concerning my buddy Mike Kenny. He turned to me with an astonished look. "Charlie, say your friend's name again real slow and spell it too." I did. He smiled. "Well, son, you're not gonna believe this, but my best friend in the navy was also my best man at my wedding. His name was Mike Kenny!"

I was so surprised by that that I called Mike. He chuckled and said, "Put your dad on the phone." I watched my dad as he spoke to Mike. My dad kept on smiling and looking at me as Mike was speaking to him.

My dad ended the conversation. "Mike will call you later," he said.

I asked him what Mike had told him that was so funny. My dad replied, "Oh nothing. All he said was that his dad's brother, who was in the navy, stationed on a destroyer in San Diego and that his name was Mike."

CHAPTER 71

AFTER I GOT back from 'Nam, my life at home was great. Well, not right away. It did take a month or two for me to get readjusted to everyday doings. From July 1970 to July 1972, I was on a learning curve especially when it came to women. Some of my relationships got as hot and heavy as some of those rocket and mortar attacks I'd been subjected to in 'Nam. I found myself having to take cover every so often not to be caught being with someone else. That's some scary shit. (I should have applied for hazardous duty pay.)

As I kept up with this stupid charade of mine, I realized there were way too many demands from all the girls I was going out with. I slowly started to separate myself from most of them. I started to recall how I was with that amazing woman I spent time with in Sydney and what she said about me. Unbeknown to me, some of them were having me take a different course of action but in a much nicer way.

After going through this lesson in life and earning an A+, I felt ready to apply for a certificate of accomplishment by finding my one and only. I knew I'd recognize her just by her smile. She did indeed have a great smile, and she was good looking and smart. She loved to speak her mind. She made a great impression on me. (I didn't tell her that her great-looking body also made an great impression on me too.)

Her name was Margie Orlich. I asked her to marry me. She's Margie Kaczorowski now, and she's been that perfect woman in my life for quite some time. I call her Margie or Marge. I'm very proud to call her my wife. I'm also very proud to say she means so much to me, more than she knows.

We got married at 3:00 p.m. on September 29, 1973, a beautiful sunny Saturday. She'd decided on that date, and I went along with her. She didn't know that many interesting things had occurred around that date in that month.

Before I met Margie, almost all the girls I'd gone after or dated and even went out with for some time usually were blondes with blue eyes while Margie was a striking brunette with beautiful brown eyes and had this great, sexy smile. I never told her this nor will I ever tell her this, but I'll always consider myself the luckiest guy in the world to have her as my wife and the greatest woman to be by my side through thick and thin. She's also a fabulous mom to Noelle.

This would be a good time to give my wife a few medals; she deserves them for all the good deeds she's done in our marriage. You might have to wait for my next book if I decide to write another one to tell you more about her and Noelle. I'd received a few medals for the good deeds I did in 'Nam, but they don't carry over and get the same recognition for the good deeds that one does in one's life today. Sometimes, your luck changes. It has nothing to do with any kind of great deed you might have done; it just happens. My life with Margie started out great. Numerous times, I hoped and prayed she'd never have any kind of death or destruction in her life similar to what I experienced and saw in 'Nam. But things happen.

My life came to a crashing halt figuratively and literally about seven years later in 1980 on September 14—again September. I was in a near-fatal head-on collision. (That was not the type of impact I was referring to.) It happened of all places on a sidewalk. I was driving a '73 Pontiac Gran Prix, and the person who ran into me was driving a '73 Pontiac Trans Am. Both Pontiacs. What are the odds?

I had just turned onto Hempstead Turnpike and saw a car shooting out of a side street about six blocks away, the block I was headed for. I'm guessing he was trying to turn onto the turnpike but was going way too fast. He tried to avoid smashing into cars parked across the road by making a sharp right. He spun out on the wet pavement. His spinning was causing him to take up two lanes. No other traffic was around. I quickly drove over and onto the sidewalk and stopped in front of my town's fire station. With my foot on the brake, I just watched him. He regained some control, but he veered off the road onto the sidewalk, where I had thought I'd be safe from him. Instead of hitting a pole, he was coming right at me. I saw his eyes; he was in a state of shock. I had no place to go. This all happened in a matter of seconds. I was a sitting duck. We both knew impact was imminent.

It was so powerful that it slammed my chest into the steering wheel and my face into the dashboard. I was thrown back into my seat and then forward again. I fell over the console into the passenger seat leg area. (I know that only because someone in the fire station parking lot saw the whole thing; I was conked out.)

Somehow, his front bumper locked onto mine causing his car to slam against the huge metal door of the firehouse and smack me again broadside causing all the windows to shatter in both cars. The foot I'd had on the brake was no longer on the brake. My car was in drive. I guess the throttle was stuck. I left the front of the firehouse and traveled until I hit a building adjacent to the firehouse. Someone said he'd seen flames shooting out from under my hood.

Luckily for me, the volunteer firemen who were at the station for some meeting came running out. Seeing the situation, they doused the flames with fire extinguishers while others looked in on me and the other driver, whose car ended up going back onto the turnpike and heading over to the other side of the turnpike. How he ended up there is beyond me.

I was being lifted out of the passenger side of my car; the driver's door had been crushed. Two EMTs and two firemen treated me while I was out cold.

I'd been going to pick of Margie from her sister's, which wasn't far away. When I didn't show up, Mary Ann, her sister, and Frank, Mary Ann's husband decided to drive her home. As they came up to the scene of the accident, they saw my car in flames and me being placed on a gurney. I'm sure they were in total shock.

Frank stopped and told them the wife of the driver of that blue Gran Prix was in his backseat. The fireman told them where I was being taken to, Mercy Hospital in Rockville Center, where Marge happed to be working at the time.

At the ER, Marge learned that I'd suffered facial, head, chest, foot, and arm injuries and that they were still removing shards of glass from the top of my head.

It wasn't until about an hour later that I finally got to see Marge, Mary Ann, and Frank. They said I didn't look good but thanked God I was alive. Marge and I spoke for a while till she was told to leave so I could rest. She came back three hours later when she learned something had happened to me. A nurse that Marge knew told her that when I tried to get out of bed to use the bathroom, I was screaming at the top of my lungs about an unbelievable pain in my lower back. I'd fallen on the floor and couldn't get up. The nurses had come running in, and the doctor had sent me for further tests. Turns out I'd suffered a hairline spinal fracture that was close to being totally fractured. When I learned this, I considered myself to be one very lucky guy again on another September day.

But the next five years were extremely painful. I was on two medications and a muscle relaxant. You know how much I hate taking drugs of any kind. I also had to wear a corset-like brace that covered my chest and back from just below my armpits to my waist.

I went back to work about a month after the accident. I told my boss I could get back to work flying all over the country for Mother Merrill. I wouldn't let some stupid brace get in my way of doing what I liked doing. I wore the brace over my undershirt and under my dress shirt. The only major problem I had was having to use the bathroom. I just kept on telling myself, *Bite the bullet, Charlie. You've been through worse than this!*

Ever since that accident and especially when there's a drizzle, my hands automatically grip the steering wheel so tightly that my knuckles turn white. But end of story. No need to go any further than that. I guess when you experience a head-on collision, your subconscious kicks in and your body reacts to the trauma by going through the motions one more time.

The other trauma I had to deal with was when I found out that my $1 million lawsuit that had been pending for almost five years in the courts went right down the drain. I was informed by my lawyer that my orthopedic surgeon had skipped town with my X-rays. Apparently, I heard from my lawyer that the kid who had hit me, his family, and my surgeon's family came from the same village in Croatia and it would have devastated the kid's family to pay out what I was asking for, and I believe the insurance company couldn't cover it or whatever. I'm not sure of all the legal details as to why, but the judge was nice enough to award me enough money to buy a set of floor mats for the front and back of the next car I purchased, a Ford Pinto. My lawyer took his 33 percent, the doctor bills ate up a good portion of the money, and whatever was left from the grand total of $96,000 was mine.

La-de-da.

CHAPTER 72

GOING BACK TO that day that I had my first near heart attack that occurred on September 28, 1990 has me wondering if I was meant to have it for a special reason. As I was lying there in the hospital late that afternoon, I thought about what was to happen the next day. Margie and I had a scheduled home visit interview the next day, our final step in the adoption process. If all went well, I'd planned to take Margie to her favorite restaurant in Manhattan, the Four Seasons, to celebrate our seventeenth wedding anniversary.

We were looking forward to the day; it had been a year of paperwork. Neither of us wanted an infant; we didn't want to change diapers and all the other stuff that goes along with an infant, so we had asked for a girl between the ages of three and five from a Colombian orphanage.

Sometime around 11:00 a.m., I was abruptly removed from my cubicle at the construction office I was working in at the time. No, I wasn't being fired. I was being placed on a stretcher by paramedics who told me I was having a heart attack. I was rushed to a hospital in Midtown. I recall hearing the term *code blue* before I blacked out for the second time.

I spent close to eight hours in the ER; Marge had to drive in from Long Island. She arrived around 8:00 p.m. and whispered, "You're going to sign yourself out of this hospital so we can go home and get things ready for our interview." She knew what to do as far as getting out was concerned; she had me sign a bunch of waivers stating that I had agreed to have myself admitted to another hospital (the one I'd been in for my car accident) within twelve hours.

A trio of doctors wanted me to reconsider, but I didn't want to be there. Because of what had occurred there and what Margie had noticed when she arrived, let's just say I wanted to go home so Margie went to get the car and when we left, having gone about two blocks, Margie got out and I actually had to drive home for she was too upset and doesn't like driving in the city.

I was released. I had to drive home because Margie was too upset after what she had complained about to the doctors and for the real reason why I signed myself out. If all went well at the interview, we'd be flying to Colombia to meet and bring home our child. It was nerve-racking having to drive through Manhattan around 11:00 p.m. Margie couldn't see that well at night, and she was stressed out enough.

When we got home, I tried to help Marge get the house ready for the home visit. I was overly exhausted, but I stayed focused on the mission at hand, the interview. The next morning, I showered, got dressed, and had a light breakfast. I sat in my chaise lounge in the backyard as if nothing had happened and waited for the social worker to show up.

The interviewer came and left within an hour. Margie took me to the hospital. We never made it into the city to celebrate our anniversary. Three days later, I returned home, and we got the call that we'd been approved for the adoption. My boss called and told me to rest the next three weeks and a fourth week if necessary.

I stayed out for three weeks. When I returned, I was transferred to handle only one project rather than the six I'd had that had had me traveling all over the city. I went to work at the American Express headquarters in the World Financial Center across the street from the WTC. I felt right at home again and was happy I wasn't running around to other sites. I think my heart was happy as well.

Ten months later, our lawyer called. "It's time to get your baby!"

Baby? We hadn't wanted to have a baby, but after hearing my lawyer's reasons for adopting this baby, I told him I agreed with him and would call Marge with the good news. She couldn't understand why I'd had a change of heart and wanted a baby instead of a three- or four-year-old.

We flew to Colombia to see our baby. The orphanage was across the way from the prison that was holding Pablo Escobar, the cartel drug king. I bonded with our daughter the moment I saw her. I knew she was meant to be in my heart from the day she was born. I wanted to name her, Noelle, thinking we would have her home for Christmas, and Margie picked Elizabeth for her middle name.

The things a person does for love … I believe what I'd done for love by leaving the hospital for the interview on September 29, 1990 was an absolute blessing for Margie and me. I'd had my first near heart attack at 11:00 a.m. on September 28, and I was back in the hospital the following day for my heart to mend. On the same day in Colombia, a baby was born on September 29. I guess my heart went all a-flutter preparing itself to give me this special gift we brought home in November 1991. I wondered if this was a surprising coincidence too.

CHAPTER 73

S o I was working at the American Express headquarters right across the street from the North Tower. I was overseeing all the renovations for the corporate division and the executive floors and any work for the building management company. My office was on the third floor of this beautiful office building.

One day, I took lunch a little earlier than normal. I hadn't had much breakfast that morning. I walked across the bridge that connected the WFC complex to the WTC complex and took an escalator down to the concourse of the North Tower. I'd done that a thousand times before and could probably have done it blindfolded. I went to a place that I knew served some pretty good open-faced sandwiches, down in the sub-Concourse, but it was packed. I went back to the escalators and headed back up to the Concourse to meander over to a deli up on Broadway. I thought I should have gone there in the first place in spite of the inclement weather and taken a sandwich back to my office, where I could eat and read a book written by my buddy, Nelson DeMille, that I was looking forward to finishing.

I never made it to the deli on Broadway. I never had my lunch. I never went back to my book. While I was traveling up the escalator that was close to the wall of the garage below the concourse, I heard an explosion and felt a tremor that came from the other side of the wall. My mind and body went into combat mode. I thought that a transformer had blown or a Path train had derailed in the station.

I was wrong on both assumptions. The explosion at 12:17 p.m. that

Tuesday afternoon on February 26, 1993 was caused by a van filled with explosives—the first terrorist attack on the WTC.

When I reached the concourse level, I realized few people there realized what had happened below. Most of the chaos and havoc, unbeknown to me and everyone else, was occurring outside and up on the West Side Highway along the North Tower. I headed over to the bank of payphones on the other side of the escalators to call Herbert Construction's main office to let them know where I was and that something had occurred in the garage. I told them where I was calling from and where I'd just come from; I said I was okay. My boss, an executive vice president, came on the line and told me he'd heard about what had happened.

I was to go back to the office at American Express and wait for further instructions, which I did. I was called about an hour later and told that I should round up any and all construction personnel who were carpenters and laborers working for me in the American Express building and be ready to head over to the plaza in the WTC complex by the North Tower. There would be a truckload of plywood delivered to board up any windows that had their glass blown out. I'd looked out the window and had seen FDNY and NYPD personnel evacuating people out of the building. I saw black smoke streaming out of the building on the plaza level. I heard that one of the security officers who worked there had said what had happened in the garage had caught them off guard. Somehow, someone had gotten that van into the garage and had detonated the explosives.

I was so preoccupied with all this that I forgot to call Marge at work to tell her I was okay; she knew I walked through the WTC daily. I went over to the plaza and saw some of the guys who were still working on a renovation I was doing in the North Tower who were now boarding up the blown -out windows and sweeping up the glass metal, and other debris.

When I got home later that evening, Marge said, "Thank God you're okay! Did you hear six people were killed, mostly Port Authority employees? Also, as many as a thousand were injured." A feeling of uneasiness came over me about going back there the next day; I was afraid other vans or vehicles with explosives could have been there to cause another catastrophe. I'd never thought something like that would happen in the WTC or in the whole city for that matter. I was lucky that the blast hadn't ripped through the wall of the garage which I'd been next to.

In 1996, three years later and on a warm July evening, Mr. Luck was with me again. I was involved in another major car accident; divine intervention or a really strange occurrence saved me from death again. It happened on the same road, Hempstead Turnpike, where I'd had my first accident, and it was around the same time in the evening. It happened two blocks from my home in the opposite direction on the turnpike. This whole thing started prior to me getting home; I believe it occurred for a very special reason. It definitely came at the right time; it saved gut-wrenching heartbreak for Marge and Noelle.

Lucky for me, I did what I did instead of doing what I would normally have done. At the time, Noelle was five and a half. One of her biggest thrills was to go with me to the supermarket. She liked singing along with me to tunes we'd hear on the radio, and she liked riding in the shopping cart up and down the aisles. We had a lot of fun doing that. She was very good at wiggling herself into making me take her even when I was extremely tired. I had this big soft spot for her in my heart, and I could never say no to her.

That evening, Margie asked me if I'd mind going for a few things from the supermarket before I changed. I wasn't in the best of moods that evening. I was exhausted from the work I'd done and having stood on the subway for a good forty-five minutes. Then I'd waited thirty minutes for my bus and had had to stand for the forty-minute ride home.

Marge was sympathetic, but she still needed some things. I wanted a minute or two to unwind and not let Noelle I was home. I went into the bedroom and sat. Out of nowhere, I felt this weird burning feeling. It brought about a very powerful kink in the back of my neck, a kink that was more like a twisting of my head from one side to the other. I felt a tightness in my neck I'd never felt before. I was having a hard time dealing with it. The tightness went down to my chest. I first thought I was having a heart attack, so I tried to relax. I hoped the nonsense would stop and leave my body.

Margie asked me how soon I'd go. The tightness in my chest made me lie on my bed. I let myself go limp. A minute later, I got up and started walking out of the bedroom feeling even more wiped out. Noelle called me from upstairs. I knew if I took Noelle with me, the tightness might start again especially when I had to secure her in the car seat. I didn't want to be grimacing in pain when I'd strap her in. I decided not to take her with me; I didn't want to scare her if I was in pain.

I grabbed the short list and headed for the door. Marge asked, "How come you're not taking Noelle?" And Noelle came into the kitchen, saw me, and figured I was going somewhere. She of course wanted to go with. I said, "No, not tonight, honey, Daddy's tired. Maybe tomorrow."

Noelle headed for the door as if she hadn't heard me. "You always take me, Daddy! I know you're joking with me!" I walked past her and out the door. Margie yelled, "Charlie, you always take her! Why aren't you taking Noelle with you?" I gave Margie this look hoping she'd see there was something bothering me. I wasn't feeling well. I kept my mouth shut, got into the car, and backed out of the driveway fast. I was so pissed off that this stupid neck pain had come out of nowhere and that I'd become a pain in the neck by not taking Noelle.

I saw Noelle standing next to Marge on the back steps more upset then I'd ever seen her get. She was in tears. I yelled out the window, "I'm sorry!" They were mad at me, but I figured I could explain to them later why I hadn't taken Noelle. I've always had a soft spot in my heart for Noelle; I'd made her cry.

I drove over to Poplar Street and made a left. I gave it the gas to make a green and get on the turnpike. I figured the sooner I got there and got the stuff, the sooner I'd be home. I thought about going back for Noelle, but by then, the supermarket was very close. All I had to do was wait for the green to take a right into the lot. I was still wondering what had caused that chest tightness. I don't know what made me look into my rearview mirror, but I saw that my face had this unusual glow around it. It was coming from these bright, glaring headlights behind me that were bearing down on me big-time. I pressed hard on the brake and grabbed the steering wheel with both hands as I'd done in the last accident and prayed for the best. I was once again a sitting target. Seconds before the impact, I saw three guys in the van that hit me so hard that I was knocked unconscious. My seat back broke where I was shoved into my steering wheel. I don't know how much time passed before I heard voices. I didn't know where I was until I saw these volunteer firemen from my town who were trying to speak to me. I could see I was still in my car and the firemen were asking me, "Where does it hurt? Do you have trouble breathing? Is there anyone in the backseat?"

Someone was trying to tell me I wasn't bleeding anywhere; I told them my chest was killing me. I tried to turn around to look into the backseat but I couldn't because I was pressed up against the steering wheel and my seatback wouldn't go back. I tried to look into my rear view mirror to see the backseat, but my mirror was gone. I started crying. A police officer asked me, "What's wrong?" I said, "Oh my God! My daughter! Is she okay? She's in her car seat!"

He told the firemen what I had just told him and asked me if there was someone he could call. I gave him my home number and told him I lived three blocks from there on Spruce and Fairlawn. I told him my wife's name. I started yelling, "Noelle! Talk to me, honey!" The firemen were trying to tell me that the impact had crushed the rear of the car and that there was no backseat. They said they couldn't see any car seat. I tried to get out of my car chest pain or no chest pain, but I couldn't budge. The pain I felt in my heart was due to my thinking my daughter was dead. Considering all the times I'd taken her to the store, in my panic, I thought she was with me.

As the firemen were putting a brace around my neck, I saw that I'd ended up in the middle of the intersection. There were cars on both sides of me, but they hadn't hit me—a miracle. A huge crowd had gathered. As I was being prepared to be lifted out of my car, my mind suddenly came clear that Noelle wasn't with me, that she was home with Margie. She would have been sitting right behind the front passenger seat and wouldn't have been in sight for any firemen to see her.

They eventually got me out and put me on a stretcher. I saw I'd traveled twenty or thirty feet due to the impact. I saw that the trunk of my Olds Calais was crushed and in my backseat. I started to feel light headed. An officer and a fireman grabbed me by my arms and asked me if I'd been drinking. A fireman said, "Take him to Mercy!"

As I lay there, I imagined how horrible it would have been if Noelle had been with me. They said they'd called my wife. How she would get to the hospital was a mystery; I'd been driving our only car. I don't remember asking about the three guys in the van. I wondered why I had an unusual painful kink, a burning sensation in my neck. All I knew was that it had convinced me not to take Noelle that evening. I wondered if it had been divine intervention. I thanked God and my angels.

At Mercy Hospital, a nurse told me Margie's sister was driving her over. Three hours later, after all kinds of X-rays, I was admitted to the hospital. I finally got to see Margie, Noelle, and Mary Ann. I complained about my chest pain and headaches, but I kept quiet about the much greater pain I was feeling about almost having lost Noelle.

Every time I mention this accident, I get this pain in my heart and one hell of a lump in my throat to remind me how close it had been. To this day, I still ask myself, *Why did all that stuff happen to me that day and evening that caused me not to take Noelle?*

CHAPTER 74

I ALWAYS THOUGHT I'd had my share of death and devastation; I'd seen it in 'Nam, I'd been in two unbelievable automobile accidents, came close to losing my life due to my liver ailment, and was just on the other side of the garage wall when that truck bomb went off in the WTC in February '93.

But all that didn't come close to what I saw on 9/11 and during the ten months I worked on the site afterward. I tried to convince myself I'd enjoy the rest of my life in spite of all the visions I had about the Twin Towers. My feelings manifested themselves in a very surprising way that evoked almost every one of the wondrous, beautiful visions from my wild heart that I depicted in all the 9/11 memorials I designed. My wild heart kept telling me that all my submissions to competitions in New York City and in Pennsylvania were the right stuff.

All my designs were surprising coincidences that had come out of my subconscious after having waited for quite some time; I put them down on paper on my drawing board one by one. I submitted them to competitions sure one would be selected. Seeing it built would be an unforeseen dream come true. I thought I had the most wanted and needed honor bestowed in a beautiful tribute to those we lost on 9/11.

I'm thankful for my knowledge and background in architectural design and construction and for the people I worked with at the WTC site and the skills that had allowed me to develop. All my deep respect, emotions, and feelings went into my first design for what could have been built on those sixteen acres—a beautiful new complex and a stunning memorial. It would have been a very surprising coincidence if someone who had seen the original design and proposed conception in the late '60s for the WTC, worked for years there, was there during the first terrorist attack and then on 9/11, and who supervised the removal of all the debris ultimately designed something great to replace it. People would notice the great respect I had for the place and the honor I'd had being involved with it in so many ways. Simply amazing.

I got my first job in that architectural firm in '65 thanks to what I had learned in the technical and vocational classes I'd taken at Sewanhaka High School in Floral Park, New York. I completed three years in architectural drafting and building construction. In junior high and my first year of high school, I attended Floral Park Memorial; my teachers told me I was artistically inclined. (I should have asked them if I was inclined 60 degrees to the right or 45 degrees to the left. I mean, fifteen degrees is fifteen degrees after all.)

As I wrote earlier, I met Marc Chagall while I was working for Harrison & Abramowitz, the architectural firm at the Metropolitan Opera House in Lincoln Center, which Harrison designed.

Chagall told me when he lived in Paris, Picasso, and Matisse, who were living nearby, would work together on their art but never got along. I didn't have the nerve to ask him why. Our conversations were colorful but very abstract. He was an absolute gentleman whose artwork was well received. I truly enjoyed seeing his two murals, "The Sound of Music" and the "Triumph of Music" at the Met having met the man.

Mr. Harrison gave me a personal invitation to attend the Met's opening on September 16, 1966, but I had to be honest and let him know that I wasn't into opera that much and that he should give my seat to someone who would appreciate it more than I would. I believe he was impressed by my gesture. I'm still the same way today about opera, but I've learned my lesson—never turn down any kind of invitation to something as important as that.

The following week, Mr. Harrison inquired about my schooling. I told him what I had accomplished and how much I loved architecture; I guess I impressed him. He asked me if I wanted to work after my regular nine-to-five job in the plan room as a junior draftsman. I'd be helping out making some minor corrections on some major projects.

Of course I said yes. I started brushing up on my architectural lettering and mastered it.

I worked a few hours a night on the contract documents for projects at the Albany South Mall, the state capital, and Columbia Law School. Two months later, I was asked to start working full-time as a draftsman—no more deliveries, no more trips to other companies. I was overwhelmed. I bought a three-piece suit and a shirt, shoes, and a tie that cost more than the shirt. I was in the big leagues at that point in my life, for sure.

Then came a day when Harrison himself walked over to my drafting table and told me to follow him to his office. I thought I had screwed up on some of my notes. He told me to take a seat. Nothing was said until his top interior decorator/designer, Edith Queller, walk into his office along with Max Abramowitz, Harrison's partner. The two new arrivals had been working diligently on the Columbia Law School project; she was also the interior designer for the opera house.

It just so happened that it was the day before my birthday; they surprised me with a gift. It was more like a shock than a gift. I was told I'd no longer be working on any more drawings. I was so sure I'd screwed up somewhere, but I was totally wrong. They said they wanted me to take a shot at something different; they wanted me to build a scale model of Columbia Law School's entire first floor out of Plexiglas to scale. They said that I was a creative and honest worker who loved what they and I were doing and that I had a flair for that kind of work. Of course I said yes.

I was transferred from my drafting desk on the fifth floor of 630 Fifth Avenue to a small, one-window office on the mezzanine level of the RCA building overlooking Sixth Avenue. My move to this new location for the new job was eventful. To get to my office, I had to take a private elevator. Someone in the building who wore a grey uniform told me I'd be sharing the elevator with some pretty important VIPs including Johnny Carson, Ed McMahon, and Skitch Henderson of NBC's *Tonight Show*. We became instant buddies. We'd talk about the weather or if I'd happened to have seen the previous night's show as we waited for the elevator. I'd make some kind of humorous remark about something that had been said; they called me witty and said I had a great sense of humor. We ended up on a first-name basis. I admit I mingled with some of the great ones back then!

The time I spent with Harrison & Abramowitz gave me my first true vision of the field of architectural design. It also gave me an unbelievable opportunity of a lifetime to have worked side by side with some of the best architectural designers in the country and to have worked on projects and attended meetings once or twice with Governor Nelson Rockefeller, Harrison's brother-in-law.

You're not gonna believe this, but one day, I called in sick and instead of convalescing went to Jones Beach with my brother and our best friend, Bob Pagano. While we were getting some snacks at one of the pavilions, who of all people shows up but Nelson himself with a slew of people. It was for something that had to do with Jones Beach State Park. Another time, I had to deliver drawings to Rockerfellers' office over on West 55th Street off Fifth Avenue when I was in for a really big surprise. I was stopped by the NYPD as they quickly placed some wooden barricades leading up to the then Peninsula Hotel when I saw the Beatles stepping out of a limousine where I was able to reach out and shake hands with every one of them. *Oh, these fond memories of* 'Yesterday' *never seem to want to leave me.*

Turns out someone took a photo of the governor there that showed up on the front page of the *Long Island Press*. Guess who was also in the picture? Lucky for me, they showed only my left side, which was not my good side, and I was wearing a ridiculous-looking striped bathing suit.

While I worked at Harrison & Abramowitz, I saw two designers there sketch out two buildings on yellow tracing paper that later became the two buildings next to the Time & Life Building on Sixth Avenue. Life was grand, and I was falling in love with architecture.

It wasn't until some thirty-five years later while I was working at Ground Zero overseeing the removal of the Trade Center that I became more curious about the Twin Towers. I never really knew much about the architect who had designed them, so I did some research, actually a lot of research, and I learned about Minoru Yamasaki.

I was surprised to learn an interesting fact about him that I think made me realize why I'd been so drawn to these two towers. Minoru and I had two things in common—we both liked sushi and playing ping-pong. (Sorry. I needed to slip a bit of humor here.)

Seriously folks, you're not gonna believe this, but my dear friend Minoru worked for Harrison & Abramowitz in the late 1930s, and it was about thirty-five years later that I went to work there, the same number of years I worked in and around the Twin Towers.

The time I spent in that private elevator with Johnny, Ed, and Skitch might have been the foundation of my broad sense of humor that had been locked away in me. Whenever I hear "Here's ... Johnny!" I think of how they told me I was funny and witty.

The time came for me to say good-bye to all my wonderful, dear friends at Harrison & Abramowitz; that was two weeks before I joined the navy. Mr. Harrison took me aside and told me, "Stay sharp, do your best, and when your four years are over, come back and work for me. I see great things in your future. You have a keen eye for design and a good, vivid imagination in architecture. Don't let it go to waste! Good luck and safe sailing!"

CHAPTER 75

I 'VE INCLUDED FOUR photos in this book of the designs I submitted for the sixteen acres at Ground Zero. The cloverleaf pattern included four towers in an arc pattern (allowing me to eliminate one glass elevator tower). The photo rendering of the four memorialized towers have façades of a different colored glass showing respect and honor to all who died that day and project a meaningful and powerful statement to all the damn terrorists out there that we are way stronger now and more united than before!

My having my office complex spread out across the sixteen-acre site would be much more noticeable to everyone than in my original cloverleaf design seeing four distinct colors of glass: grey for the civilians, red for the FDNY, green for the NYPD, and blue for the PAPD. I also removed one large reflecting pool and replaced it with two pools for each footprint of where the towers once stood. It being hallowed ground, I placed a pedestrian bridge to transverse diagonally across each footprint, and I included an eternal flame centrally located between the two. (Please take a minute and try to visualize what I was trying to convey there as a true dedication to all the lost loved ones.)

Look up on LMDC's website to see the design Daniel Libeskind first submitted. Doesn't it look somewhat similar to mine? Which would you rather have seen built there?' I believe that if the public had a say in it (and not just LMDC), we might have seen something along my design being built there on the site and people coming out and saying, "You're not gonna believe this, but that design is by Charlie K, a survivor of 9/11 who was also involved in the overall operations at Ground Zero!"

Anyone who has seen my design prior to the final selection by LMDC have all told me my design was absolutely great. So I sent it over to Silverstein again (my revision) and mainly to LMDC, the Lower Manhattan Development Corporation, a quasi-state/city organization that was in charge of overseeing the designs and development completion of the WTC site. They had a design competition coming up, and I figured I had nothing to lose, so I sent my design in. If I had made any changes, omissions, or additions to it, I made sure I had forwarded a copy to them as well and by doing this was able to leave a paper trail of what they were getting from me.

You never know what life has in store for you. My changes had been prompted by my wild heart, not my head. I even felt so kind as to send off copies of my design to two popular local newspapers, the *Daily News* and the *Post*, and the NYPD, FDNY, PAPD and the PANYNJ as well. I thought it would be to my advantage to have everyone involved see my creation, the best damn idea for the redevelopment of the site and more than likely one that would have been the least costly to build. I didn't care what was being said in the newspapers; my wild heart had confirmed that I had the right design—simple and symbolic.

I guess my wild heart was good to me after all. I knew what I was talking about. My efforts paid off. After sending off my latest and greatest revision of my design, I finally heard from someone at LMDC; the firm thanked me for my submissions in a letter dated July 26, 2002. LDMC wanted me to sign an actual agreement that read, "(1) No compensation will be due, to you, in connection with your proposal, and (2) that you reserve no patent, trademark, copyright, trade secret, or other intellectual property rights in any other material that form or is contained in your proposal. (3) Also, when they receive my signed agreement, LMDC will maintain my proposal, in a file, that may be consulted as we develop the reconstruction concepts for the World Trade Center site and adjacent areas."

Wow! After all the submissions I sent to them, they send me this! What the hell were they thinking? No reserve, no trademark, no patent, no copyright? Of course I signed it! But before I sent it back, I wanted to protect myself. (No, I didn't put on a condom. I'm talking about protection in the legal sense of the word.) I called a very good friend of mine and asked him, "What do I do?" I told him I needed some good, sound, and honest advice. I valued his to the utmost. We set up a date and time to meet.

Robert Palermo, an architect, had seen all my designs and revisions for the site. He admired my work, and he knew my background. He also thought I had the right and best idea for the site. I'd been to his office once or twice, and after seeing some of the designs and renderings he had done for the projects he'd worked on, I figured he could help me and guide me with my reply to LMDC. I'd worked with Robert on projects in Brooklyn and East Harlem that he'd designed.

I saw no harm in asking for his off-the-record advice on what he would do if he'd been me. I didn't think there would be any harm in what I was doing for I didn't think it would be a conflict of interest since there was no exchange of money for his services, which were simply sound advice and common sense.

I read him the letter. "What can I do or say about this agreement to protect myself and my submittal?" I asked him. I showed him my design, and he thought it was a great concept. He suggested I stick to it and don't let anybody change it even though I was going up against some top-named architects in the city and possibly from around the world in this design competition.

"Don't give up!" he said. "You have the right idea, and most of all, you have the truest, most heartfelt respect for the site. It's been part of you for so many years."

We talked about the letter. We kicked around some ideas as to what I'd want to add to my response to protect myself. Robert referred to it as stipulations. We came up with a few good words that I wrote down. It was short and sweet. I wrote, "I did this out of my compassion and professional feelings for the site and the 9/11 incident. I never expected nor do I expect any remuneration. I would appreciate public acknowledgement of my design efforts if my concept is selected for design implementation." I signed it, dated it 8/15/02, made two or three copies, and planned on delivering the letter to LMDC.

You're not gonna believe this, but LDMC was in the same building I'd worked in for Merrill Lynch in the '70s and '80s—One Liberty Plaza at 165 Broadway. Small world. I went to the meeting they were having on the twentieth floor and gave my letter to the person who had sent it to me.

I didn't know what to expect. I didn't receive any word from them for some time. Robert kept asking me, "Any word from LMDC?" I had to say repeatedly, "No letter or calls from them whatsoever. Not even a response that they received the letter I'd signed and given to this certain person who was high up in the executive level of LMDC." (He'd put it in his inside suit pocket. Maybe it's still there.) It was as if I was off their radar for good. I thought that my stipulation could have broken the camel's back and that my letter was in one of their legal files covered with camel shit.

You're not gonna believe this (I know, that's the second time you've read that in this chapter), but my design was shown to a lot of people who were at the Listening to the City Forum on Saturday, July 19, 2002, a town hall meeting at the Jacob Javits Center in Midtown Manhattan. They were there to discuss the proposed design development for the WTC site, and a design submitted by a local architectural firm, Beyer Blinder Belle, was up for discussion. (It was also my mom's eighty-first birthday, and I was carrying her gift with me.)

I was approached by this young reporter, Gregg Gittrich, of the *Daily News*; he'd probably spotted my Ground Zero T-shirt. He asked me what I thought about the design being discussed and shown on a huge screen. I said, "It looks like Albany!" He gave me a weird look. I continued. "It's total nonsense. I worked on the Albany South Mall Project in '65 designed by Harrison & Abramowitz, a very prominent architectural firm. So BBB takes H&A's design of this office complex and simply rotates and quirks it a bit to make the buildings fit inside the WTC site? That's no design to me!"

I showed him my design I happened to have with me and told him it was a gift to my mom for her birthday. He loved it. I said thanks and walked away. I found it odd that my comment "It looks like Albany" was the title for his article covering the town hall meeting in Sunday's edition of the *Daily News* the next day but my name wasn't mentioned even though we'd exchanged business cards. That's okay with me. I know and Gregg knows who said it and why, and that's why he used my words.

As I was walking away from him, someone who said he was with CNN grabbed my arm. He'd overheard what I had told Gregg. He wanted to interview me. We swapped cards. I asked, "Okay, Phil Hirschhorn, why do you want to interview me for?"

He said he wanted to get me on tape after seeing and hearing about the design I'd shown to Gregg. He thought it was way better than what was being discussed that day and what everyone was seeing up on the large screens as we spoke. He also told me that I might be hearing from Paula Zahn to talk more about my design after she has a chance to see the tape of my interview.

So I did my interview. His staff loved it. Just as I was thanking him and his crew, someone in a wheelchair ran over my sneaker-clad rather than my usual steel-tipped, workboot-clad foot. I wondered why the wheel just sat on my foot and noticed another reporter but not just any reporter. He apologized for what he had done; he said he hadn't wanted me to get away. He wanted to talk with me about my design. "Aren't you Chris O'Donoghue?" I asked.

He handed me his business card, said he was with UPN Channel 9 News, apologized once again, and said he'd been impressed with my design and had heard some of what I'd said to the CNN reporter. "I got to have you talk more about it with me!" he said.

I said okay, and off we went to his area. He wanted my business card and cell number. We did the interview. He thanked me for my time at Ground Zero and what I had done there and for my great design. I was on cloud nine. I spoke with some very prominent people in the field of architecture, including this nice gentleman I met, John Whitehead, who it turned out was truly impressed with my design. I was still on a high from my three interviews, and it made the gift I had for my mom that much more precious to give her. I felt as if I'd just met the three wise men and had given them a gift. I felt reborn!

I left the forum, and on my way home, I stopped to get a birthday card for my mom. When I got to my parents' house, my mom was extremely proud of my special gift for her. She told me that I'd be famous one day as a designer with original ideas. My dad said, "It's more than a birthday gift to your mom. It could very well be my good-luck piece."

I told them about my interviews and said I wished the whole world could see my design. I said, "Who knows? Maybe we'll get to see it on TV one day."

My dad, knowing I had just finished ten months at Ground Zero, said to my mom, "Tania, our son Charles has made us very proud, and even if they don't select his design, we know his heart was in it from the get-go and he's reached a major milestone in his life and in our lives too!"

He tacked my design on the dining room wall where it would be in full view.

That evening when I was still in my driveway, I got a call. "Hi, Charlie K! It's Chris with UPN News. Do me a big favor. Watch our ten o'clock news tonight. You're gonna be totally surprised!" He said that he and his crew had been "totally impressed" with my design and that I had the total tribute by far. He wanted to "get it out there to the public."

I called my mom and dad and told them to watch the news on channel 9 as an additional gift to her. When I walked into my house, Marge asked, "How was the meeting? Did you see your mom?" I told her all about the meeting, my mom's gift, the interviews, and the phone call I'd just gotten from Chris. She couldn't believe it.

We called a few of our close family members to tell them to watch the same news and waited. At ten, I turned on the newscast. When it came on, they mentioned there would be special segment on the town hall meeting at the Jacob Javits Center for the design for the WTC site. I gave Marge a look. She said, "Don't get your hopes up high. You might not be on it."

It was a good segment that got better. Chris said, "Now here's a design that they should consider." There I was holding up my design with my name mentioned below and spelled correctly too. I described my proposed tribute for the site. I couldn't believe it! Wow! At first, it was three reporters, but then the whole city was seeing it. Possibly the entire world! This viewing became my copyright, my patent, in living color, and I did not need LMDC anymore!

A few months passed. For some reason, I was drawn back to my latest revised design. I really looked at it. I got down and into it so much than before that I was looking at it but from above. I was staring at the tops of my buildings as if I were being summoned by all the lost loved ones who had died that day. My wild heart was telling me my design needed a special detail, an inspirational addition on all four rooftops. It would be a truly outstanding tribute and honor by lighting up this new symbolic gesture so it could be seen at night. The three uniformed services' shields would be on three towers, and the fourth tower would honor the civilians having a single rose. That would be the right touch from above. The four images could be placed on some kind of metal mesh material suspended above any rooftop equipment.

I didn't care what LMDC or anyone else thought about my latest addition to my design. I sent it out to everyone again. This is another one of my photos I have included in this book. If my design were selected, those flying over the site day or night would see my tribute to those who had died there.

Take a look at my final design proposal and at the winning design LMDC chose on December 19, 2002. Don't you find it odd that five months after my design was shown on TV, LMDC decided on one that looked similar to mine? That happened five months after my design got out there on the news. I consider that a really surprising coincidence.

I think I made a very big mistake when I was working at Ground Zero and had my design posted all over the walls of the cubicle I shared with a fellow DDC project manager, Ted Frank, in the American Express tower. I believe David Childs himself of Skidmore, Owings and Merrill, the architectural firm that worked in conjunction later on with Daniel Liebskind for the design of the redevelopment of the WTC site, had walked through our floor with a few other architects from the same firm. I handed him a copy of my design and said, "This is what I envision being built here. It's not just another office complex; it's also a memorial."

I find it ironic that someone I'd given a copy of my design to was later on involved in the very design that was chosen. Oh well, such is life.

CHAPTER 76

MONTHS LATER, I spilled my wild heart into another design competition for which LMDC was in charge—the WTC Memorial. I believe it was another surprising coincidence. My wild heart led my hand when I drew something that went well beyond my mind or brain's capabilities.

When it was completed, I was amazed at what I had drawn; it went above and beyond the honor and tribute in my previous design submission to LMDC for the overall site redevelopment. It showed respect to everyone who had died there. I included everything else that related to 9/11 except those frickin' terrorists. I showed dedication to all those on the four flights and for those involved in the first bombing of the WTC. It would be seen day and night from above.

I submitted my design to LMDC before the deadline and later went to its website to see where my design was being shown among the other entries. I believe my design had symbolism that went beyond that in the others. I asked myself, *Have any of these people ever been to a memorial and really see what was being displayed there and why?*

Of the 5,200 submissions, only about twenty-five or thirty designs had a chance of becoming finalists besides mine. Maybe there were one or two that I would say were meaningful, but they were not as meaningful as mine. I am not bragging about my design, but I believed once the judges saw it, they would come to an honest decision.

Each entry was given a number; my design was number 409883. I hope you go to the LMDC website and see what else was submitted and compare them to mine, which is depicted and described in this book.

Family members, coworkers at DDC, fellow Ground Zero workers, and hundreds of volunteers knew I'd be submitting a design for the competition. The majority of them thought I had the best design for the overall site and that it would be one beautiful memorial park.

I tried to make it a place of total respect for all who had died there, civilians and first responders alike. I wanted visitors to learn what had occurred that fateful day and see and feel the beauty and honor I'd bestowed there by all the different tributes and dedications.

New York City suffered such a great loss that day—people from fifty countries perished that day, and I wanted to make sure they were all remembered. I wanted the memory of the Twin Towers included in the overall tribute as well. My wild heart knew what it wanted and has spoken to me to include the following tributes.

- the Tomb of Unknown (remains)
- a shrine for the 1993 bombing of the WTC
- a shrine to the Pentagon
- a shrine to United Airlines Flight 93
- a tower of lights
- a (much needed) wall of acknowledgment
- two reflecting pools where the towers once stood
- a sphere
- a place to rest and take it all in, a Valley of Valor grandstand

Below, not shown, would be a museum, gift shop, restrooms, and one remaining piece of steel that we all idolized and saw every day at the site during recovery/cleanup— the Ground Zero Cross.

I had walkways wide enough for the throngs of visitors and an EMS bus if needed. I had benches along the walkways that honored American Airlines and United Airlines symbolically given tribute having the walkway appeared as an *A* and a *U* to give remembrance as well to the crews and passengers on the flights.

I hope my memorial will shed some light on a dark day in our history; I don't want anyone to forget. I wish I could learn how you feel about my design in this book. I even included a rendering of what it would look like if you were standing next to one of the reflecting pools at one of the tower footprints having a façade section of that particular tower placed directly in the center of the pool.

The pedestrian bridge that transverses one corner of the footprint diagonally across to the other corner is to honor the hallowed ground. I placed three flagpoles flying Old Glory in the farthest corner away from the center of both footprints. Along the top surface of each low wall that encompasses the footprint is a planter with a colorful assortment of flowers for the four seasons.

My Valley of Valor grandstand is a seating area of total respect where people could reflect and give tribute to all the lives lost. Each of about 3,000 seats would have a plate with the name of one of the lost. The white seats would be only for family members during the anniversary ceremonies. The grey seats would be for the civilians that died that day, the red ones for the FDNY, the green ones for the NYPD, and the blue seats for the PAPD lives lost.

These seats would have no seats in the traditional sense because the loved ones they represent are no longer with us. I placed a metal vase in the center where the seat would otherwise be. The vases are suspended by wires to the chair bracket and would hold flowers or mementos a family member might want to place there.

I wanted at least one or two white seats to be on each side of one of the four colored seats, which I thought was truly needed there. I'm sure all the family members of the lost loved ones would appreciate seeing this. Having been a participant in every 9/11 anniversary ceremony as a standing member of the honor guard in the Pit, I've seen family members having to stand every time for the ceremony. That gave me the idea to place these seats there. I had to swallow lumps in my throat seeing that. I had to bury these feelings inside of me until I got home later that night to where I would let the flood gates open. I've cried in public about it as well. I didn't give a damn who saw me.

On Thursday, November 11, 1982, Veteran's Day, I was sitting only a few feet from a very prominent structure in Washington, DC, when it was inaugurated—the Vietnam Veterans Memorial known as the Wall. I cried for almost three hours as I looked at the Wall. I read the names from start to finish—58,000-plus buddies who died in the war, my war.

It was too much to take in. I was dying inside. I took a breather when I came across the names of my buddies.

The hours I spent there before and during the ceremony wiped me out. I was thinking too much of just the bad times there. I wiped away tears when I thought of a rocket and mortar attack that occurred on September 22, 1969 at the Bridge Ramp. I relived that night as if it were yesterday. I couldn't stop crying. I kept telling myself that all those lives had been lost as well as that fuckin' war, and we were hated when we came back. That was probably the first time I'd ever felt like a loser.

Then, some twenty-three years later, in 2005, there I was down in the pit for the fourth 9/11 anniversary ceremony standing as honor guard for DDC and listening to the names being called off. That got me thinking about my 'Nam buddies who hadn't made it back and the 168 who had died in Oklahoma City inscribed on the backs of the "chairs" at that memorial. Every one of these major events had me thinking of all the survivors, especially those who are close and dear to me. I know that if I have to deal with another major sorrow in my life similar to any one of the events, I might not have any tears left to shed.

CHAPTER 77

I N THE SUMMER of 2003, I was asked by a dear friend of mine, Janice Cilento, LSMW, who at the time was a social worker with the St. Vincent's Catholic Medical Center–WTC Healing Services and also Behavioral Health Services, if I could get about fifteen to twenty people, survivors who had been in the towers that fateful morning, to go to the Pit at Ground Zero for a private visit.

I was surprised to learn that a majority of them hadn't been able to go to the site or even anywhere close to it; the trauma lingered in their hearts. She said it would mean a lot to them, her, and me since I was a survivor as well. How could I have said no?

I told her it would take one phone call to a very good friend of mine who was working on rebuilding the site. He had lost his brother on 9/11. "For you, Charlie K, anytime, anything!" he said. He gave me two dates and times and asked me to firm them up. I told him it would take place with no media coverage. The people involved would be going back to a place that still left them on edge.

I called Janice with the news. She told me that a few of the people were very apprehensive about going there but that she had reassured them that they would be in very good hands—another survivor of that morning who had also survived the terrorist attack of '93, ten months at Ground Zero, and Vietnam. She had told them I'd be honored to take them there and would stay close by their side. The date was set.

I was to meet Janice and the survivors at Albany and Greenwich Streets, enter the site, and go down the ramp into the Pit. I felt a surge of emotions; we bonded. I sensed that every moment I'd spend with them there would be important to all of us, especially me. I planned to take them to the Pit and let them take it all in. When they were ready, I'd take them to where the North and then the South Towers had stood.

It was a powerful and memorable time. I saw them as a group and then as individuals reliving their time at that place that morning. I was standing across the street. I couldn't imagine what it must have been like to have been trying to get down the stairways that morning. I wondered if any of them would ask me how I was able to come back there and do my job. I felt for them as I saw tears flowing down their cheeks.

We spent some time at the first footprint. I asked them if they were ready for the other footprint. They said yes. One survivor put her arm around mine and asked me where I'd been and what I'd seen that morning. I told her but left out the gory details.

After a while, they said they were ready to leave. They thanked me and gave me hugs for making the day possible. We shed tears. When we got back up to street level, no one said good-bye to the others or me. We simply knew we were all connected. I felt I'd be seeing them soon.

I was right. One week later, Janice called me with the news that the groups' president, Tania Head, wanted me to join their organization, the WTC Survivors Network Organization. I felt deeply honored. Tania had wanted me to share my experiences of being a survivor with the group. I wished I had had someone like Janice Cilento to talk to when I came home from 'Nam; I needed to express what I'd gone through there that had left a huge hole in my stomach and heart. Some of those experiences were still bottled up deep inside.

During my meetings with the organization, I learned about what the survivors had experienced. Tania told me to share anything I wanted with them. I felt that she was someone who really cared what I'd been through. I open up about a lot of things that had affected me about that morning, and she did the same. After hearing what she had been through, she went up on a pedestal in my mind. As I was leaving our fourth meeting, I looked at everyone there and wondered why there wasn't a memorial to honor all the survivors of that horrific morning civilians and first responders alike. They should be honored and recognized for what they had accomplished there. I started visualizing a simple but symbolic and meaningful (and inexpensive) memorial to honor them. My mind told me, *Don't forget about all those volunteers there as well!*

I figured my wild heart would once again lead me. I started sketching a fountain that would honor everyone who had been there with human shapes staring at the fountain. I wanted to call it the Living Memorial. I remembered the Oklahoma City memorial that honored survivors there.

I enjoyed seeing my memorial take shape more than I had the other designs I had come up with probably because it was on my terms, no one else's, and I didn't need a mission statement to relate to it because I felt my memorial by itself expressed and displayed its own mission statement, no words needed. I've included it in my book, and you can also find it at www.survivorsnet.org. I wish there was a way of knowing what you thought of it.

Try to envision what I was trying to convey in my Living Memorial. to millions in Manhattan and across the country. Since that horrible tragedy, most of the members in the WTC Survivors Network Organization have worked diligently to educate, inform, and inspire hope and healing in New York City, across the country, and around the world. Maybe some have forgotten how hard it must be to move on with life especially for the 2,792 families who had lost their loved ones. We will never forget them. The thousands of survivors in the complex that morning have had to struggle finding a new normal. Maybe some have forgotten the heroic efforts of hundreds of first responders and the uniformed services who gave their efforts once more at Ground Zero and at the Fresh Kills site on Staten Island. My Living Memorial is for them as well as the civilians who were in harm's way that morning and all those who were involved in the recovery and cleanup operations for ten months 24/7 up on the Pile, at the barges, and in the Pit. Maybe some have forgotten all the military personnel who spent their time around Ground Zero and elsewhere providing security; this Living Memorial is for them. Maybe some have forgotten the thousands of thousands of volunteers (it has been stated that they numbered over 100,000) who put their ordinary lives on pause and devoted countless hours to helping wherever was needed; my Living Memorial is for them as well.

On the morning of September 11, 2001, thousands of people were already working in the Twin Towers and the other five buildings that made up the beautiful WTC. At 8:46 a.m., American Airlines flight 11 struck 1WTC, the North Tower. At 9:02 a.m., United Airlines flight 175 struck 2WTC, the South Tower. At 9:59 a.m., 2WTC collapsed. At 10:28 a.m., 1WTC collapsed. The WTC no longer existed.

To ensure that all the survivors of these events will not be forgotten, I offer this respectful tribute to every one of them. My Living Memorial has two distinct features among its three entities that complement each other: the fountain and its base are surrounded by numerous three-dimensional figures. These three entities will somehow unify the symbolic elements of that day. The lasting image we've seen for so many months are symbolically represented by the seven shapes on the fountain. They are there to remember the victims in a special way though my memorial is to honor the survivors.

The three-dimensional silhouettes honor each individual, and the base of the fountain represents the strength and remembrance that holds all New Yorkers together. I would like to see this memorial placed in an area in the site not near either of the towers' footprints. I want survivors to share their incredible stories of hope and survival in first person in a separate setting and be able to educate the people who will visit the memorial and feel its impact. If you ever meet one of these honored individuals while you're there, they might come out and say who they are and what they did), then my memorial will truly be a Living Memorial.

Frank Lloyd Wright said, "Architecture is the relationship of visual and spatial perceptions to conceptual abstractions"; I'm hoping my design for this memorial captures what I saw that fateful morning and will continue to preserve all the feelings that stayed in me during my time at Ground Zero and have them reflect onto the visitors. I wanted a dedication plaque close to the fountain and the silhouettes that resembles the façade of the lower floors of the Twin Towers; I wanted stainless steel "forks" or "trees" with clear glass panels between them and supporting another piece of clear glass above. The glass will be lit in in this plaque, but the glass will be frosted instead symbolically representing the dust that was everywhere after the collapse of the Twin

Towers. The inscription on the glass will read, "Ye Are the Salt of the Earth".

The base of the fountain has a deep meaning. The silhouettes in black represent you. There will be twenty of them (nine plus eleven) to represent the survivors; they will appear to be standing still in awe of what has just occurred. They will be from four foot ten to six foot three and be from two feet to three feet wide. They will be four inches thick, and their sides would be frosted-white glass lit from within. The glass will glow from dusk to dawn symbolic of the line, "Ye Are the Light of the World".

I attended the tenth anniversary tribute to the victims of the Oklahoma City bombing of the Alfred P. Murrah Federal Building. On the eve of the anniversary, I took part in a beautiful and moving vigil. When the ceremony was over, I walked over to the 168 "chairs" that honored their loved ones. They were beginning to glow brightly. I came upon two survivors standing by one of the lost loved one's chairs talking to two local first responders. When they saw me, they stopped talking and looked at me. We stood like statues in that light given off by the chairs. Our feelings were mutual; they knew I was a survivor of 9/11 and had spent months at Ground Zero. We were reflecting on our fateful days.

At that moment, my wild heart gave me the finishing touch I'd wanted for my silhouettes. When I got home, I went to my design and made a slight change—I changed the black marble I had wanted for the fronts and backs of the silhouettes to mirrors. So now, as you stand in front of a silhouette, you'll see yourself as a survivor whether as a Ground Zero worker, a civilian, a volunteer, or any military person who served there. Each of the silhouettes will have a plaque dedicated to a civilian, a NYPD, FDNY, or PAPD personnel, or a construction worker. There were many fire fighters and police officers from other municipalities; they will be noted by a special plaque.

The fountain will be nine feet eleven inches tall. The seven pieces of glass became an abstract collage symbolizing the seven buildings that made up the WTC complex. The two elongated, glass blocks will represent the box beams that made of the façade and were seen leaning in opposite directions, projecting outward and upward, symbolizing the façade sections of 1WTC and 2WTC that were left standing once the dust had settled. That image has been embedded in our minds and hearts forever.

The other five glass blocks symbolize 3WTC, 4WTC, 5WTC, 6WTC, and 7WTC. The surface area of the overall collage on the base is within an eight-foot-six-inch square; those 102 inches symbolize the 102 minutes that shocked the world. The placement, shapes, and sizes of these five glass blocks symbolize these five buildings as the way they were. The block that represents 7WTC (which stood across Vesey Street and not in the sixteen acres) is in the center of the other four glass blocks in the fountain. When 7WTC collapsed, it was the last remaining building of the entire WTC. I had this block in particular display a flow of water filling the top surface and flowing over its sides to the base.

All the glass blocks will be lit from within as will be the silhouettes, symbolic for the second line inscribed on the dedication plaque, "Ye Are the Light of the World." The base of the fountain is also very symbolic; its height of 20.01 inches represents the year, the width of 9.59 feet symbolizes the time 2WTC collapsed at 9:59 a.m., and the length is 10.28 feet, symbolic of the time 1WTC collapsed at 10:28 a.m.

The water that will flow down the sides of the 7WTC block represent our tears of joy knowing that we survivors can carry on with our lives; it also represents our tears of sadness for those we lost. The water will collect in the base and be recycled to the top.

The base will be constructed of materials in a concrete mix—stone, brick, wiring, marble, tin, glass, steel, wood, paper, and cloth that symbolize the ingredients that was constantly kicked up in the ash composition that covered the site. Not shown is a flower bed approximately twenty inches wide that will display flowers from all seasons and represent the cyclical nature of healing and life.

I hope my Living Memorial will be a lasting beacon of hope, understanding, and inspiration to all who gaze upon it. I have this one last inscription etched on the side of the base: "For Those Who Did Not Survive That Fateful Day, We, the Survivors, Will Always Remember You, for You Live within Our Hearts Forever."

The time I spent on this Living Memorial stirred many fond and overwhelming emotions in me about the forty years I worked in and around the WTC. Hell, I recall something else I did in August 1966, when my boss, Mr. Harrison, told me to go the area where these towers were to be built and get as close as possible to watch the groundbreaking. He said I shouldn't miss it. Four years later, I was flying over the same area in July '70 where I flew over the North Tower seeing it almost being completed as I returned home from my tour of duty in Vietnam. Five years later, Margie and I visited the observation deck when it opened. If this Memorial Fountain ever gets built, my human-figure 3-D silhouettes could be placed somewhere in the WTC Memorial possibly by eliminating just one or two of the 200 oak trees that are proposed to be planted in the plaza. I believe this could be a fitting tribute to remember what once stood there and what we all experienced that morning. My twenty silhouettes could be in a counterclockwise spiral out and away from the Memorial Fountain going through out the plaza nearby where they could be approached by visitors and survivors alike. I believe it would be a very symbolic tribute to life and an unspoken vow from us survivors to the lost loved ones that "I was there then, and I am here now."

On October 11, 2006, the WTC Survivors Network Organization (I'm on the steering committee) and its treasurer had a special meeting with Alice Greenwald, director and curator of the National September 11 Memorial Museum. It was held at 199 Water Street in Lower Manhattan. Alice gave us a presentation of the floor plans and layout for the proposed museum. She explained how it would tie into the visitors' center and the remaining area of the memorial. Her detailed presentation was well received by the group.

I present my memorial plans to her. I showed her my poster-sized color copies of my two renderings of my design and an enlarged copy of the memorial site. I mentioned to Alice what I thought was the ideal location for my fountain and the silhouettes—one of the two voids among the trees that were as big as football fields. I made it clear that I did not want my memorial near or within sight of the two reflecting pools; that would take away from or disturb the tribute or honor that the concept of reflecting absence gave. Don't you think my Living Memorial would be something to see?

I want to acknowledge the members of the WTC Survivors Network

Organization, all of whom I consider near and dear friends. They include Janice Cilento (who first told me about this group), Richard Zimbler, Lori Mogol, Linda Gormley, Peter Miller, Brendon Chellis, Elia Zedeno, Mickey Kross, Tom Canavan, Manuel Chea, and Anne Samachson. I became closely involved with the group for most of the anniversaries at the WTC site.

It's also where I met Tania Head, the person who hoodwinked every politician in New York when the truth came out that she was a total fraud and that she hurt a lot of people in so many ways, especially the members of this wonderful organization. I was deeply hurt, but over the years, I've gotten over it and have moved on. Enough about that.

CHAPTER 78

O N JANUARY 6, 2004, the winning design for the WTC Memorial was selected—"Reflecting Absence" by Michael Arad. Go back and see what Michael Arad originally submitted in the design competition. It's not what you were shown in the newspaper or on TV, but it's still there on LMDC's WTC Design Competition website. The design shown to the public was modified and had all these trees thrown into that bare, stark, dark plaza to bring "life" to Arad's design.

After you've compared the two designs, whose would you say has more remembrance and tribute to the lost loved ones of 9/11? Which one do you think would have been built by now at far less cost and would not have required major involvement in the infrastructure below due to the majority of my entire memorial was primarily at street level? I knew the WTC site so well; I saw no need to disrupt the infrastructure in the area to build my memorial versus Arad's memorial.

I know someone who is extremely close and dear to me who was greatly affected by what she saw there and was there for only about an hour. She saw the immeasurable amount of devastation there; it was too much for her. It was on the last Sunday in October 2001 when I had Margie drive me in to work the extra shift to cover for a DDC worker who had had a family emergency. Coming out of the Brooklyn Battery Tunnel, I knew in a heartbeat that Marge's demeanor would change drastically when she could no longer see the Twin Towers.

It got kind of quiet in the car the rest of the way. We approached the armed military personnel and NYPD cruisers at the checkpoint. I took out my DDC ID and my official Ground Zero authorized pass.

I'd had to let them know I was coming and the type of vehicle I'd be in and who was with me. I figured there would be some questions about letting Marge and Noelle into the site, but I got the wave through once they saw my IDs.

As we I made our way closer to the perimeter on West Street, I saw more security guards knowing they had just gotten the okay call from the NYPD at the previous checkpoint; I didn't have to show my credentials again. Driving onto the site affected Marge. West Street was very hilly; it was covered in debris. The actual West Street was way underneath us. She looked over to where the towers had stood. She had a very strange look. I said to her sharply to get her full attention, "Marge! Once you drop me off, all you have to do is turn the car around and drive the same way out. Go back to the tunnel to get home."

She said, "Charlie, I can't drive on this! I can't do this!"

I said, "Okay, calm down. I'll turn the car around for you. Are you going home the way we just came, or do you want to go back the way you know?"

She was scared. "I want to go my usual way through the Midtown Tunnel!"

Marge, who is normally strong in stamina, surprised me. She stared out the window toward the center of the site. She looked at the façade sections of both towers leaning in different directions and asked, "What's that?"

I told her what she was looking at. She became more and more nervous by what she was seeing only a few yards away. She blurted out, "Stop!" Her comment startled Noelle, who was also gazing out the window. I stopped. "Where are we?" she asked. I slowly turned off Vesey Street to park in front of the American Express tower. I told her my office was on the thirtieth floor. She was looking at the site as if it were a set on *Twilight Zone*.

I got Noelle out of her seat. "Come on, let me take you up to my office. You'll see a different view of the site."

Ron Vega approached us driving one of our golf carts we used to get around the area. I introduced him to Marge and Noelle. Margie hardly spoke on the way up the elevator. Ron asked why I was there so early. I explained the call I'd gotten from Lou. I led Marge and Noelle to a conference room across from where the North Tower once stood. The view from the thirtieth floor was spectacular. It was Sunday, and most of the staff was off except for the field guys who were probably out on the site.

I called Marge and Noelle to the windows and pointed out what was what. Marge was trying to take it all in without saying much. I moved closer to her, and she said, "You never said it was like this! You said it was bad, but you didn't say it was *this* bad!"

Lou had walked into the room and heard Margie's comments. He said, "Uh, Charlie K, how you doing? You got a minute?" He stepped outside the room. I told Marge and Noelle I'd be right back.

When I got out, Lou asked, "Is everything okay? If you want out, just say the word."

"It's okay. She'll get over it. I'm just going to take them back down to the car. Would you like to meet my wife and daughter?"

We walked into the room, and I made the introductions. We walked back to the elevators. It was a quiet ride down and out to the car. I opened the door to the driver's side and let Noelle into the backseat. "Charlie, how do I get to the Midtown Tunnel from here?" she asked. Noelle was on her knees looking out the back window not having the slightest idea of what was going on in her mom's head or heart or mine for that matter. Marge was overwhelmed not knowing what was where. Noelle asked, "Daddy, aren't you going to work? Isn't Mommy going to take me home? Are you and Mommy staying here?"

Marge was mesmerized at the sight of the façade of the North Tower just leaning there. She was probably recalling that we'd once stood there to have our picture taken when Noelle was about six. I put my hands on her shoulders and turned her away from the very strange place she was in. I walked her over to the driver's side and helped her get in. I told her to buckle up. I leaned in and gave her a quick kiss on the lips. Noelle came forward to get one too. I buckled Noelle into her seat and said, "Mommy will take you home now."

Marge was still staring out at the site. "Charlie, is it worse out on the site? I really didn't realize the magnitude of the destruction here compared to what we've been seeing on TV."

I said nothing. I gave a wave good-bye and said, "Safe trip home. Call me when you get there."

I watched them leave the site at about ten miles per hour heading north onto the Westside Highway. When they got beyond the security gate, I waved again, but I don't think Marge looked back. I think she'd seen enough. I felt I was wrong to have brought them to the site. I knew the horrible image would leave a lasting image in Margie's mind and most definitely in her heart. I'm still mad at myself for letting her take me into the city that day to see what I was seeing every night I was there.

There's one lasting image I'll always have with me; it's one of many photos I took at the site. I took hundreds—possibly thousands—of photos to document DDC's work there. I took the photo about two in the morning on February 9, 2002. The entire scene I saw screamed out, "Take this shot!" The magnitude of what stood before me—the lighting, the surroundings, and the people in the photo—became a well-known photo. I remember when I was finishing up navy boot camp; I'd gotten orders to attend the Naval Intelligence School. They'd tested me and discovered I had what's called stereoscopic vision as well as 20/10 vision. I was told I had this Superman power to see and hear things in stereo whether I wanted too or not. (Come on! That was a joke!)

Stereoscopic means I can see the height, depth, and overall shape of a building and can estimate the distance between objects in a particular—usually an aerial—photograph. It's like having some kind of 3-D binocular vision without the binoculars. I was told that my ability would be quite useful to the navy when it came to aerial surveillance. I was told that if I'd get shot down on any aerial reconnaissance mission and captured, I'd have to swallow a certain kind of pill to shut me up for good. I simply said, "No thank you! Not for me." Instead, I was assigned to the Aircraft Maintenance Division in Pensacola.

Getting back to this amazing photo. Maybe I thought that I had the best perception and visualization and that this would be a perfect photo. It exudes the uninhibited feeling of what it was like to be down in the Pit among all that devastation. It depicts one of the many grapplers on the site. The operator had let the jaws open up completely as they hovered above a team of rescue workers and first responders wanting to remove the remains they might come upon after a load of debris was lifted. I remember exactly where I was when I took this man vs. machine shot at the perfect time. I signed a release so my agency could submit it and some other photo to a photo contest. It was the first photo contest ever for *ENR—Engineering News-Record*, a worldwide construction industry magazine. Well over 800 photos from around the world were submitted to the contest; they had to be great shots that touched the judges artistically and told a story.

On January 23, 2003, I received a package in the mail at DDC from that magazine telling me I was one of the TOP TEN Photos. The letter stated that out of the 800 photos, many of which were very good, the judges thought mine was one of the best. It appeared on the cover of *ENR*'s December 30–January 6, 2003 issue. They also sent me a copy of the issue and a certificate of achievement for my photography award, an acknowledgement of my success. I was totally surprised by that awesome honor. I'm proud of the photo, which is included in this book. Everyone who's seen it has said, "Wow, Charlie! That's one powerful photo you took!"

CHAPTER 79

I N JANUARY 2005, I heard about another design competition for a
memorial to be built as a tribute to United Airlines flight 93, which
crashed in Shanksville, Pennsylvania, on 9/11. It was to be built in the
field where the aircraft crashed and killed forty crew and passengers,
American heroes, and there was no mention of the terrorists thank God.

The passengers had stood up to these terrorists as their airliner
was heading for Washington, DC, and they probably saved the lives
of many on the ground. I refer to my memorial design as a prominent
memorial that could be seen from the sky and the ground. The crew
and passengers deserve the honor; they courageously did what they had
to do in the sky, an unusual battlefield in today's world. I wanted my
memorial to exemplify the honor and respect due them. I wanted it to
be an inspiration to all who visited it. The memorial would symbolically
merge ground and sky. I wanted everyone who visited the memorial to
think, *Here lie our heroes with the wind beneath these wings.*

The wings would have been made of clear polyurethane the same
size as the wings on the Boeing 757-200 airliner. They would have red,
white, and blue stripes, and *FLT #93* would be stenciled across the wing.
An American flag would wave from a short, angled flagpole at the tip
of the wing.

The dimensions of my memorial are also symbolic. The height from
the ground to the tip of the flagpole is 911 inches—75 feet 11 inches
tall—for the date. The wings would be oriented to the direction the
airplane was going. Each wing would be supported by forty-foot-wide

circular bases, the forty representing the lives lost. The bases would be forty-two inches tall, the height of the plane's tires.

I added some very important features to symbolize the separate seating areas—first class/business class and coach. Family members would sit in the first class/business section and visitors in the coach section. I also have a visitors' center, an archives and collectives storage facility, and a maintenance facility. I knew I needed to include an eternal flame there as well.

I designed it this way because I wanted all flying over it to see it's *A* shape that includes a fountain, a huge American flag in the family seating area, and a huge *U* (for United) in the visitors' seating area. The letters *FLT* (for flight) will be sky blue, and *#93* (the flight number) will be white. They will be on the illuminated panels that will conceal the three buildings.

My tribute to this hallowed ground will be my Memorial Fountain that will be forty feet long and forty feet wide; a frosted-glass shaped fuselage will be ninety-three inches long (for the flight number) and 10.10 inches wide (for the time it crashed). The fuselage will be lit from within.

Under and to the rear of the fuselage will be four tear-drop shaped pedestals representing the four locations of the crashes—the two in New York and the one at the Pentagon in addition to this one. Below these four pedestals are six hexagonal tombstone slabs symbolic of the events that occurred that morning: 1WTC attacked, 2WTC attacked, the Pentagon attacked, 2WTC collapsed, 1WTC collapsed, and United Airlines flight 93 crashing to the ground. Each slab will be nine feet eleven inches for the date and twelve inches high—symbolic of the nine letters in September and the total of the year 2001, three. All of this will sit atop a forty-inch-high base with a multifaceted, bluish-glass façade symbolic of the color of the cloudless sky that morning.

I was expressing my deepest feelings by having my "tears" (drops of water) when I first heard about this incident, and the continuation of tears producing more water can be seen coming from the bottom rear of the fuselage and watching them spill down onto the first pedestal. As the tears increase, more water will flow down onto the next pedestal representing all the tears we'll be shedding. The flowing water continues down to its final resting place, the fountain's base (where it is recycled). If one was to stand at the foot of this fountain base and look down into where all those tears gathered they would see their reflections and the clarity of each hero's courage.

As people leave this memorial site, they will notice a heart-shaped stone approximately forty inches high standing on its point with a plaque in the shape of the aircraft in the middle. It will be lit at dusk and bear the inscription, "Although no aircraft may ever fly over this sacred ground again and have the ability to see its dedication and honor, something far greater than anything man can make will always have perfect sight looking over it … the resting place of our nation's heroes."

My design was never considered, but that's okay. The thought I put into it and the words I wanted inscribed there will live in my heart forever.

I hope the design chosen will be the utmost tribute to these heroes who did their best by sacrificing their lives for every one of us. God rest their souls.

CHAPTER 80

APRIL 3, 2005, was sunny and beautiful. Mike Kenny, Ron Vega, and I attended a special ceremony in Manhattan in honor of the medical examiner's office whose personnel performed a very arduous task working at Ground Zero. The ceremony took place at the Church of St. Francis of Assisi at 135 W. 31st Street in Midtown Manhattan; Fr. Brian Jordan, a Jesuit priest who was constantly at the WTC site, presided.

The three of us wore our DDC Disaster Recovery Team jackets (rust-colored, zippered, L. L. Bean jackets) to show our respect by letting people know we were there to acknowledge their work. We also thought we would get some recognition too for our time working at the site.

I picked up Ron at his house in Astoria, and we took the 59th Street Bridge in lieu of going through the Midtown Tunnel. Mike drove in from West Nyack, north of the city. We stayed in touch over our radio-equipped cell phones; whoever got there first was to save a parking spot for the other.

Ron and I got there first. I took up two parking spaces. (I know what you're thinking, but can anyone please tell me why they placed fire hydrants throughout the city right by perfectly good parking spaces?) Ron and I were watching for Mike. Ron called him on the radio. "Mike, what's your twenty?" Of course we were both ready for his comeback. "Hell, I didn't bring any money with me, but I'm four blocks away!" We chuckled to let him know we appreciated his humor and most of all being on time and close.

A van pulled up alongside of me; the driver thought I was leaving.

The driver motioned to me that I should move up or out so he could park. Most New Yorkers would do something like that without saying a word thinking we know the sign language. Most New Yorkers would have ignored him, but I had a little more class than most people. I motioned with my hand that he should move along little doggie. I happened to notice there were three others in the van with him all dressed up. I tried to spot Mike. I heard someone trying to get my attention. The driver was being persistent about parking there. "Excuse me," he said, "but could you please move your car so I could get in? We're running a little late for a function."

I replied, "Sorry, but we're also running a little late for our function. This extra space is for my buddy, who will be here in two seconds."

"You can't save a parking space for somebody who isn't here, so please move!"

Before I could answer him, my radio chirped. Mike said, "I can see you, Charlie K! Don't you dare give my spot to that van! Tell him I'm on my way down the street."

The driver gave me this most disgusted look; he was thoroughly pissed off at me (which I guess is worse than being just pissed off). He looked at Ron's and my jackets, mostly mine, since I was only a foot away. I know he noticed the name of our agency, which was in block letters. He gave me another disgusting look and said, "Thank you very much, Charlie K!" in a funny kind of way. I was tempted to say "You're welcome" but didn't.

I still can't figure out why New Yorkers have all this anger stored up inside over parking spots. That's why they have parking garages all over the city. He drove off with that pissed-off look still on his face. Mike pulled up and blew his horn. "Move your car! Come on! Who the hell are you to take up two parking spaces? And who the hell were you talking to? We're running late!"

I gave him one of my looks and said, "Beats me!" I moved my car up, and Mike parked. We beat feet to the church across the street. Mike said, "Doesn't that guy know who he was talking to? I thought everyone knew Charlie K!" I said, "Now he does."

We entered the church and sat in a pew. We saw Fr. Jordan at the pulpit. The church was about 80 percent full. I noticed four chairs on the altar. He said, "I'm waiting for our main guests to show up." He pointed down the aisle. "Okay, I see they've arrived!" Everyone turned when he announced that the chief medical examiner was in God's house, but I didn't hear the rest of what he said. My brain (and I think Mike's and Ron's also) got a huge blast; it felt like it had exploded. In came the pissed-off gentleman and the three who were in the van with him.

Have you ever wanted to become totally invisible? I have. Right then. I felt I was a dead man. I'm sure Ron and Mike were thinking the same. I was more concerned that there I was sitting at the end of the pew with this big bull's-eye on my face. I knew once he got up to the altar, he'd spot me. He already knew my name. I started praying to God and all the saints including the number-one saint out there, H. F. Saint, who wrote *The Invisible Man*. God knew I wanted to turn into a caterpillar right then. Where's God when you need him and especially when you're in his house? I should have had first dibs on him. He was probably visiting Mr. Lucky and didn't even drive!

I think my prayers were answered. The men sat at a spot where they didn't have a clear view of me. *Thank you, God.* I was ashamed of what I'd done in the street. I asked God for forgiveness. My palms were clammy, and I had this pain in my stomach. I was preparing myself to have a coughing fit that would allow me to cover my face if the chief medical examiner decided to walk down the aisle.

I noticed a woman behind me who reminded me of my mom, standing there and gazing at me. I got this feeling that she was glancing at me numerous times. I thought she might have been in the van earlier. I turned and gave her a smile. She looked at me radiantly and smiled beautifully. It seemed to be an acknowledgment of something I'd done for her. I'd never seen her before, but her endearing look was the type my mom would give me when I'd done something she was proud of. She was trying to tell me something. I asked, "Excuse me, but do you know me? I would definitely have remembered you if we'd met."

She grasped my hand. "I couldn't help myself, but you and your two friends right now are like guardian angels to me." I was taken aback by her comment and more relaxed that she wasn't with you-know-whom. "Were the three of you working at the WTC site? I see the words on the back of your jackets, DDC Disaster Recovery Team."

I smiled. "Yes. My two buddies and I were there till the very end!"

Her eyes were getting misty. Ron and Mike turned around to see whom I was talking to. They all shook hands. She said I had looked deeply worried before. (Boy, she had me pegged right.) I told her whatever it was would pass. She told me, "I'm Allison Crowthers, Welles's mom." I was thinking that it was another surprising coincidence that I was meeting another woman named Allison in a church again that I felt related to 9/11 and Ground Zero. I wanted to talk with her. It was as if I should have known who Welles was.

"Hi, Allison. I'm Charlie K. Did Welles happen to work at the site?"

Allison's eyes were starting to tear up. "No, but he was there that morning." She paused. She tried to swallow. She gave me this real faraway look.

I said, "So was I."

She told me he'd been in the South Tower doing everything he could to help others get out but never made it out himself. I got a huge lump in my throat. I couldn't have said anything if I'd tried. She asked, "By any chance did you see him?"

I looked at her feeling her loss and pain. I leaned over to give her a comforting hug. "I'm so sorry for your loss, Allison. My deepest condolences to you. Yes, I was there that morning, but I was across the street from the North Tower."

She hugged me and whispered, "I know you and your two buddies did the best you could do while you were there. And to be there for all that time must have been hard on your families. I know that my son, Welles, would want you to have this, Charlie K."

She reached into her bag and pulled out a red cloth. I could see some kind of white pattern on it. I started to unfold it and saw it was shaped into a bandanna. That's when I knew who I was talking to. I thanked her for the lovely gift.

Her son, Welles, was the Man with the Red Bandanna. He was noted as being a very courageous young man who was leading people to safety that morning at the WTC. He was seen wearing a red bandanna over his mouth to protect himself from the smoke and dust. Many survivors mentioned his heroics and how he helped numerous people down the stairways and showed people the way off some floors to get to the stairways. He tragically died when the building collapsed. I was honored to have met this hero's mom in a peaceful setting, a place of worship, and receive his red bandanna. Welles Crothers was a true hero.

The ceremony ended. The three of us got while the getting was good. I didn't want the chief medical examiner to lay eyes on me. I wiped down where I'd sat with a paper towel I had in my back pocket to wipe any of my traceable DNA away just to play it safe. But I knew the medical examiner could have traced me; he knew my name and that I worked for the DDC.

We said our good-byes to Allison and left peacefully before our jackets could be seen. It was a very exciting and memorable day. I somehow knew I'd see Allison again.

CHAPTER 81

IN APRIL 2005, I felt proud and honored to meet some of the survivors and family members of the Alfred P. Murrah Federal Building bombing that had occurred on April 19, 1995, in Oklahoma City. I was invited to attend their tenth anniversary ceremony by becoming a member of the nonprofit organization September Space run by Lisa Orloff.

When I got out there, I realized we all had something in common—we had all survived horrible events perpetrated by terrorists. I had the utmost respect for these people; I'd heard what they had experienced at 9:01 a.m. that day. The attacks on the towers had taken place at 8:46 a.m. and 9:04 a.m.; the times somehow bonded us. We felt like one big extended family, and we truly love each other.

I want to acknowledge some of my extended family, dear friends of mine. They have made my journey so special and have given me the answer that I've been searching for to make my Living Memorial more powerful. I wish all my readers knew some of the survivors, family members who lost loved ones—the first responders and those who worked in the building. They are all in my heart and will remain there always: Richard Williams; Susan Walton and her husband, Richard; Dot Hill; Joanne Hutchison; Betty Robbins; Paul Howell; Kimberly Ritchie; Tom Brewer; Jenny Parsley; Vicki Hamm; Doris Jones; John Cole; Ken Thompson; Calvin Moser; Steve Fields; Brad Robison; and Phyllis Poe and especially her husband Jack.

Jack O'Brian Poe is a chaplain with the Oklahoma City Police who works with the Department of Homeland Security and the U.S.

Secret Service, and is a retired army colonel. Jack is one hell of a guy. If someone were to ask me what Jack Poe was like, I'd say, "I'd have to take all the wonderful and unforgettable traits and personalities of my closest buddies I had in 'Nam and put them in a blender. I'd purée them and pour them into a mold. That would be Jack O'Brian Poe."

I'm sure all my friends in OKC know I love them dearly for a special reason. I'm especially grateful for having been there on April 18, the evening before their tenth commemoration; as I mentioned, that's when I got the idea for my Living Memorial.

I still hope my Living Memorial will be displayed somewhere in the plaza or perhaps elsewhere. I believe it was on May 1, 2005 when I finally put the final touches of colors into and on my memorial rendering and some closing words needed to complete my write-up describing my design. It felt as if a great load was lifted off my shoulders. All my emotions were at peace and merging my life into another world filled with serenity.

I was there again for their fourteenth anniversary ceremony. Compared to the previous four years, the weather that day was something to be reckoned with—damp, windy, and cold. I sat on a stone seat that ran the length of each one of the raised, grassy, stepped levels that led up to the plaza where the Survivor Tree is located. I looked at the reflecting pool and at the two gates at both ends. I saw a couple standing nearby. They looked about my age. I figured they were tourists, visitors, or just locals like myself being that I'd been going there for five years. They seemed unsure of where to sit. So yours truly, Mr. Friendly, spoke up. "Excuse me! By any chance are you looking for a place to sit? If you are, I insist you join me right here!" I pointed to the empty space beside me.

They thanked me, smiled, and sat. We shook hands, and introduced myself as Charlie K. I said everyone in Oklahoma City knew me as that. I mentioned why I was there, how I got to go there, and how I loved coming there especially to see the most beautiful memorial in the country. I'd been sharing my time and life with my extended family, the survivors there—first responders and rescue recovery workers who toiled there in 1995 every April 19. I told them about being a 9/11 survivor who had spent ten months at Ground Zero. I felt I should be there too. I told them

I was there with some of my buddies, two DDC Ground Zero volunteers and a WTC survivor who had been injured from the rubble in the plaza.

They introduced themselves as husband and wife, Ian and Cari Burnett. They were from Palos Verdes, California. I told them I'd been born in San Diego. They said they were there for the ceremony too. The ceremony was about to start, so I said, "Nice to meet you!"

I had my DDC Ground Zero jacket on, and I was so glad I'd worn it. Ten minutes into the ceremony, my dear friend Joann, a 4/19 survivor, was shivering. I offered it to her, but she declined. I knew she was cold; all she had on was a dress—no jacket or sweater, and she was shivering. She was family to me. I took off my jacket and put it over her shoulders. That made me feel warm.

It was a beautiful, emotional, and touching ceremony as always. It was fourteen years later, but I could still see and feel that the people, the family member and survivors, were still greatly affected.

After the ceremony, the 4/19 Outreach Organization hosted a breakfast at some country club. People were told to make sure anyone from NYC got a ride. I told Ian and Cari that it had been nice to chat with them. I headed to the parking lot for my ride. We arrived in about twenty minutes; we were in a room big enough for five hundred. A huge table that could seat forty was in one corner. But before I could get to it, I had to pass a massive table covered with everything you could think of having for breakfast, and it all looked delicious.

I made my way to the table and was surprised to see Ian and Cari near Brad Robison. *What are they doing here?* There was plenty of laughs, conversation, and picture taking going on. I asked Brad about Ian and Cari; he said that he had seen me talking to them and thought I knew them.

Brad insisted they join him and us for breakfast. Brad is a great guy. He reminds me of someone else. Me! Breakfast was memorable. After breakfast, we were scheduled to go to the Memorial Museum, which I was looking forward to visiting again. I find it hard to walk through the room there dedicated to the nineteen children who had died there that day. I was hoping for the stamina to read about each one of them. That room breaks my heart.

I talked more with Ian and Cari at the museum. Ian had been

there on April 19, 1995. He'd been a fireman with the Torrance Fire Department who had flown to Oklahoma City with another fireman because of their knowledge of rescue/recovery operations in heavily damaged buildings. They had brought a new tool then, something that could cut through rebar like butter. They could cut it with one shot that would slice like a blade through metal. Pull the trigger, cut the rebar. It sounded like an amazing tool.

Ian told Tom and Sam more about this tool; Cari listened to every word. Her eyes were getting a little misty. A small crowd was gathering around us. Ian and Cari stepped over to look at another display in the room. I saw Tom and Sam talking with two women and a group of junior-high girls. Tom called me over. They were talking about the bombings in Oklahoma City and 9/11. Tom said, "Charlie K is also a survivor of 9/11 and Vietnam."

As I was talking, I saw Ian and Cari close by. I motioned Ian over and told the group that Ian had been a fireman in California who had flown to Oklahoma City to help with rescue and recovery. Before you knew it, a group of ten or more were listening to us four guys talking about the bombing and 9/11. The women and girls weren't from Oklahoma City and were finding it interesting to hear from survivors, rescue recovery people, and a 'Nam vet.

They thanked us for what we had done. The four of us guys and Cari went into the next display room feeling great about what we'd just done. Ian walked around this glass display case in the middle of the room and exclaimed, "I don't believe it! That's the tool I brought here!" He said it had been lost hours later and he'd never gotten it back. He explained to us how it worked. It was an amazing tool. We told him to let the museum staff know about that. He looked so happy and proud about finding it fourteen years later. I thought that was a big surprising coincidence. I mean, to be in OKC and meet someone out of the blue, invite him to sit down next to you at a memorial service, and he turns out to have been a rescue/recovery worker as I had been. He goes there for the first time in fourteen years later and finds a tool he'd been talking about earlier on display. What a fantastic visit. We had tickets to see an NBC interview given by Anne Curry, so we said our good-byes.

Those were precious moments talking about the Oklahoma City

bombing, 9/11, Ground Zero, and 'Nam. I didn't want it to end. I have a photo that was taken at Joann's house after her delicious Italian Night dinner she's given every year since then. This group photo has starting from the left, standing, Rick Lawson; his wife Kelly holding their son, Teagan; Jack Poe (OKC responder); Beverly Rankin (OKC survivor); Tom Canavan (WTC survivor); Susan Walton (OKC survivor); her husband Richard; Jim "Mack" McDade (WTC volunteer); Joanne Hutchison (OKC survivor); Ian Burnett (California responder); Tom Brewer (OKC responder); Janet Beck (OKC survivor); Mike Kenny (WTC responder); Ian's wife, Cari; and Sam Knedum. Kneeling on the floor is Jack's wife, Phyllis, and of course yours truly.

Those who didn't make it into this photo were Ron Vega (WTC responder) and his wife, Judy; Dot Hill (OKC survivor); Joanne's Mom, Irene; Joanne's husband, Gary; Kimberly Ritchie; Paul Howell; and Brad Robison, who had to go and get another piece of Joanne's delicious chocolate cake.

Every one of these Oklahomans are now whom I refer to as my extended family, and I love every one of them dearly. Also, my dear friend and good buddy, Richard Williams, who was not present this year in Oklahoma City, is also a survivor of the April 19 bombing and a 'Nam vet.

CHAPTER 82

It's May 18, 2007, and I'm sharing a ride with some of my fellow members of the WTC Survivors Network Organization to a school in Montville, New Jersey. We were scheduled to be there by eight thirty for breakfast before we spoke to the kids there. We were to meet the school principal and a few of the teachers at the Robert M. Lazar Middle School for their Living Lessons program in which kids learn from and interact with survivors of all types. The kids are encouraged to learn tolerance, acceptance, and understanding. The school is made up of mostly fifth and sixth graders.

We were to receive a packet when we arrived at the school parking lot entrance as to the time we were to show up to various classrooms. There was a school floor plan with highlighted areas of what was in what location. After the greetings, the entire group was directed to the library to relax, have some breakfast, and ask any questions that may come to mind to the teachers there who were serving the breakfast.

I was looking forward to talking about whatever they wanted—9/11, my time at Ground Zero, Vietnam, or others. Due to all the commotion in the school lobby signing in, filling out name tags, picking up our packets, I somehow got lost when some of my fellow survivors who I had walked in with hustled off to get some breakfast. I assumed they had headed over to the library. It wasn't a big deal—no eggs benedict, I mean—but all I wanted was coffee and a donut.

I looked over the floor plans and figured like any new student there I'd get lost but would probably meet some interesting people on my way back to where I should have been in the first place. I took the first corridor I came to hoping it would lead me to the library. I saw some teachers in the hallway. I had ten minutes to get to the library. "Could someone please direct me to the library? I'm lost. I'm one of the survivors, and I don't want to be stranded here with no food!"

One teacher, who didn't show his face, asked, "What the hell do you mean you've lost some survivors and you need some food? What the hell are you doing here in the first place?"

I was shocked at his outburst, and I thought some of the other teachers were too. I did a double-take and asked loudly enough for the entire school to hear, "What am I doing here? What the hell are you doing here?" I couldn't believe I was seeing my nephew, Derek Lynn, my sister Marianne's youngest son.

He approached me with an outstretched hand that I humorously brushed off in my usual humorous way that I've always done with him and gave him an embrace and a soft pat on the cheek. "Cut the crap, Derek. I may be one of the speakers here today, but I'm still your uncle! Where the hell's the food?"

The other teachers had no idea what had just taken place until Derek and I broke out laughing. "Hi Uncle Charlie!" He introduced me to the other teachers and led me to the library. I'd known he was a teacher in New Jersey but had no idea he was at that school—a surprising coincidence!

I made it to the library and saw the rest of my group enjoying a beautiful arrangement of assorted breakfast treats. Someone asked me, "What happened to you? Where did you go?"

I said, "Detention. I didn't have a hallway pass!"

Everyone laughed and went back to their treats.

A teacher told us to review our packets and find out what classroom we had to find first. I was set to go on this learning adventure for these students. I wondered if my nephew would be in any of the classrooms I was speaking in. I had a pretty good idea about what I'd talk about— being there on 9/11 and my time at Ground Zero.

I first talked to a class of fifth graders. They stared at me as if I had a bull's-eye on my chest. Everything seemed to be going great; they were respectful until I started my story. As soon as I mentioned that my first night at Ground Zero reminded me of my time in Vietnam, they stared at me intensely. Many hands shot up. Everyone wanted to be called on first, which gave me the impression they wanted to know about Vietnam more than they did about 9/11. I wasn't prepared to talk about that or for that matter express my feelings about the war especially to a group of fifth graders.

Derek walked in. I gave myself a little breathing room before I started by pointing to the back of the room and asked if anyone there had Mr. Lynn for a teacher. Everyone's hands went up again as they turned to look to where he was standing. Derek said, "I'm honored and proud to say this is my Uncle Charlie!"

The students turned to me and gave me their undivided attention whether I wanted it or not. (Hell, I knew I should have been a teacher. I probably would have been a damn good teacher at that.) I must have answered about fifteen or twenty questions about 'Nam and one or two about the WTC site.

It was time for me to leave for my next classroom. Before I could even make it to the door, a lot of the students wanted to shake my hand as they went about saying thank you. I even had one student salute me. The session I had with these kids was absolutely great; their questions were easy, but at times, I had to restrain myself from going there with my answers. (Some things should remain and stay locked up in the vault and one's heart.) But I found the session somewhat therapeutic.

My next class was twenty minutes later on the other side of the school. My last class was after lunch. I was greeted by a cool surprise; before I had the chance to tell the class who I was, the entire class greeted me with, "Good morning Uncle Charlie!" I guessed word had traveled fast around the school as to who I was.

During the break, I was saying to myself that I was extremely glad I was able to find the time from my busy schedule of the construction projects I was involved in back in NYC to get away for this event. I spoke for about fifteen to twenty minutes to each of my classes. I got a little choked up seeing two girls to my right tearing up as I spoke about that fateful morning. One asked me if I'd thought I was going to die when the towers came down. I smiled and said, "Yes, but not there and not that morning. As I was running for my life, I thought I'd be living to be at least a hundred and twenty." That cracked up the class. I said thank you to the class and walked out.

I'm sure Judy Gothelf or Joe Keiser had no idea that Derek Lynn was my nephew. I'll just blame Derek for speaking up to me in the corridor early that morning; if he hadn't, I might have spent the day there not knowing he was teaching there. I hope Judy and Joe know that it was an absolute pleasure to share the gifts of my story participating in their Living Lessons program.

CHAPTER 83

IT WAS ON a beautiful Saturday morning, September 20, 2008, on Long Beach Island when a slew of some pretty amazing and totally surprising coincidences occurred to me that pummeled me one right after another; it seemed that they were never going to stop, and it was the on a Saturday of our Festivus.

I never thought something like that could happen to me in a thousand years. Just think about this for a minute. How was it possible that one guy, meaning me, among a group of guys who were totally unrelated to one another but somehow related because of who we were, where we were, and what we did together traveled a good distance to an island, Long Beach Island, a place that I and the guys truly loved coming to, would have this amazing thing happen to me?

It was four of us who arrived three days earlier on a Thursday evening to check the house out to make sure there was no damage done by the previous renters and if so, I would have to notify Susan immediately of what had been done.

The only I could find wrong was that the gas grill I had always cooked on was nowhere in sight. It was gone, poof, missing in action, nada. Right then and there, I saw that our wonderful event that was scheduled for Saturday was no longer looking so festive to me.

But it was what had occurred on Saturday morning when I met this woman, one who I have seen from time to time who was completely unrelated to me but somehow related in other ways to me, had traveled to her beach house right next door for some strange reason that day. That turned out to be more of an absolute blessing than a stroke of luck.

I was about to go and ask her if I could use it. I truly believe she was meant to be there for a reason to be at our Festivus, and because of her, I am here finishing up my book, which actually started out with the simple short story I wrote about our meeting. And all of this due to a missing gas grill! That's right. So sit back as I raise the heat and get you all fired up with lots more stuff as to what happened there that weekend.

See, we had this great gas grille to use at Susan's beach house that ended up being incognito for me as I looked around to see who in the immediate area had a grill to use. I saw one on the deck of the beach house next door and if need be one in the backyard of the beach house on the other side of me. Two possible possibilities for me to cook on; they were reaching out to me and saying, "If you want me, come and get me!"

If our gas grill had been there as it always had been, right out on the deck when we come every September, I truly believe I never would have met this woman and would have learned nothing about her. I'd still be giving my usual hi or hello to her with a wave of my hand toward her or her family members as I'd been doing over the years, and that would have been the end of it. If that had been the case, I probably wouldn't be here writing this book, but that wasn't the case.

Since our grill was gone, and we (meaning me mostly) desperately needed one to cook the food for our event on, I was calamatized. I decided to take a breather and chill out by grabbing one of the chairs on our deck and just let my mind sort of drift as I sat there looking over at her grill.

I started to think about the past seven years during which my life had truly changed from what I had experienced that fateful morning, but I didn't think a simple gas grill would have had that much effect on me. I was snapped out of my thinking when I heard a loud siren coming from up the street and was coming in my direction turning down our street and was going past the house. I kind of chuckled. I didn't think a missing grill had caused such a state of emergency. And I hadn't called 911 either.

I opened my eyes, got up out of the chair, and walked off the deck. I took one more long look at that gas grill over at my neighbor's house and headed for the front of our house. This beach house we'd been coming to is located on E. Delaware Avenue (or 133rd Street) in an area called

Beach Haven Terrace; the Atlantic Ocean sits approximately 150 yards away. The homes on either side of the street going toward the ocean are a big mix of big and small, expensive and inexpensive houses that make this community so interesting and homely.

Our trip there from New York City took about one to two hours depending on the time of day, time of year, and of course the traffic and the weather conditions. The island is approximately eighteen miles long and a quarter-mile wide; it sits about eight miles off the mainland. It is connected by two bridges, one long and one short, that cross over Barnegat Bay and Manahawkin Bay. No tolls in either direction. And no public transportation to the island whatsoever.

The majority of the residents, approximately 20,000, are mainly there from Memorial Day to Labor Day even though the island does have plenty of year 'round residents. It has been called Long Beach Island for the last hundred years because the entire length of east side of the island is one long beach. (I'm wondering if the island had only a few hundred feet of beach; would they have called it Short Beach Island?)

The only reason why I'm stating this is because I know for a fact that each hand on the Statue of Liberty is only eleven inches long; one more inch to each hand and she would have had four feet.

Toward the north end of the island, the historic Barnegat Lighthouse gets visitors year 'round. They can climb this circular stairway to the top and have a great bird's-eye view of the island. The island is much more than a premier beach resort island with lots of great restaurants, bars, nightclubs, excellent lodging, interesting shops, and boutiques. It's a great place to bring the entire family—the kids can enjoy a huge amusement park, plenty of miniature golf courses, and of course frolic to their hearts' content on the well-kept, beautiful, and clean beaches.

I love going there mostly to go surf casting and enjoy a less-crowded beach than going to Jones Beach back on Long Island that is only a fifteen-minute drive from my house, as the crow flies. Plus, if I'm not getting lucky fishing off the beach I could take a fifteen minute walk up the street and hit the bay side to try my luck. I've been told by a local fisherman here one day that when I wasn't getting any hits or strikes to my bait to hook something, my time spent doing this was referred to as "fishing." But if you've been doing the same thing over and over and you finally get a hit or a strike to your baited hook and you land a nice fish, that's called "catching." Pure poetry. I had never looked at fishing or catching that way, but now I do. And I've been telling the same info to any fisherman I meet on the beach whether they want to hear it or not ever since I learned that distinction.

I've found that no matter where I go on the island, the majority of the people I come across, or meet, or stop to talk to are always cheerful and friendly and love to say hi or hello to one another but not to me. Only joking there. I actually think I do more talking to others I meet there than anyone on the whole island does, and I do so about anything that comes to my mind.

I know my wife, Margie, and our daughter, Noelle, love going there. I always tell them as soon as we step foot on the island, "Trust me—it doesn't get any better than this!"

I'd love to tell you more about the island, but if I did, I'd never get to finish this book of mine. So on to the next chapter!

CHAPTER 84

L ET ME TELL you a little about this beach house I stay at and its owner, Susan Howland. Susan is the kindest, sweetest, and dearest person you'd ever meet. She is one of my closest friends of the female persuasion; that's a sentiment the guys I work with at DDC all share.

As I've mentioned, she gives us free run of her beach house on Long Beach Island (which makes me wonder if there's a Short Beach Island somewhere). It's paradise to us; in spite of all the bars and restaurants on the island, we're content to stay put there on our post–Labor Day weekends. We do our own cooking, swimming, surf fishing, and chilling out on the deck; we don't subcontract any of those jobs. We hear the waves way more than we hear traffic on the main drag, Long Beach Boulevard.

Her property has a wide driveway with enough room for four cars. The garage has been converted into two lovely apartments up and down, and there's an outdoor shower we love—plenty of hot water. The main house has a deck and a good-sized yard. The first floor has a big living room, a walk-in closet, a sun room, a dining room, a decent-sized kitchen, and a vanity bathroom. There's central air for the first floor and window units for the three bedrooms upstairs as well as what we call the "chalet" bedroom, a small one, and a large bathroom.

Back on the first floor, there's a glass sliding door that leads from the kitchen to the deck positively festooned with chairs and tables with umbrellas and of course that gas grill I mentioned that was missing one year.

For all the times I've been on the island, I never really never knew the neighbors on both sides; we've never gone beyond a hi or hello and a wave of hands. But we've been there for only one weekend a year.

One year, our gracious Susan stopped by late one Friday and shared a meal and drinks with us. Later, she asked if we could give her a hand moving some furniture from one of the garage apartments to the main house. Mind you, this was after we'd polished off one or two bottles of tequila above and beyond everything else we'd been drinking. To this day, I can't recall what we carried up or who "we" was. Neither can the other guys though we all swear we were there. It was probably due to those damn limes or the small shot glasses we were drinking from. Maybe the salt, which is bad for you generally speaking.

At any rate, the address of the garage, considered a separate residence, was 9 E. Delaware Avenue while the main house's address is 11 E. Delaware Avenue. What are the odds of 9 and 11 in such a situation? I think pretty amazing.

As I wrote about earlier, I'd met Susan at that trauma seminar she'd held for Sky Help in 2003, where Mike Kenny, Ron Vega, Loan Dinh, and I met former FBI agent Jim Horn, Chaplain Joe Williams, and therapist Kathy Thomas who were all from Oklahoma City and had been through the bombing at the federal building on April 19, 1995.

When we were at Ground Zero, Loan met a NYPD officer, Rob Murray, while she was working there. One night, Rob was there to comfort Loan when she saw something that made her uncomfortable. On August 16, 2004, a day before Marge's birthday, Loan and Rob got married, and Ron, Mike, and I with our wives attended their lovely wedding in New Jersey. We were all having a fantastic time when a surprising coincidence occurred to me. Loan brought over her father to our table. We were enjoying the music, food, and drinks when Loan introduced Thomas to us.

While she was making the introductions, her father kept looking at me—more like studying me—to such an extent that when Loan introduced me to her dad, something told me to stand. I was giving him my hundred and ten percent respect while he kept giving me this very powerful look.

Loan said, "Charlie, my dad served proudly in the South Vietnamese

Army. He was assigned to the 3rd Marine Division in Da Nang, the group you were assigned to the same time you were there!"

I clasped his hand in a heartfelt handshake. We embraced. Loan's face was glowing as she looked at her dad. She was teary eyed when she said, "Charlie, my dad's been looking forward to meeting you after all these years. I told him about you, and he wants to thank you for what you did for his country and our family."

I couldn't believe what I was hearing. Thomas and I realized that we'd been brothers in arms many years earlier though we hadn't known that. We were embracing one another as two lost souls who had fought side my side and had survived a war. We'd been reunited thirty-four years later at his daughter's wedding. That was a memorable wedding and an eventful day.

Excuse me, but did I just hear you say, "Wow! It truly is a small world"?

CHAPTER 85

"**D**DC WHO?" THAT was the typical response we got at Ground Zero whenever we were asked by anyone, "Who are you?" Our agency was not that well known, so we went through such questioning often for the recovery/cleanup operations we were engaged in at the WTC site.

It's the city agency I proudly work for—New York City's Department of Design & Construction—DDC. We have about 1,600 personnel in our headquarters at Long Island City, an area in western Queens, but it's hardly known to those outside the New York City government or to some of the construction companies.

But after the disaster struck the WTC on September 11, 2001, we became known to the world. I'm proud to be part of a team of professionals and civil servants made up of mostly architects, designers, engineers, project managers of all types of construction, skilled and knowledgeable personnel in the infrastructure of the city, auditors, tech support, and people who know their way around permits and approvals, bid estimators, bid dispositions, budgeting, creative services, and other support staff.

We took on the role of managing, supervising, and coordinating recovery/cleanup operations at Ground Zero. Our commissioner at the time, Ken Holden, was prepared later that day to ask for volunteers from his staff. Once he had the names and they knew what they had to do at the site, the staffing plan was prepared as to who was assigned to what. The time spent there for each individual could have been a day or two, a week or two, or months, as was the case with me. It didn't matter—we were there!

We worked side by side with first responders and anyone from any of the federal, state, or city agencies and thousands from the construction trades. We and thousands of volunteers and hundreds of military personnel got the job done. Though we worked in different capacities, shifts, and roles, we all served our tours of duty and left as a proud band of brothers and sisters.

We accomplished what we did under extreme, unheard-of conditions worse than any we'd experienced at any other demolition site. The DDC personnel became well known there. We're so proud of our accomplishments; the bonds we formed those days and months will never die.

That's the genesis of our Festivus celebrations. That's why I put a sign out at one of our yearly celebrations (or commemorations if you will), "Please Stop In and Meet some Ground Zero Workers and Have a Burger or Beer at our Festivus—For the Rest of Us." (The whole Festivus idea was based on a *Seinfeld* episode in which Frank Costanza, George's father, celebrated a made-up festive holiday he called Festivus. Google it if you have to.) I thought it was a clever way of pulling in passers-by. (And people have been stopping by every year since!)

Now I think it would be a good time to tell you a little about some of the guys who came out two days early on a Thursday evening, September 18, to enjoy an extra day to relieve the stress of our jobs before the big event on Saturday, September 20, at noon.

By Friday afternoon, we already had seven guys at the beach house. Six of them were from DDC, and one had been a volunteer at Ground Zero. The six DDC guys were Luis Mendes, Ronaldo Vega, Michael Kenny, Edmund Di Blasio, John Romanowich, and me. The seventh guy was our good buddy, James "Mack" McDade. Luis Mendes, who has since left DDC, is now with the September 11th Memorial & Museum for the WTC site as director of construction for the memorial. While he was at DDC, he was an assistant commissioner, third in command at Ground Zero He hired me to work at DDC back in February 2001.

That was actually Lou's first time attending our event, and he looks forward to being at every year coming up. Everyone who came later that Saturday, were surprised and happy to see Lou there. (I guess after hearing about the past ones from Ronaldo Vega, Lou had to come.) Lou partied with us till the cows came home by suppling some of the best refreshments we had ever had there. As to those cows, there are none on the beach whether it's high tide or low tide or cowhide unless you were there polishing off some special drinks and think you might have seen a cow.

Ronaldo Vega, Ron, also has left DDC. He is an excellent architect and is now working at the September 11ᵗʰ Memorial & Museum. Ron worked the four-to-midnight shift at the site along with Michael Kenny, Edmund Di Blasio, and John Romanowich, who were the other guys at the house. Ron, whose nationality is Puerto Rican (but we don't dare tell him that) can out-sing any Irishman in the world when he sings "Danny Boy." The world should stop and listen to whenever Ron sings that song. About Ground Zero, Ron said, "Every day there was a funeral!"

Michael Kenny is a deputy program director at DDC. He worked one of the quadrants at the site and became pretty well known at the site on a very important and particular night of April 13, 2002, as you read earlier in the book. What occurred that night would have made bigger news than all the news trucks that were there covering the last night for the Tower of Lights before they were turned off; those two spotlights that went shining up toward the heavens were reminders of what once stood there. His story did make the news weeks later. That night, I believe, I proclaimed to myself and the rest of the world that Mike was my very best friend. He may not know it, but I do! We have become real close buddies almost like having another younger brother. By the way, my younger brother, who is two years younger than me, is also named Michael.

John Romanowich, J-Ro, is a construction project manager at DDC. Most of the guys worked in different quadrants overseeing and managing different contractors since the site was divided into quadrants each with one big major general contractor who reported to DDC. I believe J-Ro started out in one of the quadrants, but as far as I remember, he spent most of his time in the FDNY headquarters, known as 10–10, that was right across the site on Liberty Street. When you meet and greet J-Ro, he gives you one helluva handshake you'll never forget. J-Ro and

I did most of the fishing at the beach whenever we were there. Yes, we did get lucky catching fish!

Edmund Di Blasio was a construction project manager at Ground Zero for DDC; he has since retired and gone back to work in the private sector as a design project manager with STV. He works on projects for the Schools Construction Authority for the City of New York. Ed is also a great Toastmaster and a fabulous cook; he's known for his dry sense of humor, which is as good as mine. He is also one great storyteller at our gatherings regarding some memorable times at Ground Zero.

Our good buddy Mack McDade had been a volunteer at the site who prepared and served meals at a nearby church. He worked at the temporary morgue at the site with the medical examiner's personnel. He is a retired teacher in Pennsylvania and a minister, and he works or devotes a good portion of his personal time with the NYPD in Brooklyn at the 73rd Precinct.

I'm Charlie K, a construction project manager at DDC; I've been involved mostly with all new precincts for the NYPD. (If you wish to know a little bit more about me, go on the web and google my full name.) The other supervisor with me on the graveyard shift at Ground Zero was Mike Alacha, now with the Department of Buildings.

Susan says that whenever she hears the song "Calling all Angels" by Train, it reminds her of the time that we guys from DDC spent at Ground Zero. When I met Allison Crowthers in church on April 3, 2005, she told me we were probably watched over by guardian angels when we were there at the WTC site. Now I've received two compliments—about being an angel from Susan and Allison, who are actually to me more like angels themselves. Boy, do I feel blessed!

But if you really want to get down to some nitty-gritty religious accolades, there's no one better than Fr. James P. Hayes, pastor at St. Andrew's in Lower Manhattan, a few steps from One Police Plaza, NYPD's headquarters. Father Jim, as he is known by all, was there at the WTC that fateful morning and was constantly seen in and about the site for months. After he had met a few of us at an event in the basement of his church, he made a point to learn more about us as to our roles at the site. He would show his concern and respect for us if we should happen to attend one of his masses by doing one simple thing during his homily.

He would say "the usual suspects," his way of letting us know he saw us among the congregation. (Yes, a very nice gesture, Father Jim, but what about dinner?) Trust me; someday, we'll all get together and have dinner with this buddy of ours God willing.

Another gentleman I met on two of my projects in Brooklyn and up in East Harlem showed great interest in my designs and still praises me today for them. Architect Leroy Garriques was a consultant with an architectural firm I worked with while at DDC. We worked together on seeing through a total renovation of the eighth floor at 210 Livingston Street in Brooklyn for another city agency, HRA, and a project in East Harlem for ACS. Leroy has remained a loyal, true friend and is a constant gentleman.

CHAPTER 86

I TOLD YOU about what took place on my drive out to the beach on a Sunday morning when these pretty amazing and very powerful occurrences happened; they were the icing on the cake and prompted me to write that short story I wanted to send to *Reader's Digest*.

What occurred a week earlier with a woman I met on Long Beach Island has to be the cake, the whole cake, and nothing but the cake so help me God. It happened during our Festivus on Saturday, September 20, 2008. It always started promptly at noon on Saturday, and we were getting ready on Friday.

That's when I discovered the grill Susan had told was there was actually not there. That was a problem for sure considering the number of people we were expecting. Ed was busy preparing his Friday night pasta dinner, a true work of art. We were waiting to hear his usual "Come and get it while it's hot!" The other guys were on the deck drinking and talking about who knows what while I was asking myself, *Who knows what I'll be cooking on?* I knew damn well I wasn't going to use the eighteen-inch-diameter charcoal grill in the shed out back. Come on. It was 2008. Who cooked on a charcoal grill after that? I know I haven't ever since Al Gore proclaimed we had global warming, and I didn't want to contribute to that at all even for just six hamburgers and six hotdogs.

So I started walking around back toward the deck thinking I might have heard Ed yell out "Come and get it" and—surprising coincidence— saw this big, beautiful gas grill staring at me from the deck next door. I stopped dead in my tracks. My prayers had been answered. But then I wondered, *Is this a mirage?* Of course it wasn't. Didn't I just tell you I saw it? Did I ever mention the words *desert* or *palm trees* or *oasis*? No, I didn't. Please pay attention.

I decided to take a gander over at the other neighbor's backyard and—*ta da*—saw another gas grill. It wasn't as big as the one in the other neighbor's house, but it was a pretty close replica of the one we'd always had on Susan's deck. This was too good to be true. I was envisioning placing burgers and hotdogs on one or both of them and my eyes being filled with smoke. I wondered if it was "our" grill that had been borrowed but not returned.

I went inside our place and almost bumped into Mack and J-Ro trying to get beer out of the fridge. Lou and Ron were already at the table holding their forks and looking as if they were waiting for the main course. Mike said loudly, "Charlie K! Where the hell have you been? We just finished dinner. Nothing's left but some ends of the garlic bread. We're about to have dessert!"

I knew he was joking; he always joked about food. Everyone else was getting a seat at the dining room table looking like hungry wolves ready to tear into the garlic bread Ed placed on the table next to the huge salad bowl. The next thing we would see would be the large brown bowl filled to the brim with Ed's delicious pasta dish. I got a beer, sat, helped myself to the garlic bread and salad, and waited for the pasta. I tapped my beer bottle with my fork. Everyone thought I was about to propose a toast or say something incorrigible (Ed's favorite description of me) about the dinner. Instead, I proclaimed, "Guys, listen up! I think my prayers have been answered!"

Before I could get another word in, Ron or maybe Mike said, "Hell, we haven't said grace yet, and he's got his prayers answered. Who the hell does something like that?"

I disregarded that of course. I said, "I just found two gas grills, one at each neighboring beach house, and lucky for me, both houses are deserted. I don't think either one of the owners will be here this weekend or for that matter the rest of the season since they haven't been for the past four years!

"What I'm planning to do is place my camouflage Vietnam blanket over myself and sneak over to the big house next door in a covert kind of way by the tactical (black ops) maneuvers I learned in my survival training by the navy SEALs in Little Creek, Virginia, prior to going to 'Nam and simply infiltrate the huge deck and overtake the grill by surprise, quickly covering it with my blanket, and quietly bringing it back to our deck. Then after everyone departs on Sunday after the big event is over, I will clean it and slip back at dusk once again being camouflaged and return the grill to its rightful place as if it had never left there. What do you think of my very creative plan to solve our problem?"

The guys appeared shell shocked. Before I knew it, half of them tried to persuade me not to go through with this crazy mission of mine while the other half were toasting me by raising their drinks for which I thought was for my one hell of an idea except that Mike kept on saying over all the talk, "PTSD!" That's when everyone started laughing, including me, as Mike grinned at me.

Ed chimed in loudly. "Listen, Charlie K, the sheer possibility of you getting caught doing this and getting arrested by the local Long Beach Island PD is about a hundred percent. Who's going to do all the cooking?"

We all laughed. Everyone clinked bottles and said, "To Charlie K's arrest!"

"Charlie K, why don't you just call Susan and see if she can help us out," Ron reasonably asked. He is a very smart architect, and that right there was a very good plan of attack that was better than my plan of attack. So I called Susan and left a message about my secret mission to rescue a grill. I asked her to do me the favor of possibly calling the owners of her two neighboring houses, tell them of our dilemma, and ask if I could use a grill. I told her I needed an answer a.s.a.p. I concluded my message with "Thank you, love you."

Things were looking up. I was feeling a lot better and got into a festive mood. I had seconds and thirds of Ed's pasta. (He has never asked for a dime from anyone of the guys to chip in for the food he bought and the amount of beer he would bring with some hard liquor too.)

Around eleven thirty that night, we were on the deck drinking, laughing, telling stories, and enjoying the night air and a few cigars. That went on until our newfound friend, Mr. Patrón, a member of the Tequila family, stopped in for a visit that lasted until about 2:00 a.m. We decided it was lights out for all of us whether we knew it or not.

CHAPTER 87

EARLY SATURDAY MORNING around seven thirty, Ed, as usual, was preparing his famous blueberry pancakes as well as scrambled eggs and bacon. I was coming back from a newspaper-and-donuts run when Ed said, "Hey Charlie, I just saw someone, a woman, walk back inside her house next door. You know, the one with the big gas grill you wanted to steal."

Ron and Mike said, "Charlie K, go over and get the attention of whomever it is in that house next door and see about borrowing her grill!" I thought they were all pulling my leg. But then they started chanting, "Go, Charlie K! Network!"

I looked over and saw a side door was open. I yelled out, "Hello!" I stepped off the deck and began to wave my hand toward the house hoping someone would respond to my voice or see my hand. I felt sheer excitement growing in me as I neared the fence that separated the properties. I was thinking it was unreal that someone was in that house that day of all days because in the past, there had never been anyone there.

Mike and Ron loved to play tricks on me; they were egging me on. "Go! Go! Charlie K, do you're networking! Talk to that woman! Get her grill! Start it up!" But I also heard Ed declare, "Come and get it! The pancakes are being served! Get them while there hot!" I was thinking they'd sent me out on this quest so I would miss the first batch of pancakes, but I was hungrier for that grill. Having that would make the pancakes all the sweeter with or without syrup.

I didn't want to disappoint the guests who were en route and would be there in a few hours. So I was desperate to talk to her or anyone else who might be in this house next door about the grill. I was Don Quixote on a quest. Maybe more like Don Knotts shaking all over in anticipation of getting that grill.

I saw her walk out of her house smiling at me and waving. She was an angel about to answer my prayers. As I approached the chain link fence, I felt some kind of electricity in the air that made the hairs on my arms stand up and look like a field of hay. I thought that some strange, invisible aura was about to surround us as we approached the fence. My body was pressed against it as was hers as if we were a well-rehearsed movie scene. We both said, "Good Morning!" "Hi, I'm Charlie K." "Hi, I'm Helen!" I don't know why, but we shook hands and smiled as if we were happy to see each other again. I think it was the hand of fate that grasped ours hands together. I felt this unusual connection to her when she said, "I think I know you. Susan's mentioned you."

"You mean Susan called you and told you about my situation and inquired about your gas grill?"

"No. I have numerous messages on my phone, but I didn't get to them yet. Why? What about my gas grill?" Before I could explain our situation, she said, "Wait a minute. I believe I've seen you here before when you were with your family for a week or long weekend in the summer about two years ago. Am I right?"

She was. I'd been there with Margie, Noelle, and other family members. I said she was correct, but then I told her about our Festivus events and our need for a grill because Susan's wasn't there. I told her about all the other people we were expecting. She looked at me with caring eyes, so I figured I'd tell her about who was with me in the house—my buddies from DDC—and what we were commemorating—our time at Ground Zero.

She smiled. Her face was glowing like a warm sunset. She coaxed me closer even though the fence separated us. She hugged me. I felt that electricity go through my body. Her eyes were getting misty. "What's wrong?" I asked.

"Oh my God. Are you telling me the guys in the house with you were all at Ground Zero?"

I nodded.

"Charlie, have you seen our flagpole and marker out in our front lawn over by the driveway?"

"Yes, but I haven't had the chance to read the marker yet. Why?"

She held my hands. Tears were running down her cheeks, "It's there to honor my younger brother, Stephen, who was working there that morning on the hundred and fourth floor of the North Tower for Cantor Fitzgerald. He was caught in the collapse and died there."

I gave her a comforting hug and told her how sorry I was for her terrible loss. "Helen, I was there that morning too!"

She stepped back and looked at me. "You were there when my brother died?" She gave me another hug. I'm sure she knew that my feelings and condolences were there for her, and she was feeling sorry for me. I felt this unbelievable magnetism that was bonding us. It was so powerful. I reacted to what she had said in a special way.

She told me about Stephen; I was experiencing so many surprising coincidences that I didn't dare interrupt her. It seems Stephen and I had crossed paths in a way. I wished I had known him.

CHAPTER 88

I KNOW I'M speaking for all the guys who were at the house that Saturday morning when I say that we all felt the same way having been at Ground Zero and having walked through the dust that contained the remains of those who had died. Whenever we met family members of those lost, we let them know we truly felt for them.

It wasn't the place or time to ask Helen again about her grill, but she said with a huge smile, "Of course, Charlie K, use the grill! I know for sure that my boyfriend, Ed, and I won't be using it. Help yourself! Besides, Ed's still sleeping."

I gave her a hug. "Your Ed may be asleep, but our Ed has been up for quite a while. If you'd like to come over for some of his pancakes and meet the guys, leave a note for your Ed as to where you'll be and tell him to get his ass over when he wakes up to have breakfast too. I'm sure the guys would love to meet another Ed. And the two of you are invited to join us for Festivus this afternoon. It'll be fun! See you in a bit."

I started to walk toward an opening in the bushes. I wanted to see the marker and the flagpole in front of her house. I shouted back to Helen, "Go wake up your sleepy boyfriend! It's almost nine! Seriously, who sleeps this late?" I hoped there were enough pancakes left for her, her Ed, and me.

I read the plaque that had a short and sweet dedication to her brother, Stephen, I couldn't believe what she had told me about him—he'd lived on Long Island and had been an avid surfer who'd surfed Long Beach on Long Island at Neptune Avenue as I had; it was my favorite East Coast place to surf. Those were some pretty surprising coincidences between Stephen and me. I said to myself, *Stephen, I know you're up there in*

365

heaven and having the rides of your life on all those perfect waves. So enjoy them till I get there. I'm with you in spirit, buddy. I touched the flagpole and planted a kiss on my fingertips and tapped the marker as if to say hi to Stephen.

I went back to our beach house and told the guys about Helen and Stephen. I told them that Helen had said that she'd felt she had to come here (having this odd feeling to get to the island) minute for some strange reason and that she was glad to help us out with her gas grill. I felt we were meant to use her grill. I said, "I feel kind of lucky, guys, so I also invited her and her boyfriend, another Ed, to join us for Festivus. Ed, I hope you have some pancakes leftover. I'm famished."

"Another Ed. You're famished. And you got us a grill," he said. "I think that deserves another batch of pancakes!"

The guys were totally surprised to hear what I'd just told them especially about her brother, Stephen. I didn't get into the stuff about surfing; I figured it had nothing to do with them. I thought about having seen Helen from a distance the previous four years but then actually meeting her seemingly by chance. I excused myself and headed upstairs to use the bathroom. I told Ed I'd be right down for breakfast. I realized that if Susan's grill had been there, I might not have met Helen and learned about our close connection to 9/11.

Ed yelled something about fresh pancakes coming up with whatever blueberries he had left to put in them. I came downstairs and saw him placing them onto the pancakes as if he were plotting column locations for a building. Mack said he was starting another pot of coffee for Helen and her Ed and got two cups from the cabinet. I was eating some pancakes after buttering and syruping them when I heard two distinct voices coming from the front door—Charlie Jimenez-Hernandez and Julian Misuriski the III, two more DDC guys who had also worked at Ground Zero. Both of them are or were project managers

"Why isn't there anything on the grill?" Charlie asked. "I'm hungry!" (He's just plain Charlie while I'm Charlie K.)

Before I could get a word out, Mike shouted, "Charlie K is going to jail for stealing a gas grill from a neighbor. The woman is coming over to press charges, so there won't be a Festivus this year. We won't have a chef!" (That was Mike trying to make the day more interesting.)

When Charlie and Jules saw Lou sitting at the dining room table, Charlie blurted out, "I can't fuckin' believe it! Look who it is—Lou! What a surprise!" Everyone shook hands and hugged each other. Ed tried to announce over all the loud talking and laughter, "I got more pancakes coming, so have a seat!" Ron said, "I thought I heard a woman's voice!"

Standing out there out on our deck was Helen trying to be very cordial. "Hello, Charlie K, it's Helen!"

Mike yelled, "She's here to press additional charges on you for having her wake up her boyfriend and all your loud networking!"

I have to admit that was funny. I swallowed my laughter and a bite of pancakes. "Come in, Helen! You're just in time for some fresh pancakes!"

Ed introduced himself and gave his condolences. He said, "Please come in" and showed her into the dining room. The rest of the guys all stood. I mean, we're gentlemen most of the time, and we knew our place when a woman entered a room, especially one they hadn't met at that point but knew a little bit about based on what I'd told them about her. They showed her the utmost respect as she entered the room. All the guys introduced themselves; they gave her hugs and handshakes.

Charlie and Jules had no idea what was going on when they heard, "Sorry for your loss," so I filled them in. They extended their condolences to her.

We made room around the dining room table; it looked as if we were playing an adult version of musical chairs. We welcomed Helen into our family circle. Mack offered her coffee, and Ed handed her a short stack of pancakes and a fork. She told us how honored she was to be in the presence of people who had been, in a way, with her brother and possibly when they found his remains. That was a bond. She was getting a little misty eyed.

I told her who of us had worked where, when, and with whom. I mentioned how Lou and Ron were involved with the memorial, and she gave them a very comforting and respectful smile. I decided to change the subject by asking her where she worked.

Do you remember me telling you about this amazing roller-coaster ride I've been on ever since 9/11 and what had occurred to me on the bridge later that afternoon? And how all these amazing, unbelievable, surprising coincidences kept occurring to me? Well, that roller-coaster started picking up speed. You're not gonna believe this, but Helen said, "I work at Merrill Lynch." I nearly fell out of my chair. Every head turned to me.

Ed blurted out, "Charlie K worked there!"

I don't know who was more surprised—them, Helen, or me.

I said, "Helen, you're not going to believe this, but I worked at Merrill from '78 to '89 at One Liberty Plaza. I did a lot of traveling for them all over the United States."

She asked what division I'd worked in. I told her the facilities department on the fiftieth floor and then the third floor in the WFC. Helen smiled and said, "Small world, isn't it? I work in a pretty nice office in a building in Forest Hills, Queens."

Again I felt like I was knocked out of my seat. "Don't tell me—is it the office at 71st Street and Continental Avenue?"

She replied, "Yes of course. Why?"

I chuckled. "I can't believe this. That's the only office I ever did in the New York City area before I started to travel. Unbelievable!"

We started naming people, and it turns out we both knew about ten or fifteen we'd worked with over the years. I told Helen that I'd stopped traveling when Mother Merrill moved into the World Financial Center. I'd been assigned to the Investment Banking Division and made sure the chairman and all the executives had the best of the best when it came to their offices; it was a prestigious position in the company.

Jo-R jumped up and spread his arms as if to change the subject. He got everyone's attention with his smooth but commanding voice. "Enough about Charlie K. So Helen, where do you live? I mean, that is your beach house, right?"

"My boyfriend and I live in Westchester. The beach house belongs to the Hoffman family."

Here comes another one of those drops I told you about that I get on this roller-coaster ride. Almost in unison, Lou, Mike, J-Ro, and Ed said, "We all live up in there in Westchester!" They named the towns they lived in, and it turned out Helen and her boyfriend lived within a five-mile radius of them all. Amazing, huh?

Helen asked, "So what were you guys talking about before I came over? I hope it wasn't about me!"

CHAPTER 89

J-Ro started to say that they had been talking about his possible upcoming retirement from DDC and about his house in Westchester. Mike, Lou, and Ron said something about their homes and mortgages as Ed and Mack were talking about the real estate market. That brought Charlie and Jules into the mix. I got back to my pancakes. All the surprising coincidences were giving me an appetite.

Helen's smile became bigger and bigger. I cut into everyone's talking and told them to hush for a second. I asked Helen, "Is there something wrong? Why are you smiling so much?" She burst out with "Hey, guess what, guys? You're not going to believe this, but I'm a financial advisor at Merrill!"

"You got to be kidding! No way! Tell me you're joking!" I felt a blueberry get stuck in my throat from the excitement.

She asked, "What do you want to know? How can I help you guys?"

We were taken aback by this strange occurrence. Just then, we heard Helen's boyfriend, Ed, who had finally woken up and decided to join us for breakfast. I believe it was Mack who met him first and handed him a cup of coffee he'd just poured for himself. He invited our new visitor into the dining room. Helen wanted to show everyone she was pretty sharp in remembering who was who. She said, "This is my boyfriend, Ed." He added, "Ed Polhemus the third!"

(I asked myself, *The third of what? The third time he woke up this morning before he got out of bed, the third stop he made before he came over to join us? Maybe the third time he tried calling Helen as to where she was?* We will never know or care to know. We all know he meant the

III, but no one was counting that morning. I hoped it wasn't the number of helpings he was expecting of our Ed's pancakes.)

We were impressed with Helen's memory as she went around the room telling her Ed what everyone did. She told her Ed, "All of them are involved in construction in one form or another."

I didn't know what she meant by that until her face started glowing again and her smile got as big as the Grand Canyon. I thought, *Oh no. Don't tell me.*

"Go ahead, tell them!" she said to Ed.

Ed smiled and said, "Guess what, guys? So am I!"

He said that he worked for a company in a town up in the Westchester area and was involved in excavation work. Luis and J-Ro smiled and said that they'd heard of Ed's company. (What—another coincidence?)

We became a bigger happy family bringing everyone up to date with the goings-on in their lives and things about Ground Zero, mortgages, retirement, real estate, construction projects, and why we'd came to the island for the weekend.

Mack reminded me it was time to do some shopping for food. It was ten fifteen, and I needed to get it in gear. I always had to take into account the 30 mph speed limit on the island. I had to get back by noon. I got up and announced, "It's time to go food shopping!"

Luis stood and let me know he was ready to go. "Let's go, Charlie Cans, because I need to get a few things myself!"

(That Cans thing was Lou's new pet name for me ever since 2002. Some of us guys who were with me in the beach house were involved in a Canstruction competition—we built something out of canned goods and competed against other architectural and design firms in NYC. I was always the team captain for this event, and whenever Lou saw us doing a trial build-out in the building lobby at DDC's headquarters, he would ask, "How's it going, Charlie Cans?" It had stuck with me ever since.)

As I was heading for the door, Mike and Ron commandingly said, "Sit down, Charlie K, you, grill thief! Where the hell do you think you're going? You've got plenty of time! Let's talk some more!"

Lou and I said together, "Okay, fifteen minutes more!"

Helen laughed at the funny faces the guys were making at Mike.

"How did you get to know Susan and for her to let you crazy guys use her house?"

I was sure Helen had seen us over the past few years. Ron jumped in and gave her short overview about how we'd met and how we started coming to her beach house. He told her that for our first year, 2003, there were the Original Six—Ron, Ed, Mike, J-Ro, Rudy DiMaggio, and me. Rudy, also a project manager still with DDC, had worked at Ground Zero. He'd attended the first two events, but things cropped up that prevented him from coming to others. He was nonetheless always there with us in spirit.

Mike, with a more serious look on his face, asked Helen, "By any chance did you attend this year's anniversary ceremony? Ron, Charlie K, and I were there." Mike told her we'd attended all the ceremonies as members of the honor guard in the Pit and had read off names of the lost loved ones. Mike explained that I, Lou, Ron, Mack, and he usually attended a get-together with a family who had lost their daughter, Andrea Lyn, on 9/11. Gordon and Kathy Haberman, Andrea's parents, a lovely couple, came from Wisconsin to New York City for the anniversary. They'd invite us to a restaurant, and we'd reflect and remember Andie's life, not her death. We all have bonded with one another, so it was always great to share time with them.

I said, "You're not gonna believe this, but the restaurant we've been going to would set aside the same tables for us, but one time, we learned that another family had reserved them. Our usual tables had been roped off with some tape. We sat about ten feet away from where we normally sat."

Helen's eyes were getting all misty again, and I started to get a little uncomfortable, but before I could change the subject, she said, "We did the same thing, Charlie. My family also went to a restaurant downtown to honor Stephen. Just like you guys last year, this year, my mom was asked by the city if she would like to read Stephen's name at the ceremony. My Mom was so honored and touched to take part in it, and we were too. It was extremely memorable."

As we listened to her, the whole room took on an aura of total calmness like before a storm. Helen looked at me. We knew something was pulling us to one another just as had happened at the fence earlier that morning. The magnetism was getting stronger by the second. We were talking about the ceremony that had taken place only nine days earlier. I looked around the table and realized there were eleven of us—a surprising coincidence?

Helen said, "So there we were having a wonderful time at this restaurant sitting outside taking in the New Jersey skyline across the way and out of nowhere a complete hush came over the entire outdoor dining area. We heard some guy with a lovely Irish accent singing 'Danny Boy.'"

The hair on the back of my neck stood up. A chill went down my back straight to my wild heart. The hairs on my left arm stood up stiff as a board. Everyone there knew damn well that it was Ron who had sung.

I startled Helen when I interrupted. "My God! Were you at the Southwest Restaurant?"

"Yes! And that was us, in that taped-off area!"

You could have heard a pin drop. I exclaimed, "What are the chances that the Hoffman family reserves a group of tables at a restaurant, the same tables we always sat at each year for the last five years, and we end up sitting only ten feet away from them that afternoon? And here we are sitting at a dining room table sharing breakfast in a beach house miles from New York City where we've been actually neighbors for the past four years. I think this is totally amazing!"

Unfrickin' unreal! There we were one big happy family all because I'd asked to borrow her grill. (Preferable to being grilled by the police of course.) The surprising coincidences had happened one right after another. Maybe all that was a blessing and I'd been meant to meet Helen for a reason. Why else would she have shown up that day?

Those fifteen minutes blew by so fast that I forgot about food shopping. Lou was giving me a heads-up and pointing at his watch. J-Ro asked Helen and Ed, "Is it okay if we check out your grill?"

"Of course!" they said. "Help yourself, knock yourself out! We're family now!"

I said to Lou, "Give me two minutes. I want to check something out front and then we'll go."

Lou replied, "I'm all yours, Charlie Cans!"

I embraced Ed and Helen and said, "Please join us for Festivus.

Everyone else coming here would love to meet you. And you're family now. There's no getting away. I know where you live!"

The day was starting out perfect even with all these surprising coincidences. It was better than I had expected. I had a grill, the sun was shining, we'd met this lovely couple, and to top it off, the temperature outside felt like the warmth I'd gotten from Helen.

I went out front to check on the four sailboat masts I used as flagpoles to display the four flags I put up for our event. I had tied the four masts onto the front fence earlier that morning. I normally flew three flags, but that year, I decided to bring a fourth. I noticed something strange about it; it gave me a chill when I looked up and saw my usual three flags whipping in the slight breeze but the fourth wrapped around the mast. I thought maybe I'd put it up too hastily. Then I thought it could have been yet another surprising coincidence telling me something. I had acquired that flag earlier that year. I was flying Old Glory, my state flag of California, and the two-star admiral's flag Rear Admiral Guinn had given me.

The fourth was the Flag of Honor, an American flag that bore the names of the victims of 9/11. I found it strange that it had gotten wrapped around the mast. Could it have had anything to do with what had taken place in the house? I'd seen all the flags waving when I'd talked with Helen outside that morning. I told Lou, "This will only take a minute, Lou. If you want to go ahead without me, it's okay. I'll catch up!"

We laughed because I was the one with the list and the money. Charlie came over and gave me a friendly push. "Go! Get the hell out of here. I'll take care of the flag. You're going for the food! I'm getting extremely hungry, and Ed's blueberry pancakes didn't fill me up!"

I stepped aside. Mack had this astonished look on his face as he was walking toward me. I mentioned he was a minister. "Charlie K, can you believe what occurred this morning? I mean, her brother dies in the towers, you were there that morning, all you guys were at Ground Zero, and you come here and meet Helen, who was at the same Southwest Restaurant as we'd been. Surprising coincidences. It is a small world!"

"Mack, you're a minister! Ask God what the hell's going on here and let me know. I have to go shopping."

We laughed as I headed to Lou's car, but before I could get relaxed,

I noticed J-Ro was waving his arms over his head as he was walking toward me looking like he was ready to tear someone's head off. "John, what's wrong?"

J-Ro looked disgusted. "We have a fucking problem! The grill that Helen said we could use, well, we can't fuckin' use it!"

"Did she change her mind? Am I kicked out of the family? They didn't like Ed's breakfast? Not enough blueberries in the pancakes? What? What now?"

"No! It's the fuckin' grill! It's connected to the gas line—no propane tank, and it needs a special adaptor we don't have in order for us to use it, so we're SOL."

"Okay! So we can't use it or make it useable?" (It was like I'd just been hit in the head by a frozen snowball despite it being only the early fall. Besides, who there would have one at that time? No, not a snowball. I meant a grill.) The pain going through my head gave me a headache on top of all those powerful emotions still racing in me due to all the surprising coincidences I'd had earlier.

I was back to square one as far as cooking was concerned. *Maybe I'll just boil a big pot of water and throw in sixty hotdogs and make ten cans of beans and call it a day.* J-Ro got in my face, "Listen, why don't we do this? Each of us kicks in twenty apiece, Mack and I will buy one down the street at that hardware store, and slap it together. Then you can cook. So what if it starts late? No one's going to leave. Let them eat chips and pretzels until you cook. It'll be a nice gift from us to Susan."

Mike came over. "No problem, Charlie K. All you have to do is the shopping. When you come back, you can cook it on Helen's deck. We're family now. You can serve us over the fence. Everyone, especially, me likes da fence—*de* fence." Mike gave me this smirk and said, "Listen. You have one helluva problem, and you have your work cut out for you. It's not solving my hunger pangs or even Charlie's. He's still bitching about the pancakes. I told Ed he should have used bigger blueberries!"

That was perfect timing. Mike's comments about his hunger pangs, Charlie's pains, and my pains were on a collision course. I heard Ron yell, "Charlie K! Charlie K!" (He always said my name twice even on the walkie-talkies we used at Ground Zero, when he wanted my attention to something important.) "Susan is on the house phone for you!"

I meandered my way through the guys who were standing around and looking at me and made my way to the back deck and into the kitchen trying to figure out why Susan would be calling. Lou was waiting for me in his car with the engine running. Whenever Susan called, it was usually important. I was having second thoughts about what Mike had suggested about cooking on Helen's deck. His idea was feasible, but I didn't like the idea because every so often, someone would want to cook his or her own food, and I hadn't planned on having our big event at another house—it just wouldn't have been the same. J-Ro had the right attitude and the right solution for such a simple problem, but for me, it was a complete travesty. Everything had been going so great only minutes earlier, and now this. *What next?*

Ron was on the phone with Susan. He said, "We'll miss you. Here's Charlie K." He handed me the phone. I sat at the dining room table. "Hi, Charlie K. How's it going?" she asked. Before I could say anything, she jumped in with, "I've made three or four calls to Helen, all voice mail messages! She hasn't returned my calls, but you're not going to believe this!"

"Susan, before you tell me what you have to tell me, I thought I'd tell you that I met Helen and her boyfriend, Ed. We're like family right now, but we can't use her grill. It's connected to a gas line. Any luck with the owner of the house next door? It's my last resort!"

As I was speaking, I looked out the dining room window at the grill next door, which I swear was calling out, *Take me. Use me. I'm all yours. Use me to your heart's content.*

"Charlie," Susan said, "I got in touch with the owner of the house next door. Guess what? His name is Charlie too, but he likes to be called Chuck. I told him about your predicament, and he said for me to tell you by all means use his grill to your heart's content."

I'd just thought those same words a second earlier. Another surprising coincidence?

She continued. "I told him a few things about you, and he said, 'I know who you're talking about. I've seen him before numerous times when I was out working on my house. He always said hi or hello and gave me a wave.' He said you two never really talked much beyond that, but he enjoyed your warm greetings."

"Thanks for the good news! It comes at the perfect time. Please tell Chuck I'm—" Lou was blowing his horn. "Thanks! Gotta go. Love ya!" I grabbed my wallet, sunglasses, and the shopping list and walked to Lou's car. "What are you still doing here? Why haven't you left?" (I won't get into what exactly he responded, but it was my old boss giving me some really good a-d-v-i-c-e about myself if you know what I mean.)

I got in not making eye contact. I calmly said, "At the corner, make a right like you were leaving to go back home, but instead, we'll go food shopping." I yelled to the guys by my makeshift flagpoles and yelled, "Susan said we can use the grill at our other neighbor's house!"

Lou asked, "That for real?"

I smiled. "Yup! Homeland Security approved!"

The ride off the island was eventful. I could hear my hair growing on my head; it was amazing that I'd never heard that before. It wasn't until we were going over the first bridge that I heard Lou breathing, which reminded me he was in the car with me.

Lou cleared his throat. "Is everything okay?"

I said with a smile, "Everything's peachy keen!"

"I know that, Charlie Cans, but is everything okay with you? Fuck the peaches!"

We cracked up. We said almost at the same time, "We need a fuckin' vacation!"

CHAPTER 90

L OU AND I arrived at the Stop & Shop on the mainland. I said that
I'd grab a cart and that we should start down the first aisle we came
to. I felt as if I were home shopping for Marge when I started calling out
the items we needed.

We did pretty well; we finished in forty-five minutes. We still needed
ice, beer, and liquor to make it a more memorable feast. We stopped at
liquor store down the road. Lou grabbed a shopping cart, and we put
beer and wine in it. Lou picked up some bottles of Patrón tequila (the
exact number is a state secret), a bottle of vodka, and other fine spirits
we somehow lost count of.

I was taken aback when Lou paid for the whole kit and caboodle; I
made a mental note to inform the DDC guys of that historic moment
I was privileged to have witnessed. I called the house to check on how
things were going and find out who else has arrived. I was told that
George Thomas, another DDC Ground Zero worker who worked mostly
on payments had arrived. George was a great guy to have around for
any party whatsoever. And if there wasn't a party, he'd make you feel as
if you were at one just by his dry sense of humor. You'd wish you had a
drink in your hand to enjoy his humor, and you'd do so even more than
that if he himself had a scotch on the rocks in his. His humor became
soakin' hilarious. I'm proud to know him; he's my biggest competition
when it comes to telling jokes.

Edmundo called with the news that Ron's wife, Judy, and their friend,
Maria Noto, had arrived. Maria used to work at the WTC Memorial
with Lou and Ron. Things were looking good; some good party people

were arriving. I knew that Judy would be right in there helping out wherever she could; that's why I love her. The same goes for Maria, for it's not too often that the DDC guys help out with the setting up of things unless they're asked except for Edmundo, the "real" workhorse besides me when it came to making sure everything gets taken care of.

I was hoping someone had brought Chuck's grill to our deck with perhaps a spare propane tank. I thought about one last item to attend to—making sure someone had checked out the bathrooms. After all, we had ladies in the house. I called Edmundo and asked him to make a final check on that.

Lou and I were headed back to the island when I said we needed some cigars. We stopped at one or two stores but no luck—that idea went up in smoke. We got back and learned that everything was under control. Some more guests had arrived with coolers of beer—very thoughtful of course.

Some of the new arrivals were happy to see Lou even more than they were to see me. Didn't matter. We all respected him greatly. I yelled out to the guys to help unload the car, and of course they headed for the beer and ice. I headed for the deck with the food and saw a sight for sore eyes—our good neighbor Chuck's gas grill. Perfect timing. I set up my boom box and started cranking out the Stones' "Start Me Up!" to which I sang along.

I fired up the grill and did what I did every year—I ritually poured a bottle of ocean water over my head to get tanned while I cooked because I'd not have time to go to the ocean and jump in because I was cooking, okay? Everyone looked forward to my little ritual.

"Let the Festivus begin!" I sang out. In Swedish, it means "The party's on!" I chugged my first beer. I set my signs up to invite any and all over for our event. Trust me, I'd spoken to a lot of people on the way to and from the beach about our event telling them to join us and bring along some food if they wanted—the more the merrier. That is, food and people. I loved the folks I'd meet on the island.

The weather was perfect—plenty of sunshine, hardly a breeze, and about seventy-five. People arrived with food and drink but no gifts since there was no star in the East. They also brought plenty of good cheer because they were party people. The way I see it, if there's a party going on and I'm there and the party is going real well, anyone who's there to partake in this with me is a good party person.

Two really good party people were Janice and Larry Cilento, who had been attending our events each year. They arrived with a dessert and a nice bottle of wine. Everyone who knows them loves and respects them like family whether they like it or not. As we're saying hi and giving hugs to one another, we hear this loud commotion coming from the street behind the tall hedges. Someone was blowing his horn and yelling, "Where are the valets? Why aren't there any parking spaces available here?"

I told the others, "Let's ignore them, people. Maybe they'll go away and bother someone else!" I knew who it was—Lorraine McAndrews and Nelson Hernandez, two more DDC Ground Zero workers. Lorraine was a barrel of laughs and funny too. I spotted them through the hedges; Maria Puternicki was with them. Maria was an architect in the A&E unit at DDC who had also worked at Ground Zero.

One memorable night at Ground Zero, I asked Maria to call our DDC representative at the FDNY Headquarters, 10–10 at the site, for the night temperature and wind velocity. When she was told that the wind was 5 mph, she corrected him. "I play golf. The wind is always more than five miles per hour, at least ten" in her strong Brazilian accent. It was priceless, and we still laugh about it.

I had plenty of burgers, a couple of hotdogs, and a piece of kielbasa going on the grill. My mouth was watering. The sun was getting stronger. That and the heat from the grill were cooking me as I was cooking the food—a double dose of warm. Everyone was chatting, laughing, drinking beer, and having a good time.

Someone shouted, "Mr. Patrón has arrived." Some of us were looking forward to meeting him a.s.a.p. Edmundo came out with as many shot glasses as he could carry, and J-RO was behind him with a plate of lime slices and a salt shaker, and of course Lou came holding our special guest. He lined up shots until he had to leave with an empty bottle.

Luckily, Lou had had the common sense to invite Mr. Patrón's brother-in-law, another type of tequila. Everyone met the entire Patrón family and some of his cousins such as Ms. Tanqueray, Johnnie Walker

Red, and his old friend, Grey Goose. I never expected to see all of them the same night. We were good party people. What are good friends for?

I guess the aromas of food and beer took a breeze and ended up on the street, where it caught the noses of George Sahm, another DDC Ground Zero worker, and his buddy, Frank Cavaulluzzi. They said they'd known they were close when the caught the scent.

Their question "Is this the right place?" was so well rehearsed when they said it in unison that I just had to come back with, "No! But you can stay. Everyone else here wasn't invited either!" More handshakes, hugs, and pats on the back. When they saw Lou, there was another call for shots.

Some neighborhood people we'd seen before came over to see what was going. I invited them to join us and handed them beers and burgers whether they wanted them or not. I'm like that. I would have invited the world, but I wasn't cooking for anyone beyond the international dateline or below the equator. They'd have to wait until the next day to be served.

George and Frank had been with us before. They're excellent party people; I mean, that's what they told me. A line of folks expecting a hotdog, burger, or a slice of sausage formed in front of me. We heard a loud, rumbling noise coming from the street. No, it wasn't anyone who had just eaten a can of beans (but don't think I didn't see you take most of it). I knew exactly who it was—my supervisor, Kevin Arscott, and his lady friend, Jolelynn Gansemer. They'd ridden his Harley chopper, and what a chopper it was. When Kevin revved the engine, his Harley made the hairs of my eyebrows raise up even more and somehow face toward the tremor of each burst from the exhaust pipes. Isn't science amazing?

At the same time, Edmundo was trying to announce above the numerous conversations, the laughing, the music, and Kevin's revs, "Grab your glasses! We're going to meet and greet a long-lost cousin of Patrón Don Julio! Get your shots!" I heard him because I was only two feet away, but I don't think others did since Kevin kept revving his bike to let us know he'd arrived. It was funny watching Edmundo talking. No one had a clue what he was saying except me. He poured shots for the two of us.

I yelled out between Kevin's revs, "Come … and … get … it!" The usual greetings started all over again when Kevin and Jolelynn walked into the yard and up on the deck and saw Lou and Lorraine laughing it up. Ron and Maria were singing along with some song on the boom box while Mike yelled out to me across the deck over everything, "Charlie K, put more sausage on the grill! Did anyone bring kielbasa?"

J-Ro, who worked with Mike and who was sitting next to him, was seconding everything Mike was stating; it was an echo. Mack, who was standing at the bottom of the steps of the deck, got my attention by pointing toward the front of the house to let me know we had new arrivals. I tried gazing through all the smoke coming from the grill to see who it was—Desi Spillane, another Ground Zero worker with DDC and his wife, Yasmin, an admin liaison at DDC. She participated by helping out with other DDC personnel at the Jacob Javits Center and who are considered as having worked on the WTC project but weren't physically at the site. They had tied the knot on April 27, 2008.

Right behind them I saw KP, another DDC Ground Zero worker. He worked in the same police unit as I did but on the design side. KP is Kaushik Patel, AIA. Yes, he's an architect, or perhaps a member of Another Individual Abjecting to all food and only drinks. Thank God he wasn't an RA, a Rehabilitated Abjector who wanted only food. He was carrying a large covered tray. KP, Desi, and Yasmin had all been there before and knew most everyone.

Someone yelled, "Charlie K, where are the steaks I was told you were serving?"

What? Is he kidding? I don't remember telling anyone to get there early to steak a claim on a chair! That's what happens when you don't listen yada yada yada.

The photo labeled 'DDC GUYS AT THE "FESTIVUS"' will show you true conservative drinking partners who decided to share one bottle of beer brought by Kaushik Patel. To KP's left are Nelson Hernandez, Charlie Hernandez (no relation to Nelson also no chips), Frank, Mike Kenny, Julian Misurski III (who was eyeing the chips behind those false Foster Grants), and Lou Mendes.

We didn't have a pool in the yard, but our dear friend, George Thomas, who said he was once a pool boy, was hard at work thinking of ways to get a drink in his hands without cleaning the pool. He said he'd wait till one showed up by stirring some ice in a glass of scotch. He also said he could play valet and park cars for an hour or two but not there—instead, at a party he was told was about to start farther down toward the beach. Funny thing—he left with drink in hand. He came back fifteen minutes later to help me out with any of the chores that involved mixing ice with anything.

I believe his next course of action wore him out—seeing George having perfected the absolute way to dissolve unwanted ice cubes that were left in a bowl in a very sustainable way in a very large plastic cup. He scooped up these ice cubes that were various sizes and shapes that nobody wanted and gingerly poured some scotch on them. I believe he was trying to avoid global warming having any effect on them. George had a great sense of humor and at times was funnier than me, but I won't tell him that if you don't. Let's drink to that!

CHAPTER 91

A BOVE ALL THE laughter, music, and calls for more food, I heard Janice calling me to her table. She was sitting with her husband, Larry. I walk over. She looked happy about something. I thought it was my cooking, but she didn't have a plate in front of her, just a drink. I asked, "What's up?" She said that Ron had just made her day and was about to tell me what it was when I thought that I was the one with the good news as to what had occurred earlier that morning.

She said Ron had told her about all the unbelievable events that had taken place that morning and more so with Helen and me. All I could say was that she couldn't believe all those surprising coincidences had occurred to me on a day like this, our "FESTIVUS" because it was only Janice who really knew about the surprising coincidences I was having. I mean, c'mon! I had to tell someone!

I saw George Sahm and Desi tending to the burgers on the grill. Janice said, "Charlie, you're not going to believe this, but guess what just happened?" I was afraid to ask. Janice said that on their drive to the island from Long Island, she and Larry were trying to figure out what they could get for a warm, comforting gift for their two dear friends, one of whom had spent time at Ground Zero.

Her friend, Kevin Duffy, an FDNY battalion commander, had built a cozy house in the country with his wife, Susan. Janice said that Kevin called it therapy with dignity. She told me she and Larry were looking forward to going there the next weekend and wanted to bring a special housewarming gift. Janice knew that Ron, Mike, and I had been going to Oklahoma City for the past five years to attend the memorial anniversary ceremony there and had brought back seedlings from the Oklahoma City Survivor Tree on one trip. She also knew that wonderful friendships evolved from such tragedies; a simple seedling from the Survivor Tree was an extension of the friendship that was planted around this tree, and everyone hoped that the seedlings they took home would flourish for all of us.

I could tell by her look that she had something important to say. "What's planted in that brain of yours that you're dying to tell me?" I asked. I ignored some remarks Mike and J-Ro were making about where the chef was. I mean, how hard is it to flip a burger? Even they could handle that task. I gave Janice my undivided attention. She smiled and said, "I guess this is a surprising coincidence for me, Charlie, because Ron just told me that his seedling from the Survivor Tree couldn't be planted in his backyard. He felt his yard wasn't big enough for it to grow properly, so he asked me if I could use it somewhere. I came here hoping that I could ask you or Mike or Ron to help me out with this small request on getting me a seedling, and here's Ron offering me his seedling! Isn't that amazing?"

I asked Janice, "Isn't there a law about having too many surprising coincidences in one day without prior approval? I'm thinking about joining George over there; he's in la-la land or asleep in his lounge chair. I guess all those ice cubes got to him battling global warming." She looked at me as if I had two heads; she didn't know what I was talking about.

Janice and that seedling was mere chance, the hand of fate, or possibly a seed to life that had happened to her, for I learned something the following week when I spoke with her about all the surprising coincidences I'd had. She told me she and Larry had gone to Ron and Judy's house the previous Wednesday to pick up the seedling. They watched Kevin and Susan plant it that weekend. Janice said it was the perfect gift for them. I agreed. I told her that I regularly admired my Survivor Tree I'd planted in my backyard. It always reminded me of my dear, extended family in Oklahoma City. I was happy that another one would be growing at another Ground Zero worker's home. That made me feel connected to him.

Let's get back to the Festivus that was in full swing. Desi and Yasmin took over the grilling for a bit. They put a pan of mussels on the grill. I grabbed myself a cold beer (Corona of course) and went out to the front of the house for a breather. I saw J-Ro helping his good friend, Frank Lojec, who lives on the island year 'round, off-load a gas grill from his van. I asked J-Ro if it was a present for Susan or if they were planning on selling our hotdogs to passers-by.

J-Ro came back with a smart remark with a joking smile on his face. "Someone was throwing this out from a garage sale he was having. He said he had no use for it, so Frank and I thought we'd leave it here since it looks almost new. And about cooking hotdogs, well, we're taking over the grill on the deck to cook these three rings of kielbasa Frank got for us, and even though the three of us are Polish, you're not getting any!" All you could hear were these three hearty laughs coming from all of us.

I heard this song blasting from my boom box on the deck. Ron, Judy, Maria, and Lorraine were singing along above the volume, and they sounded good! (See what happens when you're surrounded by your best friends? The very best comes out of them including when they're singing.)

My feelings got a huge jump when I saw Helen and her boyfriend, Ed, coming into the backyard to join us. I ran up to the boom box and lowered the volume. "Could I please have everyone's attention? I'd like everyone here to say hello to Helen and Ed. Helen is now a dear friend of mine and everyone else who is here. I am sad to say Helen lost her brother, Stephen, in the towers that fateful morning. I consider Helen and her boyfriend, Ed, and her family a part of our family. They're here to enjoy Festivus, so everybody, welcome them!"

The crowd came over to introduce themselves and give their condolences. I hoped I hadn't made Helen or Ed feel uncomfortable; I just wanted them to feel as a part of us. Besides, I felt that Helen and I had been meant to meet after all those years even though we were already connected in a spiritual way but hadn't known that before then.

There was another photo that should have been taken—a photo of Lou and Lorraine dancing cheek to cheek to a '60s song. I shouted, "Could someone get that shot of them dancing so I could send it to page six of the *New York Post?*" Hearing me say that, Maria, who was still singing with Ron, came over and grabbed me while I had a Corona in each hand. (I can't remember why I had two.) Very ladylike, she pulled me toward her to dance with her. I thought she'd never ask; I thought she needed a break from her singing.

You may not know this, but I'm a party animal. I had two distant cousins twice removed from the family tree (due to a fly-by-night landscaper I had used years ago) who had made a big mistake. He went to our family tree (on paper of course) where the names of Romulus and Remus—no, not the Romulus and Remus of ancient Rome—Romulus and Remus Kaczorowski of Somkraziplac, a small town in eastern Poland, which was known for throwing the biggest party in all Poland. On January 7, 1518, a huge amount of kielbasa, pierogi, galumki, babka, kruschiki, vodka, and hundreds of barrels of beer were consumed in twenty-four hours. Almost everyone who had attended passed out; they were totally wasted. When they came to their senses the next day, they declared the day before as a local and national holiday. Today, some four hundred and ninety-one years later, the holiday is still celebrated in that town. It's known as the "We did what that day?" holiday.

Look, I needed a break to humor myself, so I thought I'd throw in some Polish humor. Besides, my finger is killing me. I've been typing for almost nine and a half hours straight. I had no food or drink, and my neck is getting carpal tunnel syndrome. You can just imagine what I look like. I know, I look like shit. Be right back.

Okay, I'm back. Now where was I? Oh yes, the amazing Festivus we had that grew merrier. We ate and drank with some neighbors who came over, and some of them were bearing food. They'd grab drinks and start feeling right at home as if we'd known each other for years. I guess that was due to all my coaxing and pleading the previous two days with those I met on the beach. I'd told them the reason for Festivus and invited them to stop by.

In another photo, you'll see Charlie Jimenez, Mike Kenny, George Sahm, Desi Spillaine (standing), Maria Puternicki, Yasmin (I believe those were pine cones or baked potatoes she was trying to juggle; either way, they weren't going on the grill), the back of J-Ro, the back of Frank Lojec, and half a body of the other Frankie. (Don't ask me why I included this picture here. I know it couldn't go into another book I'm thinking of writing.)

The next book I'm thinking of writing about is, global warming, which I believe started on Sunday, October 22, 1939, around 3:15 a.m., the first day after we had our first above-ground nuclear test that added this new and strange ingredient to our atmosphere—nuclear matter—which eventually affected our whole planet. (This is my theory, not Al Gore's.)

My thoughts on this were rudely interrupted when certain words permeated the air: "We need more burgers and hotdogs! Where the hell is Charlie K? Isn't he the chef here?"

CHAPTER 92

E VERYONE WAS EATING, drinking, singing, dancing, talking, basking, smoking, laughing, cooking, shouting, thinking, text messaging, or juggling pine cones—whatever. It was looking like the best Festivus we'd ever had! I didn't know what the next Festivus would be like, but I planned on getting there the Wednesday before to get a jump on things.

I had to include this group photo of us on the deck of whoever was still there at the time others had gone for a walk to the beach. So starting on your left from the screen door: J-Ro (in long-sleeved blue shirt), Mike (in front of him), Charlie H's head and hand, Lorraine, Jolelynn, Frankie, Maria, Ed, Helen, Jules, and yours truly at the table. Far right going counterclockwise (toward your left for any Swede out there): Lou, Edmundo, Ron, Janice, Maria N., Kevin, Judy, George, and Frank Lojec. Anyone who didn't make this photo, I'm sorry. Next time, don't go for a walk on the beach. It'll always be there!

After the photo, Said Daryani, another DDC brother who had worked at Ground Zero, showed up. He's one outstanding individual no matter where he stood on the site or off the site. Late Saturday night of our 2007 Festivus after the majority of the people had left, the guys who were sleeping over or "had" to sleep over got together on the deck to talk about anything in general as we poured shot after shot of tequila and gave our undivided attention to Said, who told us about his amazing childhood in Iran. He told us how he'd met his wife and what his life was like in Iran; he said he was proud and happy to be in the United States.

His story was so amazing that whenever I see him, I always think of that night. His life would make a great book. I was thinking when everyone who was there went back to work on Monday, they'd all be talking about the weekend. The stories would get around the office, and I was sure I'd be getting calls from people who hadn't ventured to LBI but wanted to be informed about the one next year.

My thoughts were interrupted by someone mentioning that a few people had decided to stay at a nearby motel instead of traveling home that night. I wished we'd had room for them at the house. I don't know what made me walk to Helen's house for another look at her shrine to her brother, but there, I saw that her flag was slightly frayed. I don't know why, but I felt a warmth in my heart for her. I lowered my 9/11 memorial flag and folded it. I wanted to give it to Helen the next morning as a memento of what had occurred between us early that morning.

The following morning, I saw Helen and Ed come out their side door. I told her I had something to give her. "What? Are we still doing shots?" she asked.

I laughed and said I'd be right back. I went back for the flag. As I was making my way out of the house, I saw Ed making his way to me in our backyard. He said, "Charlie, I was going to ask you before Helen and I left last night where I might get a flag like yours. I think it would be a lovely sentimental gift to give to Helen and be a special keepsake for the house."

I couldn't believe it—another surprising coincidence. I said, "I thought about that last night. I decided to take mine down and give it to her this morning. And here you are asking me if I would mind if I gave you this flag for her. By all means, but if you don't mind, I would like to have the honor of presenting it to her, you know, being that I was there that morning with Stephen. Besides, after all those unbelievable and amazing coincidences yesterday morning, I feel connected with Helen and now you."

I think Ed totally understood. He gave me a quick embrace. I saw Helen making her way to where we were. I looked into her eyes and said, "Helen, I'd be honored if you accept this gift from me to fly this flag when you and your family are here on the island."

She was so touched by my offering. Ed just looked at her as she came and gave me this big hug and said, "I think I need to talk with Mr. Patrón right now!" We all stood there with misty eyes and started laughing.

To change the mood, Helen started talking about the previous night saying that Susan's deck looked like Studio 54, a very popular nightclub in New York City in the late '70s, when someone found the light switch to the deck spotlights and was casually flipping it on and off. I told her that was me and it was also me with my flashing red lights on my FDNY wristwatch that I had worn that had added a touch of flashing red strobe lights to illuminate the dancing on the deck. Then someone turned the volume up higher, so I then switched to another button on my watch giving off a bright, flashing white strobe light that brought on cheers even from the peanut gallery, which we didn't know we had.

No, we didn't have a peanut gallery, but I believe the art gallery up around the corner on the boulevard might have thought we were nuts.

Again, Helen, Ed, and I let out another hearty laugh. I sort of changed my mood real quick for there was something I wanted to mention to them before they left. It was that since they were now part of our family, I figured I might as well tell them what had occurred the previous night after they left regarding one of the guys in the house. I told them that Edmundo and Janice came to tell me something extremely important knowing already well by their facial expressions that something was up. They asked me if I knew where the nearest hospital or clinic was on the island. I told them that I didn't know of any hospital or clinic on the island but that I remembered seeing one on the bayside of the island going north. "Why?" I asked. Just by their look, I took off looking for the neighbor who lived two houses away (who lived there year 'round) and who'd I just seen walking his dog a few minutes earlier. I rushed toward where I'd seen him last, caught up to him, and asked him.

I ran back and told them that the hospital was off the island about five minutes on the mainland on the right. There was a clinic going toward the Ron Jon Surf Shop, but it was more like a first aid station. I told them that, and Janice walked away and went upstairs. Edmundo stayed with me to fill me in as to what was going on. I saw Judy walking down the stairs in front of Ron with Maria Noto behind him, and Janice was carrying Ron's overnight bag. They started to say good-bye to everyone saying that Ron wasn't feeling well, so they were leaving to go home.

Edmundo continued to tell me that Ron was complaining of having these intermittent chest pains. We both knew that Ron was under a lot of pressure working very hard on seeing the memorial open on its scheduled date. I thought maybe it was getting the best of him and the stress was overbearing. No questions were asked by anyone as to why the sudden departure; we just said good-bye, have a safe trip home, and we'll talk to you soon.

Edmundo and I looked at one another with deep, hard looks but gave each other reassuring nods that everything would be okay. Word got around the house about Ron having to leave, and that changed the entire climate in the house and outside. That was the first time we had an incident within our family; it was something we had never expected.

I went out to the deck and made the announcement; I asked if anyone needed to sleep over. We had three beds available since Ron, Judy, and Maria had left. (I won't be going into any details of the conversation that went on among us DDC guys until two in the morning.) We called it a night, and it was lights out.

I could see that Helen and Ed were taken aback as to what had transpired the previous night. We all learned that a few days later, Ron was rushed to the hospital; his chest pains had gotten worse, and he had some stents put in to clear up his heart problem.

He's doing much better today, and I know he's looking forward to this coming and every Festivus that we have on LBI.

CHAPTER 93

I T WAS AROUND eight fifteen Sunday morning. A second pot of coffee had been made. There were all kinds of cake and donuts left over from the previous day's shindig, and if anyone wanted something hot for breakfast, it was of his or her own doing because Edmundo and I had resigned from any and all kitchen duties. It was a day that everyone would have to fend for himself or herself.

I figured that since everyone was pretty much wiped out from the previous night's unbelievable get-together, I'd head down to the beach and try and make the rest of my day clear as the sky above with the sun shining down on me; I could feel it getting warmer by the minute. I was hoping I could get a few rays in before I had to leave.

I still didn't know who among those who were still there would be able to drive me back into the city. As I started heading out of the backyard to head down to the beach, I saw Lou walking down from the deck in my direction. "Charlie Cans, what time are you leaving?" His question to me was totally amazing. I was quick to reply, "I really didn't know, Lou, because first of all, I didn't drive here, and two, I came with you and Ron. Now that Ron left last night, I guess I'll be leaving whenever you decide to leave if that's okay with you."

He laughed and said, "Oh yeah, that's right, so are you going my way? I'm going into the city, but I might want to stop for lunch before we get into the city."

I gave him this real serious look. "Well, I'll be taking this fucking survey that has about a hundred and fifty questions that concerns you coming to this island and attending the Festivus that you can answer while you're driving back!"

He said, "Sure, no problem, but fuck your survey. You answer the fucking questions as if it were me! How's that sound to you?"

I responded even though I knew that he knew I was going to say this, "Well, it sounds like I will have my hands full on the drive home."

Lou gave me this look, shook his head side to side, and said, "Whatever! Other than that, how's eleven a.m. sound to you on leaving here?"

I said, "You got it! It's a date! I'll be ready!" I turned and continued with my walk down to the beach figuring that I still had a good hour and a half to spend soaking up the rays. I got down to the beach and saw my buddy Mack sitting on a blanket watching the surf. I joined him, and our conversation jumped right into the thick of things as to Ron's condition. Mack started to recall what had occurred there the previous year when I got some pretty bad, upsetting news that had hit me like a sledgehammer, which had my heart come flying out of my chest because of what I had been told by my dear friend Janice about this other dear friend of ours, Tania Head, who had turned out to be a total fraud about her 9/11 experience.

(I won't be going any further on this subject because I was deeply devastated by the news of what was stated in the *New York Times* that had me wanting to swim out to the horizon and not come back. With that being said, I'm closing the vault on that whole episode and throwing away the key. If you want to learn about this, read *The Woman Who Wasn't There*.)

So Mack and I sat there and took in the rays while we talked about the great weekend we'd had, and we were already looking forward to next year's Festivus. I could see that my time was up and I had to head back to the house. Mack said he would join me to say good-bye to Lou too.

As we approached the house, I could see that Mike, J-RO, and Edmundo were talking with Lou out on the deck. Lou saw me, and I gave him a thumbs-up. I told him I would be ready in five minutes, but all I heard him say was another "Whatever!"

I was down in six minutes stating, "Good-bye, everyone! I got a plane to catch, and if I don't leave now, I'll be stuck on the tarmac till the cows come home!" Edmundo and Mack didn't have the slightest idea as to what I was talking about except for knowing what was needed to be done before they locked up the house and left. Susan had left us a requests checklist as to what had to be done whenever we stayed at her house.

I felt bad about leaving and not staying to help out, but since I had a ride back into the city with Lou, I might as well take it for no one else was going my way. I saw Lou and said with a smile, "I'm ready when you are!" I heard him say "Are you sure?" I looked straight ahead toward the heavens, nodded yes as if I were talking to someone up there, and came back with this heartfelt reply, "Whatever!" Of course he laughed.

So there we were heading north on Long Beach Boulevard where we hardly said a word to each other for the first half mile as we sat there just taking it all in. There was hardly any traffic to talk about for a Sunday morning as far as I could see. I thought it best that I remind Lou about the speed limit there and how the local police on the island take their speed limit warnings extremely seriously. Pulling someone over for speeding would simply make their day.

I saw Lou check his speedometer and rearview mirror as I was checking my sideview mirror just to show him that I was deeply concerned as well. Lou was smiling and casually looked over at me and asked, "Are they really that strict here, Charlie Cans?" I looked to my left, then to my right, and then turned around to look out the rear window, and then looked forward as I scanned the road out in front of us then started to nod in a funny kind of way and smiled back at him as I pointed downward and made a gesture with my two fingers to my lips (hush-hush). I even looked under the floor mat before I remarked, "After a day like I had yesterday, it would be one hell of a surprising coincidence if we got pulled over after you mentioned this to me."

Lou jokingly tapped the gas pedal, and his car quickly responded by speeding up a few mphs over the posted speed limit. I don't know why it occurred, but it was as if it had been meant to be; within a second or two, we both replied loudly, "Whatever!"

Boy did we laugh as Lou began to slow down, and he and I checked all the mirrors and even the backseat before he signaled to go into the right lane and then back to the left lane for we were about to take the left turn that was up ahead that would take us to the bridge that would get us off the island.

I mentioned to Lou that I was already thinking about the next year's Festivus. I knew that the next 9/11 anniversary would fall on a Saturday that year, so more than likely, we would probably have our get-together on the nineteenth or the twenty-fifth of September. Either way, I would still have to clear it with Susan come next June or July, and the Original Six had to agree to it too. Lou replied, "Count me in. I'll be there!"

Well, I know that next year's event will be just as great if not better than that year's, so if you're around the neighborhood, stop by. You'll meet the greatest bunch of guys you'd ever want to know and who know how to have a good party. Who knows, maybe one day you'll be there on the island long before our Festivus gets geared up to start and you'll run into someone at a bar or a restaurant on the island and you happen to overhear a conversation about us. You might even come out and say to them, "Uh, wait a minute. I met a person a while ago here on Long Beach Island who was surfcasting off the beach for striped bass where we got into a conversation about California. Well, you're not gonna believe this, but it just so happens we both …"

CHAPTER 94

A FTER WHAT OCCURRED on that September Saturday morning to Helen and me, my mind was in such a tizzy that it had me recalling the time when I was about ten years old and ready to have my first piano lesson. I was finding it extremely hard and exhausting for I was being taught on this piano my dad had gotten for us, an old-fashioned piano that was made back in the early 1920s. It could have been made earlier, but I doubt it very much for I don't recall ever hearing anything made in the 1910s. Probably because it just wouldn't sound right.

Well, his piano wasn't your typical piano; it was so huge that it looked like a small closet or dresser on its side that had a section that opened up in front to insert a piano roll. I thought about putting some butter and jelly on it but it would probably have made the musical notes sound off key. (Cream cheese and jelly was my second choice.)

Anyway, these piano rolls were about ten inches long and two inches in diameter, cylinder shaped, having this perforated paper rolled up around them where these perforations (rectangular cutouts in various locations) made this magical music. (Science always amazed me, but as for these perforations, nada!) The roll was placed in the front opening that was usually concealed behind a sliding door (that James Bond couldn't even find) that had a thin shelf where one would place the music sheets to sing along as you played the piano. But in order to hear the music, you had to make the cylinder spin around causing the perforated paper to unravel as it got slowly pulled away. That was accomplished only by the constant pumping of one's legs as one sat at the piano and actually had to hold onto the piano or the bench one was sitting on (for dear life).

The faster you pumped your legs, the faster the music would play and be heard as you tried to keep your feet on these two big foot pedals. (Now there's something to ponder. Why do you always hear someone say "one's feet" or "one's legs" or "one's eyes"; don't most people have two of each of those?)

Well, it took quite a while to play one roll entirely, so my first lesson on this type of piano wasn't too successful. Ever since then, every time I hear about some famous artist from long ago or back in day had "banged" out a tune, trust me, I've been there and done that! After that first experience, I never had the desire to play the piano again, and that goes for any kind of piano including a baby grand. I took up with another type of instrument altogether, a pair of cymbals. I got into the habit of waiting for a song to end and then giving it my all. I found this line of music very traumatic for me, so I do a lot of humming instead.

Oh, before I forget, when my dear friend Janice and her husband, Larry, were there at the beach house on that Saturday in September 2008 arriving just two hours after everything occurred between Helen and me, I think Janice was totally surprised to hear that I had had numerous amazing coincidences in such a short amount of time that happened with a next-door neighbor whom I had seen over the years but knew nothing about.

CHAPTER 95

I T HAD TAKING me longer than I thought trying to complete tidying up Noelle's car for the long journey we were about to take in early August 2010. I was making sure that every little thing she gave me went into her car that was packed to the hilt for our father-daughter cross-country trip from our home on Long Island to San Diego. Noelle was going out there to start classes in marine biology at the University of San Diego. She had just graduated with an associate's degree from Nassau Community College. She had made the dean's list, which made Margie and me very proud of her. She was setting her sights on this new undertaking far away from home. Her 2005, two-door blue Honda Accord was packed to the gills to the extent that I hardly had a view out the rear window from the driver's seat let alone the passenger seat.

As I was cleaning the windows with Windex, I saw from the corner of my eye Margie stepping outside the house. She called out, "Charlie, stop what you're doing and come inside the house." I knew that when she said things in a certain way to me, something was definitely up.

When I walked into the kitchen, I could see straight into the dining room where Noelle was already sitting in her chair; Marge called me into the room to have a seat too for she had something to tell me. Margie waited till I sat to tell me that Noelle's doctor had just called to tell us that they had found three cysts on her spleen and that she needed to have surgery immediately.

Hearing that placed a totally new spin to our trip out west. Of course, Marge was completely taken aback by new and upsetting news. I realized that the two of them were waiting to hear my new course of action. I walked over to Noelle and told her that I wasn't going anywhere until she had the surgery and I knew everything had gone well and she had had a speedy recovery. I didn't even want to mention my plan B if my new course of action didn't pan out. I believe the words I said made her more upset where she practically pleaded with me, "No Dad, you got to go. Don't worry. Everything will turn out okay! I'm a big girl."

Our main goal was to take this road trip together and look at a bunch of apartment complexes out there in San Diego for her and her puppy, Jace. I told her and Margie that I had a list of some twenty-six potential apartment complexes to check out and then I would whittle them down to what I thought were the best five. At that point, Marge would fly out to meet us and help in the decision. So after we all had a good talk, the three of us agreed that I would go ahead and leave. We said our good-byes, and I left, but I let Margie know that I would call her on her cell in one hour as to what I was thinking of doing.

I then stopped off to see my parents to tell them what had taken place and that I'd be on my way to California as soon as I left their place. I left there, stopped at a Burger King for a medium fries, two cheeseburgers, and a large Coke hoping that the meal would calm my nerves and provide some nourishment to my brain more than my stomach as to how to solve this problem on going out west at a time like that.

By the time I finished my snack, I was pulling off the road somewhere before I went across the Verrazano Narrows Bridge and placed a call to my dear friend Susan Howland. I asked her a big favor. She said, "No problem!"

I'd come to a rational decision that I would not proceed with my journey out west until I explained my plan to Margie regarding Noelle's surgery. I headed toward Susan's beach house on Long Beach Island, and once I got there, I planned to call Margie (making sure Noelle couldn't hear my conversation) and explain my game plan. If Noelle happened to hear Margie talking to me, I told Marge to let me speak to her and I would tell her I was heading for Pennsylvania (a little white lie that I could tell her years later).

The plan I had come up with was that I would wait to hear from Margie as to when Noelle would be going in to have her surgery—either Tuesday or Wednesday—then I would wait till the surgery was done, hear the good news that all had gone well, and then leave and hightail it out to California as fast as I could. But when I called Margie to wish her a happy birthday on Tuesday, after thanking me, she quickly told me that Noelle was going into the hospital the next morning for pre-op and was scheduled for her surgery early Friday morning. She also added that Noelle had said she was looking forward to having the surgery done a.s.a.p. and getting well enough to be able to fly out to the West Coast with Margie in a week or two to look at the five choices of apartments I had picked out.

Hearing of the delay, I told Margie I had to leave the area and get going. I told her I could always fly back home if something changed with Noelle on Friday. I had been so looking forward to having to take my very first drive cross-country with my daughter, but I realized I had to make up for lost time for I had three scheduled appointments that coming Monday that Noelle knew about as to three great locations to move to.

I decided to drive like a bandit to Oklahoma City, where I would sleep if needed in my car in some hotel parking lot in order to save time. I called Susan that I was leaving, and I headed north to leave the island and get back on the mainland to head west when I realized I couldn't find my paperwork that contained my route to California. I pulled into a small strip mall that was completely deserted before I was about to go across the first bridge to leave the island. I called my sister Marianne, who lived in New Jersey, and asked her for the best route to take to get to Pennsylvania. Before I went to tell her what has taken place since I had left home, I told her to ask Wayne, her husband, who really knew the roads in New Jersey, to give me the shortest route to get to western Pennsylvania near southern Ohio. She relayed this info to him, and as he went on the computer to check on which roads I should take, I started to tell Marianne about what were the odds of something like that happening when Noelle and I were just about to leave on our trip together. Why couldn't it have happened earlier or for that matter not at all?

I thought I heard Wayne yelling out to Marianne something like, "Tell Charlie to take Route 78 ... Route 78!" As Marianne started repeating the same thing again to me, "Route 78 ... Route 78," I noticed this car pulling into the deserted parking lot. It was another Honda Accord similar to mine—same year but silverfish grey. It had two passengers, a woman and a girl, who was driving. I assumed the woman was her mother. They had pulled off the road to discuss something on a piece of paper the young girl was holding. In doing so, they actually went and made a big circle and ended up almost facing me, who was ready to pull out of the parking area. They stopped about fifteen feet away from me and were facing me.

You're not gonna believe this, but smack right in front of me was this Honda Accord with plates that read, RTE 78. I kid you not! I said out lout, "Holy shit!" My sister Marianne heard me say that. I said it again. "Holy shit! I don't fuckin' believe this!"

"What's wrong?" Marianne asked. I told her what had just occurred, and she was surprised to hear that in spite of the fact that she had known about the number of surprising coincidences that had occurred to me since 9/11. I could hear her telling her husband, Wayne, what had just occurred. I told Marianne that it was a sure sign of approval from the man upstairs to get going. I said my thanks and good-bye and told them I would let them know about Noelle's results in a few days.

Now, I got to ask you, was that one amazing, surprising coincidence or what? I thought, *Wow—with everything going on in my life with Noelle's surgery and it being Margie's birthday, here I am receiving this amazing gift of another surprising coincidence on the roller-coaster ride I've been on.* It took me on one hell of a spiraling upward loop in my life that somehow gave me this huge rush to put the pedal to the metal and be out in San Diego in no time at all and then back to my home sweet home.

CHAPTER 96

I MADE MY way to Pennsylvania. I stopped to get gas and found my paperwork buried under the stuff in the passenger seat. I was able to get back onto the right roads from where I was in eastern Pennsylvania and head toward Oklahoma City. I drove like there was no tomorrow, and before I made my way in toward town, I placed a call to my dear friend Joanne. I told her where I was, that Noelle wasn't with me, and my plan and schedule. I asked her that since I was passing through, would she round up some of my extended family members there and meet me for dinner around 6:00 p.m. at the Mexican restaurant we had gone to the previous year downtown.

I had driven practically nonstop from New Jersey to Oklahoma except for a two-hour nap I felt I needed to take right outside Branson, Missouri. I think I did pretty good making up lost time in getting to where I was on Thursday afternoon. I figured I could take a couple of hours after dinner and be on my merry way on Friday morning and be in a better frame of mind.

I arrived at the restaurant fifteen minutes early to pick out a nice area to sit in. Ten people had shown up with Joanne to join me for dinner—my treat—and told them what I was doing. I was truly looking forward to seeing my extended family members there—wonderful people. I was surprised to hear Joanne inviting me to stay overnight at her house. I saw her husband, Gary, and of course Mom again, and I quickly went to sleep.

I woke up next morning after having had a good night's sleep. They fed me breakfast, and I said my good-byes and left super early that

Friday morning. On my way out of the state, Margie called to tell me that Noelle had had her surgery early that morning. They had drained the three cysts on her spleen and had kept her spleen intact. They said she'd be going home on Saturday to recuperate. As to how long she would have to wait to travel to San Diego to start college would be the next step. But it was great news. Marge handed the phone to Noelle, who said, "Hi Dad! How's it going? Are you making good progress getting to San Diego?"

She was overly pleased to hear me tell her bottom line that I would be in San Diego by late the next afternoon and be ready for my appointments on Sunday. I told her I'd probably look at some of the apartment complexes close by to the university before and after my appointments to make sure they were all pet friendly for her little pride-and-joy shih tzu, Jace. I told her that by Monday, I should have a pretty good idea as to which ones were the most suitable. I said, "I love you! Happy to hear the good news!" I asked her to give the phone back to Mommy.

I went over the details with Margie. Once I'd found a good apartment for Noelle, I'd describe it to her, and if need be, because of the time frame and not really knowing when Noelle would be able to fly out to California, I would pick one, sign the lease, pay what was due, and go out and rent the furniture she needed to make it a home for her. I said that in the interim, I would stay in a motel until I signed the lease and would sleep in the apartment till the furniture arrived.

I had checked into the Vagabond Motel (maybe because of how I felt), which was just northeast of the University of San Diego. I showered and was getting dressed when I called Marge and Noelle to tell them that I was going someplace special that night for the three of us. It was a place that we had all spoken about prior to Noelle's situation. I had suggested that once everything was in place there in San Diego and Marge, Noelle, and Jace had flown out, we'd stay in the apartment for the week before classes were to start, and then Margie and I would leave for home.

Due to this big change in plans, I decided to have dinner at my favorite restaurant in the whole wide world as celebration of the fact that I had made it to California without any glitches and to celebrate Marge's birthday and Noelle's good news on her surgery. I told Marge and Noelle that the weather there was perfect and the food would be perfect too as I was going to the Marine Room in La Jolla, a restaurant that was literally on the beach.

There, at high tide, the ocean's waves splash against these huge picture windows as you sit there enjoying a fine meal of seafood cuisine. I made a mental note to myself to call them from the restaurant during my dinner and before the sun went down.

As I was getting dressed, I turned the TV on and tried to decide what I wanted to wear when I heard on the TV station I was watching, CNN, something that surprised me. I looked up and saw the teletype that was flashing across the bottom of the screen was showing the 9/11 Memorial in Lower Manhattan. The teletype was stating that "Ronaldo Vega, Director of Design of the September 11th Memorial, is awaiting the arrival of the first ten trees to be placed in the memorial."

How odd was that of all things and of all days I was having to see this while I was out in California. I was instantly emotionally touched by this news; it had me going back to get my cellphone and unplug it from the wall outlet and placed a call to my good buddy, Ron Vega, back in NYC at the Memorial.

When I heard his voice, I quickly told him that I was watching live where he was just on TV and talking about the trees being delivered. That was making my evening that much more enjoyable and memorable; I told him why I was out there, and he said, "Charlie K, why aren't you and Mike out here with me waiting for these trees to arrive?"

I replied, "Well, Ronaldo, because I'm out here in San Diego, and seeing you in the area that I've called my home away from home, I'm finding it a little ironic as to where you are and where I am."

He said, "Wow, CNN just left here five minutes ago and you saw it on TV in California!"

We had a few good laughs and talked some more, and then I told him what I was doing in San Diego and that evening for Marge and Noelle. (I just like to say that I truly honor Ron for his son, Chris, who was nice enough to be Noelle's date for her senior prom. They truly looked great together.) I told Ron that I would have a drink in his honor after the ones I'd be having for Marge and Noelle.

He said, "Enjoy your evening. Give my regards to Marge and Noelle, and have a few more drinks for the trees."

We said our good-byes, and I went back to getting dressed and left for dinner. I still had enough time to catch a great sunset from the bar in the Marine Room where I was thinking of possibly eating my dinner there to watch the spectacular viewing instead of being at a table. I arrived, parked the car, and walked in to where one had to take this staircase down to the bar and main restaurant. The place was practically empty except for a table of four in the far corner where the diners were laughing about something. I guess I was too early for dinner, but it's never too early for a drink before dinner, so I made my way over to the bar, took a seat, and waited. I saw the bartender on the side trying to finish whatever he was doing before he came over; he said "Hi! What's your pleasure?"

I said, "I'll take a Tanqueray and tonic with a twist of lime, and when you get a chance, I'd like to see your menu."

It was only me at the bar. I didn't even see a waiter or a waitress or any other customers there. So I figured I might as well start a friendly conversation with the bartender. I think I briefly covered all the important stuff with him such as my cross-country trip, what I was doing in San Diego, why I was there in the Marine Room, and that I was a survivor of 9/11 and had been at Ground Zero. I told him I was writing a book about all the above and all the surprising coincidences that had occurred to me all tied into one another. I also told him what had occurred just a few minutes earlier with my buddy Ron back in New York City.

He asked, "So what's the title your book? It sounds pretty interesting to read."

I told him the title and waited. Sure enough, he asked again for the title. I told him, "That is the title of my book!" He had a good chuckle and said, "For that you deserve another drink." I thanked him and said, "Great! Let's make it a bottle of Corona for my good buddy back in New York City, Ronaldo Vega, where right about now I should have been there with him on this historic day!" He stopped dead in his tracks and walked over to the bar and put out his hand toward me for a handshake. I said, "What did I do to deserve this handshake?"

He asked, "What's your name?"

I remarked, "I'm known by many as Charlie K! What's yours?"

He gave me this big smile and simply said, "Ron!"

I was totally flabbergasted. (There have been numerous times when I was slightly flabbergasted, but never totally.)

He then pointed toward the massive windows showing a beautiful sunset. "A picturesque scene to ponder as you're wishing you were back there with your buddy but in a spiritual way for that festive occasion. Let me get that cold beer for you!"

As he was getting my beer, I saw him making a drink for himself. I happened to catch in the corner of my eye someone appearing from behind a wall next to the bar. It was this stunning and extremely good looking woman probably in her mid-twenties—a year or two older than Noelle— wearing a striking red dress. She had this beautiful, long, curly, raven-colored hair that was not only resting on her shoulders and over the front of her but I could see it was also going down her back.

She leaned in and asked Ron what all the celebrating was about. The bartender started to tell her about what had just transpired, and then he told me to chime in anytime and I could fill her in with all the rest. He then looked at me and said, "Why don't you tell her what you told me about your book and what your title is?"

As she came over, I briefly started to tell her, and then I said, "Let me just take a swig of my beer before I continue." After taking a long swig, I told Ron that I would like to have a drink for my wife's birthday and for my daughter who would be attending USD. "Make it a Rum Screwdriver!"

I went on to tell this beautiful girl what the three of us would have been doing together there, but due to my daughter's emergency surgery back in New York, I was there having to have these drinks in their absence since my daughter was recuperating back home. "It's me, here, for the three of us."

She said, "Ah, that's so sweet, and I just graduated from USD in nursing. I'm presently on a waiting list for a job at one of the local hospitals." She turned to the bartender and asked for a club soda; she wanted to join me for a drink and make a toast to my wife and daughter and to my book too. She told me, "I have some time before my first reservation shows up for dinner, and I happen to be the only waitress on for tonight!"

The drinks were made, and as I sat there looking at this lovely waitress. I said to myself, *Wow, it looks like she has some Hispanic background.* She reminded me in a very surprising way of Noelle, except this girl was way taller and her beautiful hair was curly, not straight, like Noelle's, who loved keeping it long and straight.

She gave me a smile, raised her glass, and said, "So Charlie, what are the names of your wife and daughter so we can toast them?"

I smiled and said, "My wife's name is Margie, and my daughters' name is Noelle, not like the Christmas song, for it has another *l* and *e*."

She then came out with this lovely smile, bigger and more beautiful than the one she had given me earlier and then looked over at the bartender. He shrugged his shoulders at her and said, "Go ahead. You can have the honor in telling him!" I didn't know what he was implying by his comment to her, but as I looked over at her, she was slowly brushing her hair off her shoulder and pointed at her name tag. I could not believe what I was seeing. Her name tag had Noelle on it. I stood up and walked over to her in total amazement and said to her, "Wow, what are the chances of the two of you having the same exact names as my buddy Ron and my daughter Noelle?"

(I know what you're thinking, but trust me, this is the God's honest truth as to what happened.)

I took my cell phone out of my clip quickly scrolling down to my daughter's name and called her. When she answered, I quickly said to her, "Hi honey! It's Dad. I have someone here who wants to say hello to you."

She remarked, "Dad, I don't know anyone in San Diego!"

I said, "You do now!" and I gave my phone to the waitress. I told her, "Say hi to my daughter!"

She said, "Hi Noelle, this is Noelle" and started giggling. "Yes, my name is spelled the same way as yours! Your dad is telling me all about you." They chatted for a minute or two, and then she laughed and said, "Okay! I'll tell your dad what you said. Nice talking to you. Feel better! Bye!"

She handed the phone back to me. I looked at Noelle and asked, "What did she say to you that made you laugh?"

She smiled again and said, "Your daughter said for me to tell you, 'It looks like you're gonna have to write another book!'"

We all had a good laugh. I went ahead and ordered a platter of stuffed baked crab cakes, had another Corona, and decided to stay at the bar to enjoy my dinner with these two new friends of mine who became two amazing people in my life for this unbelievable reason of what had just occurred. I felt like I was doubly blessed when I turned around on my barstool and sat there to watch the sun get swallowed up by the horizon as I was being swallowed up by this pretty surprising coincidence that happened to me in my favorite restaurant in the whole wide world. It felt as if I had just taken one huge, spiraling twist upward and then went straight down to the bottom as I quickly shot right back up to the very top of this imaginary roller-coaster ride I've been on.

I sat there motionless, thinking of what a hell of a memorable night I was having there back in my birthplace, San Diego, on this special occasion where I felt like I came full circle. My life started out there, and everything that had occurred in my life had done so for a reason. I wouldn't have changed one single thing.

I keep on having these magical, inspirational moments of unbelievable surprising coincidences that made me feel enormously blessed. I asked Ron for my last drink, which was a Bailey's on the rocks. As I was sipping it, it had me thinking of something I had recently read in a magazine written by Stephen W. Hawkins. It was titled "A Brief History in Time." I believe he had written, "The whole history of science has been the gradual realization that events do not happen in an arbitrary manner, but that they reflect a certain underlying order, which may or may not be divinely inspired." Now whatever made me think of that, at that particular moment, beats the hell out of me.

I waved Ron over and asked for my bill. I gave him my credit card and left a nice tip in cash for both of them when I went over to say my good-byes. Noelle gave me a kiss on the cheek and said, "Looking forward to reading your book, Charlie K!" I walked over to Ron, and we shook hands and gave one another a quick embrace. I said, "See you around, buddy!" I took a slow walk out to my car, got behind the wheel, turned on the radio, and took a deep breath. I heard the Doobie Brothers on the radio singing, "You keep me running! Yeah … you keep me running!" I sat there, looked up to the night sky, gazed at all those beautiful stars in front of me, and tried to look beyond into the heavens above and smiled. I asked my wonderful angels out loud, "Why do you keep me running and having these amazing surprising coincidences? And, more than anything, why do they keep popping up and giving me the most amazing feeling in my wild heart?"

I started the engine and changed the station when the song ended to another station and I sat there and started to laugh for it was like that Sunday morning drive that I had taken out to the beach a few years ago when this very song came on the radio—"Slow Rider." The things that had just occurred to me in the restaurant with Ron and Noelle has me saying this to you for the very last time: You're not gonna believe this, but from this day forward, I am ready for everything and anything that life sends my way, and if I have another event in my life or another amazing and unbelievable surprising coincidence, they better be fucking spectacular for me to sit down and write another book.

EPILOGUE

Like I said in the very beginning of my book, there have been quite a few times when I knocked on heaven's door when an event took place and I was lucky to have survived it. I don't remember which one of these events that took place when this occurred to me while I was in the hospital. This strange vision appeared in my head where all I saw was this large copy of some sort of "LIFE WARRANTY."

It might have been when I was having either an MRI of my head or a CAT scan possibly when I had my car accidents. I saw some kind of "renewal" clause. It was the last four words that were noted on the bottom of the paper, having "when hell freezes over!" Go figure.

I had almost been killed in my very first car accident when I wasn't even in a car or on the road but totally asleep on a typical army cot that my dad had placed in the front part of this bungalow (a wood-frame cottage that was common all over the Borsht belt up in the Catskills Mountains back in the day). Unbeknown to me, a drunk driver had gone off the country road and had crossed over this five-foot-wide ditch that was about three feet deep that ran parallel to the road. His car somehow went across this ditch and kept traveling for another sixty feet before it smashed through five newly painted wood pieces of Adirondack lawn furniture and then through and over a foot-high brick-layered flower garden before it found its way to careen into the front part of the bungalow I was in with my family.

The car came to a complete stop with its huge, shiny front bumper resting not more than six inches from the top of my head. I did not awake from the sound or the brunt of the crash as it came through the front wall of the bungalow nor when the police showed up and pulled the drunk driver from the car, arrested him, and tended to his minor injuries as the car was being hooked up to be pulled out of the bungalow by a tow truck.

I didn't wake up even when my dad and my Uncle Frank took pieces of plywood to close up the opening. My dad always said that I survived that accident by the hand of God; he would illustrate where my head had been and how close the front bumper had gotten to it when the car came to stop in front of me.

I don't want to leave this little piece of information out. My baby sister, Marianne who was one at the time, was asleep at the other end of the cot by my feet. My dad also said that I was blessed not having to witness any of that at such a young age. It might have been traumatic for me, but I do recall waking up and seeing little bits of daylight coming into the room that managed to sneak around the pieces of plywood. My dad told me about this accident when I got my driver's license at age seventeen.

The time I had that inflamed and enlarged liver two and half times its normal size that could have killed me if I'd gone home and had had a beer … having those crushing headaches and not knowing I had a 104-degree fever …or the time I had that head-on collision on the sidewalk in front of the Fire Department just two blocks from home where I was almost killed … I've been lucky.

Apparently, I wasn't too lucky after having spent some 2,278 hours at Ground Zero. I'm having to deal with about twelve or so health ailments, and two of them have already taken a toll on me, cardio and pulmonary, where I thought tomorrow would never come.

I told you about my first near heart attack in 1990. I had another one in 2007, and then I actually had a heart attack on April 18, 2010; that one outweighed the first two put together for I also had acute kidney failure at the same time. I had my kidneys flushed out while I was there recuperating for my heart problem in Mercy Hospital in Oklahoma City when I went out there for their fifteenth anniversary ceremony in remembrance of the bombing of the Murrah Building.

But I gotta tell you folks, out of all the events that had occurred to me in my life which I managed to survive, I'm gonna have to say in all honesty my worst event ever will always be the one that occurred that night that, literary and figuratively would have killed me for the remainder of my life having to live with what could have been. Lucky for me, it didn't occur. It was that night I would have taken Noelle with me to the grocery store. I wrote about this earlier—the pains I had in my neck and my exhaustion after a long day had convinced me not to take her along as I usually did, remember? I had tried to sneak out of the house so I wouldn't have to explain to her why I wasn't taking her along; she loved to go out shopping with me and riding in the cart.

That van rear-ended me just as I was about to pull into the parking lot. There hadn't even been enough time for the airbags to deploy. I was pinned in the wreckage. Somehow, I survived the accident that was so bad but could have been a hell of a lot worse if I had brought Noelle along with me. When Margie showed up with Mary Ann and Noelle in the ER, I was almost tempted to say that I didn't want to be admitted to the hospital; all I really wanted to do was go home and apologize to Noelle and give her one big hug for not having been with me. Before Margie, Mary Ann, and Noelle left, they all gave me a kiss; Noelle's kiss shattered my wild heart and left me crying. I wanted to hug Noelle but the doctor advised me not to sit up or lean over, so I gave her a very long, endearing look. As they were walking out, Noelle turned around and threw me a kiss. I'm sure that kiss of hers was given by one of my wonderful angels in letting me know that they were there for me again and that God was probably the one who had given me that pain in the neck. Divine intervention.

My left arm has never really healed properly from that accident; that's a reminder to me that God had more than his hand in in what had taken place that night that had kept Noelle safe.

Turns out the brakes on the van that had hit me had failed. Not one of the three guys in the van had a driver's license or insurance, and the van was not even registered. Wow. And the accident had occurred on the same road on which I'd had my other horrible accident.

I was surprised to learn that Hempstead Turnpike is considered to be the deadliest road in the entire state especially the part of the road where I had my two accidents—another surprising coincidence. I consider myself one of the luckiest people on the planet to have survived not one but two accidents on that road only a few blocks from my house.

Whenever I drive past the scenes of the accidents, I always get a chill down my back and my palms sweat. After what I've been through, especially after what I went through and experienced on 9/11, I keep telling people whether they want to believe me or not that I deserve the right to say, "Been there, done that and that too!"

I've been asked if I planned to write a sequel to this book I don't know. But if by chance I continue to have these surprising coincidences, I will. I know what it's title will be: *What the #@&% Is Going on Here?*